Guiding Light

Guiding Light

The Collected Speeches of

John Smith

Edited by
Brian Brivati

Politico's PUBLISHING

First published in Great Britain 2000
Published by Politico's Publishing
8 Artillery Row
Westminster
London
SW1P 1RZ

Tel 020 7931 0090
Fax 020 7828 8111
Email publishing@politicos.co.uk
Website http://www.politicos.co.uk/publishing

First published in hardback 2000

A catalogue record of this book is available from the British Library.

ISBN 1 902301 62 5

Printed and bound in Great Britain by St Edmundsbury Press.

CONTENTS

FOREWORD

Donald Dewar

FIRST MINISTER OF THE SCOTTISH EXECUTIVE

If you have to find one word to describe John Smith, it would be 'formidable.' It was the key to his character. He was great company, enormously kind, loyal to his friends, entertaining and consistent in action and thought over the years. But he was always, in all things, formidable.

Determination was another defining quality – effective and forthright. Those who wrote him off as everyone's idea of a Scottish bank manager misjudged the nature of the man.

For all politicians public speaking is part of the job. For some a dramatic setting the flashing phrase, the right gestures liberated by autocue shape the end product. John was not of that school He actively distrusted and disapproved of anything that he saw as 'flash.'

For him a speech was an exercise in persuasion and logic. He was not an ideologue who knew his Marx or decorated his speeches with side references to Gramsci. His Labour Party was, above all, committed to redressing the balance in favour of those who were the victims of circumstance – the depressing, damaging, self-fulfilling expectation of failure. The aim was to create opportunity.

The social justice agenda was at the heart of the matter. He was arguing that case even in the early years when he arrived at Glasgow University from his home in mid Argyle. He was remarkably consistent – a politician committed to winning in order to act. Government in the 20th century could not be revolutionary. It was a case of working the system to improve it. He had to persuade to construct a majority and then to break down the barriers to progress.

John was not a natural phrasemaker. His technique at the Bar was to lead the jury to the wanted conclusion by dissecting the evidence and picking over the bones to justify his client's case, inviting them to draw from his selection the inference that undermined the prosecution's arguments. There was no trace of the theatrical 'murder in the red barn' tradition that some favoured.

He had the forensic skills, the power to analyse, to accentuate the essential. The Westland debates were key in establishing his reputation, concentrating as they did on destructive logic (see *Westland plc*, pp. 34–40) The same strengths served him well when negotiating the complexities of the Maastricht legislation (see *Maastricht*, pp. 223–40). John was a determined supporter of an active role for Britain in Europe and never wavered (see *European Community*, pp. 144–54). His experience as Shadow Chancellor allowed him to argue the case for linking social justice and fiscal policy with great authority (see *The Economy and Recession*, pp. 132–44) .

His trade was debate and there he reigned supreme. He had no ambition to be an orator in the grandiose sense of the word. He was at his best in the House of Commons. The crowded, tight amphitheatre with its packed benches allowed him to establish a rapport with his audience, even to dominate. The Commons is volatile. The audience is alive, built-in. Those who are there do not sit and listen. They participate.

It is an audience that can be cruel. If a speaker on a big occasion loses the thread, the hum of conversation on the benches rises. It is the final disaster, leaving whoever is at the Dispatch Box struggling and often sinking. If the speaker is in form then a momentum builds as he is roared on by his own side and silences the enemy.

The strength of the Smith armoury was the brutal ability to demolish those who attacked him. Always a master of the facts, he could destroy the irrelevant, demolish pomposity. He loved living on his wits, relying on timing and the ability to search out the chink in the opposition's armour. He fed off interventions returning every point with doubled force. It did not matter whether it was a jumped-up, sharp-suited, city gent turned politician or one of the remaining traditional Knights of the Shire. John Smith was ready for them.

In that sense – and that sense alone – he resembled Mrs Thatcher in her high days. She, too, was immensely helped by interventions from the other side of the House. Without the spice of confrontation, she could struggle, run flat. The Opposition Whips would on occasion try to persuade the backbenchers that she was best left to her own devices (and in malicious times a little talking on the benches would not go amiss). It never worked because they never learned. There are in Parliament always members who, sadly, believe that they have the devastating point that must be aired. Up they would jump only to be hand-bagged in her inimitable style.

John had something of the same ability. He was always in command and ready for the hapless, of course, but equally for those who carried reasonably heavy guns. They all got short shrift. On occasion John would go down to an important debate in the Chamber with a proposed script that was clearly short in content and might even be described as light. He was never phased by this, assuring aides that he would get by by feeding off interventions. His tactics indeed were to goad the opposition into rising, only to scythe them down in turn. In the House of Commons the last word tends to lie with the Dispatch Box. When John was there it always did. His attack on the Major Government when leading on a key No Confidence motion showed that other side of John – mischievous, rumbustious with sustained argument, very much at a discount. The speech was full of life, a bravura performance, gaining impetus from a string of unwise interventions from a mixed bag of opposition figures ranging from Kenneth Clarke to Gyles Brandreth. It was no contest and the troops loved it.

He was not so comfortable in Party Conference. He did not like a vast arena, a choreographed performance, polished and projected. He was always uneasy with the razzmatazz and any trace of show biz style. His speeches were persuasive, coherent, forceful but were not sprinkled with one liners quoted again and again. He was not happy singing 'We are the Champions' on the stage at the close of Conference for a national television audience. He delivered only two Conference set pieces as Leader. Typically the priority was practical change. He pushed One Member, One Vote in the interests of party democracy and took real risks to further that cause. Unusually the outcome of the key vote on OMOV was uncertain, even at lunchtime on the day it was to take place. Almost certainly the victory owed more to John Smith's unrivalled ability to sort out the weaker brethren in direct negotiation than any one speech delivered by him or anyone else.

The great policy area which appeared again and again in John Smith's speeches was the need for constitutional change (see *A Scottish Parliament Now*, pp. 154–9, and *Reforming our Democracy*, pp. 176–188). It was under his leadership that the settled will of the Scottish people was built into Labour's plans for Government and so paved the way for the Scottish Parliament. The template for radical democratic reform delivered by Tony Blair was cut in John's time.

At Conference and in countless speeches in the country to vastly differing audiences he argued the case for Labour's priorities and policies. He asked for trust and commanded trust. He was determined to bury the memories of the chaos and confusion of the early 80s when internal division and intellectual chaos left the Party virtually unelectable.

John Smith was in many areas a traditionalist. Family values, community and the duty of the citizen were immensely important to him. All leaders have speechwriters, some of whom become skilled at picking up even the cadence of their master's voice. John always put his own stamp on every significant speech. Some were very personal statements of conviction. His lecture to the Christian Socialist Movement on Social Justice demanded great care and involved in a most unlikely way the reading of a number of volumes on theology and social policy (see *Reclaiming the Ground*, pp 212–23). As a result it also involved a good deal of irritation, but the end product was important to hint. John, after all, was at heart a Presbyterian from the West of Scotland. He once horrified his staff and congregation of advisers by assuring, with some relish, a local radio audience in the South of England that 'we are not put on earth to enjoy ourselves.'

He was a complex man, but at his core stood unyielding principle. John argued for the social justice agenda, for redistribution of opportunity and of wealth, for his vision of a just society. It was idealism always dressed in the uniform of practical proposals that might stretch the conscience of middle Britain, but on which he believed the majority could be carried. He knew politics was the art of the possible, but on the great principles he would not give ground. He had a commitment which was unbreakable. He was a man with a sense of direction, a politician who knew what he was doing.

INTRODUCTION

The Politics of Democratic Optimism

Political careers that are cut short leave many unanswerable questions. For Leaders of the Opposition this is especially the case because they have not reached the final prize and for John Smith the poignancy is enhanced because Labour went on to win so decisively the election following his death. There is no point in ignoring the question: how would a Smith government have been different? But rather than tackle it now, so that it is in the forefront of the reader's mind, I have moved it to the end of this book as a conclusion. This collection should be a tribute to the life that was lived, not the one that was denied him by his early death.

John Smith was a dedicated parliamentarian whose speeches in the House were better than his speeches on great set piece occasions like party conference. They were better because in the House of Commons he could use the interventions of his opponents as a spur to his sharp wit and take energy from these exchanges to feed the force of delivery of the prepared text. In a conference or other major speech there were fewer interruptions and thus less stimulation for his acidic and funny ad-libbing.

Two examples will give a flavour of the range of his Commons weaponry, others are left within speeches reproduced from *Hansard*. The key combination which made Smith a great parliamentary performer were preparation and spontaneity. In the first example, we see the well prepared politician, ready to trump a hapless opponent:

Mr Smith: I will give way to the hon. Gentleman in the hope that at least one Conservative Member might have picked up the point.

Mr Brazier: The right hon. Gentleman has mentioned the rate of inflation four times already in his speech. Will he tell the House whether at any time in the future he expects the rate of inflation to reach the average level that it was under the previous Labour Government?

Mr Smith: I thought that it might occur to Conservative Members to make such a point. It occurred to me also when I was reading the Prime Minister's contribution during the Gracious Speech debate. On 21 November the Prime Minister said: When growth has been too fast, inflation re-emerges. It emerged in 1973 and it has re-emerged now. The House should note the significance of that. Inflation emerged in 1973, before the 1974 Labour Government were elected. It was there with the Barber boom, just as it is here with the Lawson boom.

Hansard, 28 November, 1989, Debate on the Address

In the second, we see a parliamentary joke. The truth is that House of Commons jokes are not very funny when read in print. Those that get the best laughs are not even funny when they are told in the Chamber; the laughter is part of the theatre of politics. Smith was brilliant at House of Commons humour and could have his own side rollicking with loyalist myth. He could also, on occasion, raise a smile from all sides of the House:

Mr Favell: I agree with much of what the right hon. and learned Gentleman has said, apart from the cheap political jibes that are part of the cut and thrust of debate. However, he should tell the country the Labour party's solution to this enormous problem. We want to know.

MrSmith: I do not intend to make expensive political jibes either out of office or in office. The hon. Gentleman might have noticed that the Chancellor of the Exchequer was not wholly free from bias in his description of the Labour party, nor wholly free from rather cheap personal references. If the hon. Gentleman were as even-handed as he would like to be considered, he might have noted that as well.

Hansard, 24 January 1991

These and many other instances earned Smith a reputation for a sharp tongue but he was also a master at the elaborate art of parliamentary flattery when it was appropriate, as in this example from the Queen's speech debate in 1993. It is a convention of the House that the mover and seconder of the Loyal Address are congratulated:

For me, it is an easy duty because of the quality of the contributions from both hon. Members. The hon. Member for Wealden (Sir G. Johnson Smith) has a long record of service in the House – 33 years as a Member of Parliament and, as he reminded us, most of it representing Sussex. Of course, he was also a London Member. He had a celebrated tussle with Lady Jeger for the Holborn and St Pancras seat. He won the seat from Lady Jeger in 1959 and then lost it to her in 1964. The hon. Gentleman made a wise decision to move to Sussex in 1965 because Holborn and St Pancras has been Labour ever since. Before the hon. Gentleman entered the House, he had a distinguished career as a broadcaster. He was a founding member of the famous *Tonight* team. Of course, those were the days when interviewers were a much more courteous bunch than they are today. '*Tonight* has developed to become *Newsnight*, but I am glad to say that the hon. Gentleman is much too stylish and urbane a performer ever to be compared with the likes of Jeremy Paxman [*Interruption*] That is probably the most courageous remark that has been made for some time and it is made in the cause of being generous to a Conservative Member. It was in a television studio that the hon. Gentleman had perhaps his greatest moment. He was the first British interviewer to question Brigitte Bardot on television. I have been told that he got straight to the point and that his opening question was, 'Apart from men, what are your other interests?'

From such great heights, the hon. Gentleman has declined to senior membership of the 1922 Committee. I understand that an election to the executive of that Committee is presently in hand. It is widely expected that it will provide yet another opportunity for the Conservative party to display its spirit of unity and coMradely affection. I wish the hon. Gentleman well. He wears his grey suit with style. He sounds and looks the part of a member of the executive of the 1922 Committee, which is a lot more than can be said for some others who occupy that position these days.

The hon. Member for Bolton, North-East (Mr Thurnham) seconded the address with fluency, flair and, if I may say so, disarming wit. His description of the adventures of the new Member will strike a chord with many Members of the House. He has not been with us as long as the mover of the address, but he has managed to get elected twice since he first came here in 1983, with majorities of less than 1,000 on both occasions – 813 in 1987 and 185 last year. He is on record as saying that concern about unemployment made him decide to go into politics. Given the size of his majority and its downward trend, that is a wholly understandable concern. The hon. Member for Bolton, North-East was bold enough – perhaps even rash enough – to tell us of the present that he received from the Home Secretary for service as his Parliamentary Private Secretary. He told us that the book was called 'Modern Fairy Tales'. He did not tell us that it was a collection of speeches to the Conservative party conference.

Hansard, 18 November 1993

John Smith's parliamentary career had started slowly after his election in 1970. He spoke little, asked questions and played himself in. Once he began to make speeches he quickly made a mark (see *Family Income, pp. 3–6*, and *In Defence of Multilateralism, pp. 11–14*). Within the Labour Party he was little known outside Scotland but he was one of those of the 1970 intake to gain Ministerial office when Labour returned to power in 1974. His time at Energy, as Under Secretary of State for and then Minister of State from 1974–1976, is important in a number of respects. First he proved in his Ministerial appointments an astonishing ability to work closely with people from very different ideological backgrounds: at Energy with Tony Benn and, most importantly, with Michael Foot, both when Foot was Secretary of State for Employment, and when Smith became Minister of State at the Privy Council office and Foot, Lord President of the Council and Leader of the House of Commons.

Smith and Foot came from entirely different wings in the party. Foot was the living personification of Bevanism, Smith, as a young student in Glasgow had supported the leadership of Hugh Gaitskell: the two wings of the party that had fought so fiercely in the 1950s and 1960s united by office in the 1970s. Their common feature was a loyalty to the Labour Party that was almost part of their genetic codes. They were wedded to the Labour Party by emotional and intellectual ties that they recognised in each other and that Foot recognised as differentiating Smith from other Gaitskellite social democrats. Even when Smith had joined Roy Jenkins and others in defying a three line whip on entry to the European Community he did it as loyally as he could. He did not make a speech in the debate but spoke earlier in the year to make clear his position (see *The United Kingdon and the European Communities*, pp. 6–11). He listened to the arguments of the front bench, including those directly from Foot, but he stuck to his guns. Foot, of all people, could respect a rebellion based on principle. Smith's natural integrity and obvious consistency earned him respect throughout the party.

The job at Energy was to create a public enterprise to exploit North Sea oil and manage the taxation structure of North Sea oil (see *The Petroleum and Submarine Bill,* pp. 14–19). The job at the Privy Council office was to manage devolution for Scotland and Wales (see *Scotland Bill,* pp. 19–29). The first was a triumphant piece of policy making; the second a political failure but one that ensured the survival of the Callaghan government. Neither of these jobs produced particularly good speeches. They were neither of them much about eloquence by the time Smith became involved, they were about intellectual competence and political management. His brief time at the Department of Trade, overshadowed by the Winter of Discontent and the general election campaign, was harder to sum up. Perhaps its most important feature was that he at least had some experience of running a great department of state, a rare and precious commodity in the Labour Party by the end of the 1980s.

Intellectual competence and political management were areas in which Smith excelled, but most importantly he had years of experience of managing a party in government. Working with Foot as leader of the House and in the many long debates that kept the Callaghan government afloat, he became an expert in the Parliamentary Labour Party. In the 1980s he learnt how to campaign in the country and he got to know the national party better. Of leaders of the party who have come from the right and centre, bearing in mind Attlee's view that the Labour Party should be lead from the centre-left, Smith and Callaghan were the most at home with the culture of the party (see for example, *Running for the Leadership,* pp. 159–63, and *A Commitment to Change,* pp. 167–76). It was said of Gaitskell that he took years to come to terms with the Labour Party. It is said of Tony Blair that he has a difficult relationship with the party he leads because he does not understand it. Smith knew the Labour Party inside out. Only James Callaghan came to the leadership with comparable experience and a comparable feel for the party. Take Smith's attitude to Clause Four of the party constitution. On a gentle stroll through the Frost programme on 10 January 1993, Sir David threw up what passed for him as a tough question:

David Frost	Clause 4 – going through the various areas where people want to know answers – Clause 4, are you going to repeal Clause 4?
John Smith	Well I don't think that's the heart of the matter actually, I think the important thing is the practical policies which the Labour Party will bring forward. We are a party of the mixed economy, we've always been a party of the mixed economy. . .
David Frost	Well why keep Clause 4?

John Smith	Well I don't think there's any great point in arguing about theology, I'm fairly relaxed about that. What I'm concerned about is. . . .
David Frost	Don't tell me you're a local pastor, worrying about, talking about theology. . . .
John Smith	Well I'm using it strictly in the sense of party politics in the sense, but you're quite right in the sense, one shouldn't be disparaging about theology at all and let me take that back, I apologise to theologians everywhere. But I believe the number of tasks we've got to do; let me just give three areas of policy which I'm very committed to. . . .
David Frost	Yes alright, you do that. . . . I think you're underestimating the degree to which, though Clause 4 may not be, may not be a dead letter in your mind but it's a litmus test for people out there. Do they mean what they're saying, do they mean to modernise – why are they keeping that? I think it's a litmus test.
John Smith	Well I've never heard anybody on the doorsteps, certainly not a wavering voter saying to me 'what about Clause 4?' Have you tidied that up yet? . . . I don't really think that is where the matter. . . .
David Frost	Alright come back to your three points.

Later that year in his Robert Kennedy memorial speech Smith gave a reminder that the Clause 4 which was being discussed was actually Clause 4, Part IV and that the whole Clause contained a great deal more than just public ownership:

The post war Labour government and, in particular, its distinguished Foreign Secretary, Ernest Bevin, played a critical role in its foundation. In fact the Labour Party is the only major political party in Britain that includes support for the United Nations in its constitutional objectives. It appears in a clause which is usually discussed by political pundits who have little idea of its real content. It is clause four of the party constitution. So the next time some worthy commentator calls for the abolition of clause four perhaps they would like to read it first.

Re-inventing the United Nations, pp. 230–241

The period at the Privy Council office, the prelude to the major, though short-lived, job as Secretary of State for Trade, was about managing the party. With no overall majority and governing through a pact with the Liberals, Smith was in the frontline of the experiment in virtual coalition that characterised the end days of the Callaghan government. This combination of ministerial experience was deep in the vein of mid-1970s politics. It was about the state's management and exploitation of a primary manufacturing industry and it was about the political management of a party firing the opening shots in a civil war that was to almost destroy it. Smith emerged with an enhanced reputation from both sorts of bruising encounters but he did not have time to push himself straight into the front rank of the Labour Party. This was, in many ways a blessing. It was Roy Hattersley who emerged as the leading figure on the right of the party that argued against the schism that was to come.

Smith became almost invisible for a time, speaking less in the House of Commons during the 1979–83 sessions than in previous or subsequent ones and taking more cases in the Scottish courts. No one, it is said, even bothered to ask him if he wanted to join the SDP. To say that it was the haemorrhaging of talent to the SDP that allowed Smith to become the leader of the centre and right of the party is to take the defector's own estimation of their importance in the Labour Party, rather than the reality. Roy Jenkins was out of British politics at the European Commission; the SDP an unexpected Indian summer. Bill Rodgers was never going to be a leader of the Labour Party though perhaps he was a future Home Secretary and the rest of the defectors were made up mainly of those that had already finished the active part of their political careers but wanted to give the left of the Labour Party a bloody nose. Then there were the Owenites who really believed that the political space existed for a new political party. Owen himself had virtually no political base in the Labour Party and certainly not in the trade unions, he was highly unlikely to have become a leader of the Labour Party and for him the SDP was a vehicle to a political future.

Shirley Williams was the biggest loss to the Labour Party in political and electoral terms and she might have been the one figure to have beaten Smith in a leadership election when the party wanted a return to the centre right. Whatever the speculation, the fact remains that Smith did not owe his rise to the flight of the social democrats, he was already in place and aside from Williams, they were not his main competition. What is more surprising is that his rise to a leading position in the party after 1981–2 took so much longer than that of Roy Hattersley. His public image was not as well advanced as the members of the gang of four or Hattersley or Denis Healey, but in the PLP and the Trade Union movement, he was a well known and well respected figure. It was under the leadership of Neil Kinnock that Smith became a star performer. Firstly, he had a series of shadow briefs in which he dominated the opposition's attack on the Conservative government from the House of Commons, most effectively of all during the Westland debates but also regularly on the economy (on Westland see *Westland plc*, pp. 34–40 and on the economy see *The Market Is Not Enough,* and *Everyone Needs Good Neighbours,* pp. 76-86 and pp. 86-99). Second, the new style of continuous campaigning forced Smith to get to know the Labour Party in the country better than he had done before (see *The Critique of Thatcherism*).

As the Thatcher governments unfolded, Smith came increasingly into the political limelight. As one the few former Minsters still in the House he commanded respect, but he was also increasingly effective in the critique of Thatcherism that he offered. He had never been a nationaliser but he was the creator of a successful public enterprise and his conviction was that the state could be an enabler, especially in the manufacturing sector.

A huge part of the Labour Party's critique of Thatcherism was that monetarism and the deregulation of the British economy had a disproportionate impact on the manufacturing sector compared to other sectors of the economy, and that manufacturing jobs were in some sense real jobs. Over and over again Smith tried to link a necessary readjustment of Labour's vision of political economy to the rapidly changing world economy. A recurrent theme was technology. In 1986 he stated that 'new technology is significant precisely because it can be applied to established industries like steel, textiles and motor cars, not simply to obvious high technology products like computers. The question is not whether an industry is 'sunrise' or 'sunset' but whether it can be renewed or not.' He also defended the notion of planning, 'A Labour Government would require a greatly strengthened planning organisation on the NEDO model to be the fulcrum of communication and implementation of industrial policy.' (*An Industrial Strategy for Britain*, pp. 40–53)

In his Macintosh memorial lecture he pulled all the threads of his approach together: 'I wish to argue the case that prosperity, broadly defined as a steadily increasing standard of living in an efficient and productive economy, is not only consistent with a socially just and caring society, but that in an intelligently organised community, prosperity and social justice mutually reinforce each other.' But, he argued the state must enable this prosperity to properly directed. 'I argue therefore that if we truly wish the better society, we must on the Left, give more attention than in the past to the business of growth, of efficiency, of economic progress. We must be prepared to be engaged in a positive sum game in which a greater cake is created, the more equitable division of which can be more effectively achieved. . . .The Labour Party must produce policies which convince voters that their own prosperity depends on a government which takes active responsibility to promote a strong economy and that their own security – and that of their families – is best advanced by a government which works for the welfare of the whole community' (*The Eighth John Mackintosh Lecture*, pp. 53–76). Or as he put it in his first speech as leader, 'I say to the people of this country – it is right that we are ambitious for ourselves and our children. It is right that we should aspire for better lives and a better Britain. But let the ambition and the aspiration of our people be matched by the commitment and action of their government' (*A Commitment to Change*, pp. 176–167).

His sharpest learning curve was over constitutional reform. He had initially been resistant to the notion of changes in the constitutional balance of power, in part because of his disdain for Scottish nationalists whom he saw as irresponsible. His experience as the Minister carrying the main parliamentary load of the Scottish and Welsh devolution legislation in the 1970s, gradually changed his mind. From this beginning the long years of Thatcherism took him further in an analysis of politics that questioned the nature of our democracy. He became more and more concerned with the concentration of power by the Thatcher governments, the abuse of government communication for political purposes and the cronyism of Tory politics and business. Some passages in the speeches which deal with constitutional reform and standards in public life, will make uncomfortable reading for the present government. For example in 1992 Smith attacked the creation of new *ad hoc* bodies which were being 'instituted to perform functions which displace democratically elected local authorities. And on these – and the whole host of other bodies in respect of which Ministers have powers of appointment – this government has placed its own partisan nominees. The purpose of course is to strengthen the range and power of central government. But it gravely weakens the plurality and diversity of our national life, if it is necessary to be a partisan adherent of the ruling party to be considered for appointment' (*Reforming Our Democracy*, pp. 176–188 and see also *The Standards and Practises of Government*, pp. 202–212).

Smith's economic vision and his adherence to the cause of constitutional reform were components of a political philosophy that put people ahead of ideas or institutions. One of his favourite phrases, was from Tawney, 'the extra-ordinary potential of ordinary people'. This highlights one of his major objections to the philosophy of the new right which he summed up in one of his most important speeches, the Tawney memorial lecture in 1993: 'The fundamental flaw in the individualism of the classical writers, and their modern counterparts in today's Conservative Party, is, I believe, their assumption that human beings conduct their lives on the basis of self-interested decisions taken in radical isolation from others. This thesis grotesquely ignores the intrinsically social nature of human beings and fails to recognize the capabilities that all people have to act in response to commitments and beliefs that clearly transcend any narrow calculation of personal advantage . . . the goal of individual freedom and the value of society, which we advocate as democratic socialists, is a theory of sustained intellectual force. When tested in the experience of humanity it can be found to be a better explanation of the lives and purposes of men and women than its rivals on the laissez-faire Right or the Marxist Left.' He rejected these reductionist characterisations of human potential and the eloquence and force of that rejection eventually carried him to the leadership of the Labour Party.

He was Leader of the Labour Party for just under two years. A very short time to arrive at a judgement on his performance. The main measure we have is popularity and on this measure his period as Leader must rank as one of the most successful since records began. Each month Gallup polls peoples opinion on voting intention and on the performance of the PM and the Leader of the Opposition. These are Smith's ratings in full:

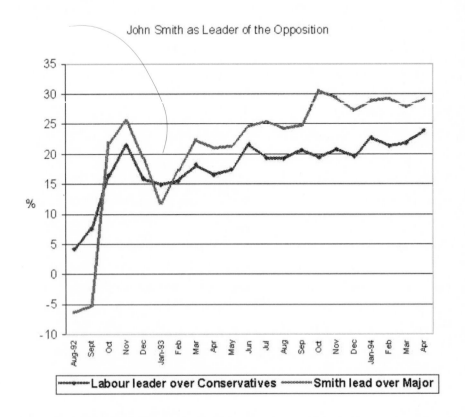

John Smith as Leader of the Opposition

Source: figures from David Butler, *British Political Facts, 1900-2000*, Macmillan, 2000, pp 277-278

The Labour Party began its long domination of the Conservatives in the opinion polls under the leadership of John Smith. Smith himself often ran a little ahead of his party and recorded quite extraordinary levels of approval, especially in comparison with John Major. The key to the ascendancy that John Smith enjoyed over John Major was consistency. One of the political strengths of Thatcherism had been its ability to force the political agenda into terms which it set and to have an easily understood response to almost every political situation. People generally knew where they were with Mrs Thatcher and her governments and surety was often mistaken for political competence. The Major government frequently appeared clueless because it did not have a consistent or well thought out rhetoric. Major's attempts to develop one, in for example the Back to Basics policy or the warm beer speech, backfired with even the core Conservative vote. In these circumstances Smith appeared not only a safe pair of hands but a conviction politician. What comes across over and over again in these speeches is the consistency of outlook and the confidence with which ideas and policies nurtured over time are communicated. It was a quieter kind of conviction politics than Thatcher's and it was often dressed in the language of consensus, but on all the major questions which faced Britain and on the central elements of Labour's reform programme, Smith could claim to have held settled opinions for a minimum of 20 years. In contrast, on key macroeconomic questions, on devolution, on the EEC and on the bomb, Neil Kinnock had had to go through very public conversions. The mantle of conviction politics, which is really a highly effective way of generating confidence by appearing competent, passed from the Conservatives to Labour as it passed from Margaret Thatcher to John Smith.

In the preparation of this collection of speeches I have read ove half a million words spoken and written by the late John Smith. In life, Smith was sometimes dismissed as merely a safe pair of hands, an unexciting politician, a likeable caricature of the conservative Scottish bank manager. He was sometimes assessed as being the beneficiary of the exodus from the Labour Party of the real talent on the centre right to the SDP. He was sometimes equated with his main political opponent as leader, John Major. Two grey men for a grey era. In death he is seen by some as simply a prelude to the main event, the leadership of Tony Blair.

I hope this collection of speeches puts paid to these views. Caution should not, in John Smith's case, be mistaken for a lack of radical ambition. Political luck and timing were based on loyalty and competence. And grey is the last colour that comes to mind when one considers the basis of his political philosophy. That basis was, in my view, optimism. In his own phrase, his were a politics of democratic optimism. In this, as in many other things, John Smith was a triumphantly unfashionable politician.

We are often told that we live in late capitalism. That these are postmodern times. If so, Smith was the last modernist. He had a faith in action, he had a faith in people and in the institutions of Britain and the European Union, that was based on a resilient and hard headed optimism about our potential to improve our country and our world. His life and career were a triumph of substance over style, content over packaging and consistency over fashion.

BRIAN BRIVATI

Muswell Hill
August 2000

PART ONE

The Early Years

INTRODUCTION

John Smith was elected to Parliament for the safe Labour seat of North Lanarkshire in June 1970. He served his political apprenticeship in the small world of Scottish Labour politics and at the Scottish bar. The seat had been Peggy Herbison's, a Gaitskellite loyalist who had been Minister for Pensions in Harold Wilson's government. Herbison passed the safe seat on to Smith who joined the slowly diminishing ranks of right and centre MPs selected after the 1966 general election. He kept rather quiet in his first couple of years in Parliament, asking questions and getting the feel of the place. He got his Maiden Speech out of the way relatively early and successfully, without making any discernable impact.

Family Income

Hansard, 10 November 1970

The Heath government had been elected on a manifesto which promised a new direction in a range of policy areas. Their reform programme was extensive and they had planned to try and tackle some of the issues relating to welfare reform which had been debated through the 1960s. In the debate on one of these measures, Family Income and Supplements Bill, John Smith made his Parliamentary debut. It was a small but significant area of policy, important in his constituency and well suited to a Maiden speaker who is not interested in making a splash. John Smith rose at 5.18pm on 10 November 1970 to speak.

The hon. Gentleman the Member for Birmingham, Perry Barr (Mr Kinsey) spoke of the trepidation which he felt in making his maiden speech. I share that trepidation and can only hope that my contribution will be as assured and as confident as his was.

It is customary for a new Member to refer to his predecessor, and I feel a special obligation to do so because my predecessor was a person uniquely respected both in the House and outside. For 25 years, Miss Margaret Herbison served the constituency of Lanarkshire, North with dignity and found great acceptance both as Member and as Minister among her constituents. She referred to them throughout her long period as a Member of Parliament as her 'own people', and this they certainly were. She served the nation, first, as a junior Minister at the Scottish Office in the post-war Labour Government, and in the last Labour Administration as Minister of Pensions and National Insurance, or Minister of Social Security, as her Department later became. Finally, having resigned from Ministerial office, she served the House as Chairman of the Select Committee on Overseas Aid.

Miss Herbison's career, which covered interests stretching from her native Lanarkshire to the furthest corners of the world, was motivated by the compassion which she felt for her fellow citizens. She recently completed a distinguished period of office as Lord High Commissioner of the General Assembly of the Church of Scotland. Hon. Members will understand the diffidence which I feel in attempting to follow in the footsteps of so fine a predecessor.

I am aware, particularly in this debate, that when Mss Herbison was Minister of Social Security she provided for one of the largest extensions of our welfare services in Britain's history. It is appropriate when considering the proposals in the Bill now before us to remember the massive extensions which were made by her and by the then Labour Government, as compared with the proposals which we are now debating.

The first and most serious criticism which, I feel, must be made of the Government's proposal is directed to the amount involved, a mere £7 million to be distributed to the working poor. That sum should be regarded as insufficient in itself, but in addition one has to bear in mind how unfavourably it compares with the £30 million promised by the Conservative Party before the election.

If a convincing demonstration were required that it is a very small sum, recourse might be had to the Speenhamland system referred to by the Secretary of State and my hon. Friend the Member for Hitchin (Mrs Shirley Williams). *The Pelican History of England in the 19th Century* notes on page 15 that in 1818, the peak year for poor relief under the Speenhamland system, the sum spent amounted to £8 million. So in 1818 the system of relieving the working poor cost £1 million more than a Conservative Administration propose to spend in 1970. That is a statistic that the Secretary of State should bear in mind when he considers how generous he is to the present day poor.

Another argument used by hon. Members opposite to justify the means-testing approach of the Bill is that they believe in selectivity in seeking out areas of need and bringing help to them. We on this side of the House find it difficult to accept that they are genuine in that desire. If in the public expenditure package, all the charges for school meals, health services and dental services and the like had been given to other areas of need, we might be impressed by the selectivity approach. But what happened was that the sum collected from the relatively poor was included in the £350 million dispensed to the relatively well-off. It seems to us that the Conservative Party is committed to selectivity upwards in giving money to the income tax payer, and is not committed to selectivity downwards in seeking out need throughout the community.

The Secretary of State referred with approval to an article in last week's *New Statesman* by Professor Brian Abel Smith. He should also remember another part of that article, where the author pointed out that the Conservative Party was likely to redeem its election pledge to allow children's income to be aggregated with that of the parents, which would mean that £25 million was likely to be given back to the children of wealthy parents. I fancy that when the Conservative Party redeems that election pledge there will be very few administrative difficulties in the way of its fulfilment. It is worth bearing in mind that we are proposing to dispense £7 million to the whole of the working poor of this country and at the same time the Government will probably dispense £25 million to the children of the wealthy and the much better-off.

Those points reinforce the feeling on this side of the House that the Bill is a niggardly attempt to solve a gigantic problem. We are not impressed by the sincerity of the Government's desire to help the poor in view of the small amount they are prepared to allocate, especially when we compare it with the large sums the Government have seen fit to dispense to other much better-off sections of the population.

Basically, for those reasons, we regard the Bill more as a piece of window dressing on the part of the Conservative Government than a real and lasting attempt to solve the problems of poverty. I thank the House for according me the courtesy of listening to my maiden speech.

The United Kingdom and the European Communities

Hansard, 26 July 1971

John Smith was not a natural rebel. He did not make a posture of his opposition to the line being taken by the Labour Party when Heath's government was pushing for membership of the European Economic Community but he voted with his conscience. He did not speak in the actual debate which preceded the vote on the membership in which 69 Labour MPs defied a three line whip to support the government, but had laid out his position in an earlier debate in July 1971.

I do not wish to follow the line taken by the hon. Member for Westbury (Mr Walters). I hope that he will forgive me if I refer briefly to the powerful speech of my hon. Friend the Member for Llanelly (Mr Denzil Davies), who argued against entry from the regional development point of view. Like my hon. Friend, I represent a constituency in a development area. If I thought that my hon. Friend's gloomy prediction for the future of the development areas would result from entry into the Community I should be a devoted opponent of entry, because any hon. Member whose constituency was to be affected in the vital way suggested by my hon. Friend would have to argue against going in.

Having gone into the matter as carefully as I can, because of the special responsibility which I, as a Member representing a development area, have, I am convinced that my hon. Friend's prediction is not likely to be correct, and I think that that was foreshadowed by the inexact example which he took from the action of the Commission, when he found that the Commission was acting against indiscriminate aid to a country, rather than to a region.

The answer to the problem about regional development is to be found in the activities that have taken place within the Six, some of them using techniques which I wish this Government or their predecessors had used. They demonstrate that it is possible to have a vigorous development policy within the EEC. We have been given examples of what has happened in Italy, in Belgium and in France. They do not exactly parallel what is going on in this country, but they indicate that the attitude of the Commission is one of permissiveness towards regional development policies carried out by individual countries, and that was the conclusion at which the previous Government arrived. It was the conclusion given expression to by the Leader of the Opposition in the debate on entry in May, 1967, and I do not think that very much has changed since then in the Commission's attitude to regional development.

The other argument that is used – and it was deployed by my hon. Friend the Member for Llanelly – is that of the fear about the free flow of capital. There is a feeling among many people that if there is free flow of capital the regional development areas will inevitably suffer. I do not take such a pessimistic view of the future. One reason which prompts me to take a more optimistic view is that it has been clear, particularly in relation to Scotland, that a good deal of the investment that has come in has come from outside the United Kingdom. If the development areas in Scotland had been dependent simply on United Kingdom investment, we should have had very little in the way of investment. We have attracted investment from outside, from Europe and from America. It is that sort of investment that has kept us going, and I think that in future we shall be able to attract investment on that scale.

One thing that I know for certain is that, unless the United Kingdom's general economy prospers, there is no hope for the development areas. I say that because of the difficulties that we are facing in Scotland. They result not from the fact that we do not have a set of tools for a regional policy to bite into the problem, but because there is not a generally strong economy to back it up and provide the mobile industry that is missing. I think that in this sense the development areas are even more dependent than other areas upon the general economic health of the community.

I cannot see how it is possible for industry to go to Scotland or to Wales unless there is industrial expansion in the whole country. Industry does not grow out of the ground of its own accord. It comes because of a willingness to invest somewhere in the United Kingdom. It is only if there is a substantial rate of growth in the general United Kingdom economy that one gets growth in the development areas, and that is one of the main reasons why we need to go into the EEC.

The question of economic growth is one which can be argued from both sides. At bottom this is a question of sovereignty, and many hon. Members are reluctant to give up some of the sovereignty which is held dear in this country. I do not take that view, and if there is a diminution of sovereignty, as I think there is, in going into the Community, I am willing to face that. A sovereignty which is not real is not worth having.

There was an interesting interlude at the end of the speech of my right hon. Friend the Member for Stepney (Mr Shore) when he referred to the speech of my right hon. Friend the Member for Birmingham, Stechford (Mr Roy Jenkins), who had talked about sitting outside meetings of international monetary bodies in Europe waiting until the Six made up their minds. My right hon. Friend the Member for Stepney asked whether he should have been there at all. I am sure that my right hon. Friend the Member for Stechford would have been happy not to be there, but he had to be there, waiting in an anteroom even when we were outside Europe, because decisions of great consequence to us were being taken. A country is not in a position to display effective national sovereignty in a situation like that. Ministers are in a better position to secure national interests and bolster up the country's sovereignty when they are inside the conference room, not waiting outside.

The key question which we as a nation and Europe will have to face is how best to use the advantages of technology. I am convinced that we shall never be able to get investment on the scale required to build up the necessary technologies on a nation-state basis, or at least on a nation-state of the size of this country. It will have to be done on a European basis.

That is something hon. Members on both sides can agree, whether, Conservatives arguing for entry for Conservative aims, Liberals arguing for entry for Liberal aims, or Socialists arguing for entry for Socialist aims. AR will agree on the necessity to obtain the advantages of technology, and, in my view, they will not be achieved unless we have the enlarged Common Market. It would, of course, be possible if we were not in the EEC. for Governments to make *ad hoc* agreements about various technical developments, like military aircraft, but they are only likely to be in the areas where the Governments are purchasers and consumers, rather than more general areas where we shall have to find our own customers throughout Europe and the rest of the world. We shall need to do it on a European scale.

Having created that technology on a European scale we shall need to devise institutions to deal with it. Here, I come to the point raised by my hon. Friend the Member for Cardigan (Mr Elystan Morgan). I cannot see how it will be possible for us to control the international companies that will increasingly dominate the economic scene if we are all working within a nation-state framework. Some international companies already have assets larger than those of many of the nation-states of the world. They can take their decisions on an international basis and steer their industry away from one area to another because they dislike the policy of a particular Government. A theoretical national sovereignty which can be flouted by the economic power of international companies is a national sovereignty which is not apt to meet the real problems a nation faces.

I am willing to give us some national sovereignty to gain a sovereignty which will be able to do something about controlling the international companies of the future. If we create a technology but cannot control it we shall not have achieved very much in the way of political and economic development. The institutions that can control it are in the EEC The Commission, derided so much, can be the instrument to stand up to and control the international companies. That is the difference between a free trade area and the EEC The EEC is not just a free trade area but has Community institutions, two of which could do the job – the Commission, and the European Parliament – at a later stage.

This is a fundamental argument about entering Europe. It is one which I sincerely put, not only because I am concerned about the problems of industry in relation to politics but, more important, because as a democratic socialist I believe that the fundamental of democratic socialism is that economic forces must somehow be brought under popular control and be fashioned towards social and political ends which the people determine. If we do not enter Europe we shall not be in a position to control them and achieve those economic, social and political ends which we on this side hold among our main political objectives.

I have strayed a little far beyond the terms of entry but some of the long-term principles are perhaps the most important aspects of the debate. Younger Members in particular should stress those long-term objectives when we are discussing this vital issue. I hope that when we look back in 10, 20, 30 or 40 years' time and some of us may be lucky enough still to be in the House then we shall recall some of the fears expressed and wonder how they could have existed when we see the real achievements of the Europe we shall have helped to build.

In Defence of Multilateralism

Hansard, 2 July 1974

Smith was not a Gaitskellite on Europe but he was on the bomb. In July 1974, following a major defence review, the House of Commons debated defence and Smith

made a politically brave speech, given the direction of the PLP at the time, in which he
attacked the unilateralist speech of his colleague, Robin Cook, and supported the
government's nuclear tests.

I should like to mention two matters which have concerned hon. Members in the debate. One is the defence review and the other is the recent nuclear test.

Regarding the defence review, we have heard, by and large, a difference of opinion between hon. Gentlemen opposite, who do not agree with any cuts in or adjustment of our defence responsibilities, and hon. Members on this side of the House who suggest that we should cut our defence cloth to meet our current economic situation. I think the latter proposition must be indisputable. The hon. Member for Shoreham (Mr Luce) said that, instead of cutting our defence responsibilities to the proportion of gross national products which other countries in Western Europe adopt, we ought to create more wealth, but there is little prospect in any country in Western Europe, let alone in ours, of creating more wealth in the next two or three years. It would be intolerable to make reductions of expenditure in social services without seriously considering whether we can have some economies in defence.

There are the hawks who think that no cuts should be made and the doves who want to make cuts for the sake of cuts. I do not know what species of bird is halfway between a hawk and a dove, but I fancy the posture of that bird. We have to take our defence responsibilities seriously, but, on the other hand, we must have regard for our economic situation. That is the approach on which the Government have embarked, and they are right to make a long-term sensible survey of the matter rather than short term, piecemeal cuts which disrupt programmes and upset defence policy.

I refer to the question of nuclear tests. My hon. Friend the Member for Edinburgh, Central (Mr Cook) advanced a number of arguments against the recent tests. He argued on the basis of a speculation which he developed and then attempted to demolish. I do not know whether the nuclear test is an attempt to make the Polaris missile into a MIRV and whether it is a test or a development. My hon. Friend was very much attracted to the possibility that it was a matter of turning it into a MIRV, but I rather suspect that he would object if it were merely a testing device, because in the closing part of his speech he advanced the argument of unilateral disarmament that has exercised us on this side of the House for a long time. But the experience of international life argues very much against that. I do not believe that nuclear disarmament by Britain would enhance our security or lead others to follow suit. I do not believe that the Russians or Americans would disarm, except by mutual agreement, and it is clear that the Chinese will not disarm in the present situation, and there is not much chance of France being likely to disarm following our example.

Whatever the arguments about the timing of the recent test, it is clear that there were differences between that test and those carried out by India, France and China. I understand the objection to a nuclear test which centres on pollution of the atmosphere. I particularly appreciate that tests by France, especially in the area in which they are carried out, can cause a hazard to neighbouring countries, particularly Commonwealth countries. We were right to protest against atmospheric tests. It is to be regretted that France is not a party to the treaty prohibiting atmospheric tests.

China has also been a great offender in this regard and the matter is grave so far as India is concerned, because it involves a spread of nuclear weapons. But I do not believe that the Indian Government would move one way or the other if Britain went in for unilateral nuclear disarmament. There is no evidence that unilateral nuclear disarmament by this country would affect the policies of other countries. If there were such evidence many people would no doubt march to Aldermaston, or to its modern equivalent.

However, if we have nuclear weapons, and they are part of our defence system, they must be kept in working order. There is not much point in having them if we do not test them, develop them and keep them in a credible state of readiness. We would have the worst of both worlds if we did not test them and keep them in a state of readiness. If we did not do that it would be better to give them up altogether. It would be a hopeless situation to have nuclear weapons but not to test them. I would not, in those circumstances, criticise the Government over our recent nuclear test.

The Petroleum and Submarine Pipe Lines Bill

Hansard 7 July 1975

When Wilson returned to government after the October 1974 election, Smith became Under Secretary of State at Energy, the newest department in Whitehall. The global impact of the energy crisis was still very much dominating politics and the discovery of North Sea oil and the beginnings of its commercial exploitation were vital political issues nationally, and most especially in Scotland. Smith was appointed to this key and highly technical job and was promoted to be Minister of State in 1975. His first major piece of legislation was the Petroleum and Submarine Pipe Lines Bill which would create the British National Oil Corporation. This was a highly technical matter which did not lead itself to oratory. For two months the Bill languished in committee before Smith took it to the floor of the House to ask for a guillotine. This speech is reproduced here to give a flavour of the long debates and the job of Smith as Minister at Energy. While not a masterpiece of speech making or eloquence it is actually representative of the bulk of the speeches made by govern-ment ministers the majority of the time and it also gives a clear indication of the pride Smith took in creating a public enterprise.

We come to the end of what has been an unusually good humoured and relaxed debate on a timetable motion. My right hon. Friend the Secretary of State set the tone for the debate by the way in which he proposed the motion. It has been not accusation and counter-accusation, but serious consideration of an important matter.

Perhaps I should say at the very start that the Government propose to accept the amendment of my hon. Friend the Member for Lewisham, West (Mr Price).

In this short debate we have had an opportunity to consider the wider question of how Parliament goes about its business. In Committee, when we had a short discussion about the Government's decision to move towards a guillotine motion, I was struck by how many Members on both sides of the Committee took the opportunity to express their dissatisfaction with the way in which Standing Committees operated and the way in which Parliament went about its business in Committee. This discussion has continued tonight and many hon. Members in all quarters of the House have taken the opportunity to express their dissatisfaction with the way in which Parliament presently organises itself.

My hon. Friend the Member for Bedwellty (Mr Kinnock), in a speech of particular note, expressed with clarity and conviction his feeling that we had to think very carefully about altering our procedures. That was echoed by my hon. Friends the Members for West Houghton (Mr Stott) and Leeds, West (Mr Dean) and by the hon. Member for Ross and Cromarty (Mr Gray), who unfortunately, had to make a good speech from the back benches, but who has now been restored to favour on the Front Bench that he generally graces. He said that he had no objection in principle to timetable motions – a thought that has occurred in many speeches.

It would not be possible for any party that has held office in this country to object to timetable motions in principle, because it would have behind it a record of its own activities when in office. That applies to my own party as well as to the Conservative Party, there is a growing conviction that to make too much fuss about a timetable is indulging in a certain amount of hypocrisy. I must say, to be fair to the right hon. Member for Yeovil (Mr Peyton), that we got a slight whiff of grapeshot when he expressed his opposition in almost uncharacteristically moderate terms.

This has been the way in which the debate has been handled. It signals the changing mood of Parliament and a much greater readiness on the part of hon. Members on both sides to question the way in which we go about our business. A welcome opportunity has been taken by right hon. and hon. Gentlemen tonight. They have seized in the best parliamentary manner on a particular matter to raise a general question.

Mr Peyton: The hon. Gentleman would be very wrong to learn from the good conduct of the Opposition lessons that his complacency is too readily teaching him.

Mr Smith: That is the first ill-humoured note that we have had in the debate so far. It is strange that we should get it from the right hon. Member for Yeovil, whose attention to Parliament is so detailed that he wandered out of the Chamber when he had finished his speech and returned only at the end of the debate, whereas other hon. Members have sat here throughout the debate. If I am to be taught any lesson in parliamentary manners, I shall require a better teacher than the right hon. Gentleman.

Mr Peyton: It has just been observed to me that that is the kind of conduct that my right hon. and hon. Friends have had to endure from the Under Secretary throughout the Committee stage of the Bill. I can assure the hon. Gentleman that he is doing his reputation no good.

Mr Smith: I should have thought that if the right hon. Gentleman were so sensitive, he would reflect that it is unusual to make the opening speech for the Opposition and then wander out of the Chamber for all the debate and return only at the end. There may be very good reasons for that – I do not know – but it is certainly unusual.

The reason for this motion is that we want to finish the Committee stage of the Bill in the House of Commons by the middle of this month so that the Bill may go to the other place and go through the procedure that is required there.

It is a very important Bill. It sets up a new public corporation, the British National Oil Corporation, which will hold the State's share, which will be achieved through participation negotiations, and which will be available to receive a share of the licensing in future licensing rounds. It also introduces very important depletion controls in the North Sea and for the whole of our Continental Shelf. Conservative hon. Members have complained that the Government have been slow to bring forward this measure given that they announced certain basic items in their policy in July 1974. Of course, as those Members who have served in Committee will know, it is a complex and detailed Bill. There was a great deal which the Government had to do and a great deal of precise legislation which had to be formulated.

I am sure that hon. Members who have not served in Committee, and who perhaps have not watched developments in this area with great care, will be surprised to know that the Government inherited a situation in which there were no depletion controls over the exploitation of the North Sea. We were told by the right hon. Member for Wanstead and Woodford (Mr Jenkin) in his closing sentences that North Sea oil is this country's lifeline. If it is such an important part of our economic future – and I accept that it is – it is surprising that there should be no power given to the Government regarding the rate at which such an important asset should be used. However, we inherited that deficiency and we intend to put it right by means of the Bill.

I find it surprising that, although the Opposition spent two years in Government reviewing North Sea oil policy, we inherited no taxation proposals, no proposals for participation and no proposals for depletion. One of the things that makes me wonder about the genuineness of some Conservative opposition to the Bill is the Opposition's refusal to rule out participation as a policy. It seems that they would adopt it themselves in future licensing rounds. We know that every producer country, with the exception of the United States, adopts a policy of participation towards the exploitation of offshore oil. Therefore, the Government have not devised a unique policy. It is a policy which has found acceptance in many countries throughout the world.

The great silence of the Conservative Party as regards future licensing rounds and whether it would adopt participation is interesting. Right wing Governments in other countries have adopted it. There is a certain amount of suspicion as to the genuineness of the opposition to some parts of the Bill.

The Labour Party was committed to the Bill in two General Elections. We have made it the basis of our policy for a long time. We believe that it is vital that sufficient public control over such a vital asset as offshore oil, which will be of such great importance to the nation's future, plays an important part in our legislation. That must be so when we are dealing with fossil fuels which can be used only once. It is essential that the Government have proper controls over their use, otherwise, at an important period in their development, we might fritter away the assets with which this country has fortunately been endowed.

It cannot be argued that this is not an important Bill. It features an important part of the Government's legislative programme. We have already had very full discussion in Committee on the setting up of the British National Oil Corporation. I do not believe that the Opposition can say that they have not had a good chance to discuss the matter in detail. However, we need to consider the rest of the Bill as well. It is for those reasons that the Government put forward this motion.

I hope that the House will be wise enough to accept the amendment tabled by my hon. Friend the Member for Lewisham, West and the main motion so that we can bring consideration of the Bill to an end during the course of this Session, and so that we can see established very soon Britain's own national oil company.

Scotland Bill

Hansard, 31 January 1978

Smith was moved in April 1976 to be Minister of State in the Privy Council office under Michael Foot. The massive debate on the Scottish and Welsh Devolution Bills took up a great chunk of parliamentary time during the 1974–79 parliaments. There were debates on the nature of the parliaments to be created in the two countries, debates on the referenda to be held and debates on the way these institutions would impact on virtually every aspect of public life. Smith carried the weight of ministerial responsibility for the passage of these substantial pieces of legislation. One of the key questions raised by the legislation was the status of Scottish MPs with respect to questions affecting English constituencies and vice versa after there was a Scottish Parliament. In this speech Smith sets out to answer the so-called West Lothian question and admits that he had changed his mind about the constitution. The debate was on a new clause suggested by the Conservative Party to refer the question of devolution to a constitutional convention.

I do not know why the hon. Member for Cleveland and Whitby (Mr Brittan) was so anxious not to answer a question from his hon. and learned Friend the Member for Kinross and West Perthshire (Mr Fairbairn), who tried throughout the hon. Member's speech to catch his eye. If the hon. and learned Gentleman wishes to ask the question of me, I shall be very glad to answer it.

Mr Fairbaim: I shall wait until the Minister has made a complete fool of himself and then take up his invitation.

Mr Smith: I cannot promise to oblige the hon. and learned Gentleman, or even to try to do so, but he has tried to intervene so persistently that I offer my condolences. I give an absolute assurance that if he seeks to intervene during my speech, I shall be glad to give way.

The new clause was moved by the right hon. Member for Cambridgeshire (Mr Pym). He told us first – and his speech was amplified in this regard by the hon. Member for Cleveland and Whitby – that he did not think that there was a case for reducing the number of Scottish Members of Parliament in the present pre-devolution situation. Throughout the debate some of his hon. Friends have disagreed with that. But we seem now to have it crystal clear that the Conservative Party does not see any case for a reduction in the number of Scottish Members of Parliament on the present basis – that is, before devolution is carried through.

I must confess that I was not always entirely clear about that, but I am clear about it now because it has been put forward so clearly – even though the hon. Member for Aylesbury (Mr Raison) differed from that view perhaps. This concept has made great progress during the debate. The second point – this is where we come to the nub of the new clause – is what would be the situation regarding Scottish representation after devolution? Some hon. Members, including the hon. Member for

Edinburgh, Pentlands (Mr Rifkind), in a very interesting speech, said that they thought that there was not a case for any reduction. Other hon. Members – more from English constituencies than from Scottish constituencies represented by the Conservative Party – tended to argue that there was a case for reducing the number of Members of the United Kingdom Parliament coming from Scottish constituencies.

Members of the Conservative Front Bench say that they do not know whether there is a case for reducing the number after devolution and that they do not know what the policy should be, so we need, in the words of the hon. Member for Cleveland and Whitby, an alternative forum. That alternative forum is the Speaker's Conference, into which the Conservatives will go without any idea of what they want to suggest and from which they wish to emerge with an agreed policy for all concerned. It is rather like the constitutional conference idea of the right hon. Member for Cambridgeshire which he puts forward whenever he is asked for his policy on devolution, because we have two varieties offered at present. One is non-legislative, non-Executive devolution, on the Douglas-Home lines, as put forward by the hon. Member for Pentlands. I do not think that it amounts to very much by way of devolution, but I can understand the argument for that. The other is that there ought to be a constitutional conference in which all other parties get together to provide a policy for the Conservative Party. I do not know whether that is the most constructive way to go about it.

Before developing the argument fully, and because I may forget to do, so, I want to refer to a question put to me by my hon. Friend the Member for Liverpool, Walton (Mr Heffer) in regard to a quotation in a speech of mine at a conference on the Labour Party in Scotland when we as a party were discussing the various alternatives to devolution. Frankly, I have changed my mind from the proposition that I advanced then. I shall give the reasons. Perhaps my hon. Friend will understand them more clearly than Opposition Members.

First, on the question of 71 Members of Parliament, it is essential that they be retained post-devolution, for two reasons above all. First, this Parliament will remain the only sovereign Parliament. It will have the override powers as well as the inherent power to legislate. It can change the devolution Act itself. Second, the devolution scheme does not contain tax-raising powers, and the conferring of money on the Scottish Assembly remains a matter for Westminster. I have come to the view that it is right that it should remain a matter for Westminster. But when these two matters – sovereignty and taxation – are reserved at Westminster, I believe that it is right that there should be 71 Members of Parliament.

The role of the Secretary of State post-devolution will be different from his present role. As is known, he is an omnibus Minister with responsibility for a wide range of functions. We propose to retain the Secretary of State, but he will have a more limited role than he has now He will be concerned with economic matters, agriculture and other matters, such as the police, but not with education housing, health and some of his present major concerns.

I have come to the conclusion that it is desirable to have a Secretary of State responsible for the decentralised, not devolved, functions that remain. That view was strengthened by the Government's decision to transfer some responsibility for regional development policy from the Department of Industry to the Secretary of State.

From time to time we all change our minds over different aspects. My hon. Friend the Member for West Lothian (Mr Dalyell) and I know that to be true. My hon. Friend was right to ask for an explanation. I hope that he finds my explanation, with which he may not agree, at least logical in its development.

Mr Fairbairn: I trust that this is a suitable moment at which to take up the generous offer that the Minister made to me to intervene. The fact is that Scotland will have to face a number of brutal realities. Devolution is not just an extra present. People must understand that if they want devolution they will have to forgo the powers that come from here, the number of Members who will go from this place and the tax and other benefits that go to individuals in the United Kingdom. It is utterly dishonest to pretend that the Minister has changed his mind. He must explain to the people of Scotland, if devolution is the round-about that they choose, the disadvantages that they must accept to obtain the pretended advantages that those on the Scottish National Party Bench and those on the Government benches imagine they will gain by devolution.

Mr Smith: The hon. and learned Gentleman raised a number of issues in that intervention. One was that there had to be some reduction in Westminster representation as the price of devolution. I think that he is the one Scottish Conservative Member today who has made that suggestion. I think that his hon. Friends are not only wiser in argument but more prudent in being reticent in the way that they have put forward the matter. However, he is stating clearly that there should be a reduction in Scottish representation at Westminster.

The only way that we can properly deal with the value of inserting a new Clause 1 in the Bill is not to take it on the basis on which it was put forward by the right hon. Member for Cambridgeshire, who suggested that he did not have a view on the numbers or the role of Scottish Members, but, as one Conservative Member said, to take it as implicit in setting up a Speaker's Conference that there would be a suggestion for a reduction in numbers. It is unlikely that a Speaker's Conference would recommend an increase. I suppose that conceivably it might recommend the status quo.

The status quo – 71 Members – does not arise from the Boundary Commission's recommendation. It arose because Parliament guaranteed

71 Members for Scotland and the Boundary Commission had to work out the division of constituencies in Scotland on that basis. In order to make sense of the argument, we must approach it on the basis that there is an implication of a reduction. Albeit those on the Conservative Front Bench cannot bring themselves to say that, I think that is at the back of their minds, and certainly it is at the back of other hon. Members' minds. I am glad that the hon. Member for Eastleigh (Mr Price), with whom I often disagree, agrees with me on that proposition.

What is the case for a reduction? The right hon. Member for Cambridgeshire dipped his sights slightly when he implied that the number of Labour Members from Scotland was a way of imposing Socialism. We should try to argue out this matter and look at it apart from questions of party political considerations. I do trust that the right hon. Gentleman meant it seriously. But the important matter to bear in mind is that the Parliament of the United Kingdom remains the sovereign Parliament, and the people of Scotland are as entitled to be represented fully in that Parliament as people in other parts of the United Kingdom.

If there is to be a reduction in the number of Scottish Members in the United Kingdom, it should be done on the basis that Scotland is over-represented, whether or not we have devolution. But if it is done as a consequence of devolution it implies that, because this Parliament does not have day-to-day legislative responsibility for housing, education health and the other matters which are to be devolved, there is less of a case for representation in matters of trade, the economy, the taxation system, industrial relations, employment and the like. I cannot see that it is right to say that, because the range of responsibilities for which the United Kingdom Parliament remains responsible in Scotland is reduced, there should be a reduction in the number of people being represented there when such fundamental and weighty matters at the heart of a political system remain with the United Kingdom Parliament.

I must stress the importance of parliamentary sovereignty. Post-devolution we shall have devolved not sovereignty but powers which will be subject to the continuing sovereignty of Parliament. This Parliament can override decisions of the Scottish Assembly using the constitutional devices which are in the Bill. In those circumstances it seems right that full representation should come to the United Kingdom Parliament from every part of the Kingdom.

The so-called West Lothian question has been asked. It implies that there should be a logical symmetry post-devolution and that every Member of the House of Commons should be responsible for the same things. It is objected that, post-devolution, English Members, because they are Members of the House of Commons, will not be able to vote on Scottish education, housing, health, and so on. It is worth noting that the net result of devolution is that what is lost is that English Members will not be able to vote on Scottish education, housing, health and the like. I do not know how many of them will wish to have a great influence over them but that is the net effect.

I do not think that logical symmetry, which is what this argument is about, is necessary. The right hon. Member for Down, South (Mr Powell) and other hon. Members – though I doubt whether the hon. Member for Cleveland and Whitby is one of them – argue that, because we cannot have a Parliament in which every hon. Member has the same responsibilities, we can make no change at all. They say, therefore, that devolution is impossible and that we can never have in any circumstances and with any range of powers any legislative devolution because each Member of the House of Commons should have equal responsibilities.

I do not share that view. It seems to be a despairing conclusion that we can never make a constitutional change which involves legislative devolution and giving law-making powers to a body other than the House of Commons simply because of our adherence to what I describe as logical symmetry.

What I find interesting about the views of the right hon. Member for Down, South is that he is saying by implication that there can never be a devolved scheme for Northern Ireland which involves legislative devolution. I do not know whether his colleagues agree with him. I should be slightly surprised if that was the unanimous view of the United Ulster Unionist Members in this Parliament. This House devolved powers to the Stormont Parliament of Northern Ireland for 50 years. It is sometimes argued, and it is argued by the right hon. Member for Down, South (Mr Powell), that the *de minimis* rule applies to this situation, but let me remind the Committee of the position.

There were 12 Northern Ireland Members – sometimes 13 – and they were consistently from one party. They voted consistently that way in the House. Scottish Members do not arrive in this House as particularly Scottish Members. They arrive as Labour, Liberal and SNP Members. What the hon. Member for Aylesbury was driving at was the situation where the party balance in the United Kingdom might be affected by Scottish Members.

Mr Norman Tebbit: The minister seemed to be saying that there was nothing wrong in having in the House of Commons Members whose responsibilities were slightly different one from the other. The other day the Lord President of the Council said that it would be wrong if some Members who were on Select Committees had certain information, which made them slightly different from other Members. Is not there a contrast between what the Minister is saying and what the Lord President of the Council said?

Mr Smith: I did not hear what the Lord President said, so I am not in a position to compare the two statements. I do not think that there is very much connection between a Select Committee and the serious matter that we are debating – not that Select Committees are not serious. Nor do I think that it helps the discussion to draw false parallels or analogies that will not bear close examination.

Mr George Cunningham: If this proposal goes ahead, the Scottish electorate will be able to get a Scottish education policy, a Scottish housing policy, and so on, by electing a majority of its peruasion to the Scottish Assembly. Does my hon. Friend accept that that is something that will not be open to the English electorate, and that the average excess from Scotland and Wales, minus the Northern Ireland reverse direction trend, in the last four elections has been between 27 and 45 Members? Does he think that that will be borne by the English electorate in perpetuity?

Mr Smith: It is very difficult for me to answer questions on the future political situation in perpetuity; I should not be bold enough to answer on that basis. I find it difficult to predict what will happen in the foreseeable future. However, if, for the purpose of this argument the hon. Gentleman accepts that there is a genuine demand in Scotland for devolution – he disputes that, but I think there is – and if that demand is such that it is consistent with the unity of the United Kingdom and the sovereignty of Parliament, he says that the demand must not be met. He says that there must never be legislative devolution to Scotland because of the need to adhere to the logical symmetry of the present structure of the House of Commons. I think that it is such a conservative, hopeless attitude to say that we can never make constitutional changes that it does not bear close examination.

It is a good debating point to say that everything will be the same after devolution. I hope not. Devolution will make considerable differences to the constitution of this country. One of the changes is that responsibility for certain Scottish affairs will be transferred to the Assembly, although some important matters that affect Scotland will be retained in the United Kingdom Parliament.

We have made a careful division, as best we can, of the responsibilities between the Assembly and this Parliament, and we have come to the conclusion that the wisest and fairest course is to keep the full Scottish representation at the House of Commons. That is also the wisest course from the point of view of maintaining the unity of the United Kingdom, which ought to be as much the concern of Conservative Members as it genuinely is mine.

Mr Rifkind: In answer to his hon. Friend the Member for Islington, South and Finsbury (Mr Cunningham) the Minister said that it would be wrong for the Government not to respond to the genuine wish of the majority of the Scottish people for devolution. How will he respond to what might be the genuine wishes of the majority of English people who will resent the idea of Scottish and possibly Welsh Members voting on purely English domestic legislation?

Mr Smith: I do not know whether English people will resent that. Apart from anything else, it is a mistake to talk of Scottish Members voting on things. There are not Scottish and English Members of the House. We are all Members of it, and the whole House votes on certain matters.

I am told that there might be resentment. The background to the argument is that the Tory Party might continue to do badly in Scottish elections. I shall be fair and take into account the Conservatives' prediction. In 1955 in Scotland there were 35 Labour Members, 35 Tory Members and one Liberal Member. The Tory Party believes that it will be the first party in Scotland to get a majority of votes, but the catastrophic decline of the Tories to 16 Members is the biggest decline for any party in the United Kingdom.

Why did that happen and why might it continue? The hon. Member for Glasgow, Cathcart (Mr Taylor) is optimistic. He frequently tells us that the Tory Party is doing particularly well in Scotland. He says that it is on the up. Indeed, he says that it may well win the majority of seats at the next General Election. He has forecast some startling gains. In that situation there is likely to be parity between the parties and therefore no English resentment. The Tory Party must choose between the optimistic view and the pessimistic view. We must try to make the United Kingdom and its constitution work.

I reject the 'in and out' system because it is not practical politics in terms of parliamentary responsibility and administration.

I do not accept what my hon. Friend the Member for West Lothian and others say. They say that we can never have devolution – not that we cannot have this Bill, but that in no circumstances can we have devolution. They argue that it would be different if there were a federal solution because that would mean that all parts of the United Kingdom would have to express a wish for a federal system. But one part of the United Kingdom does demand devolution. My hon. Friend the Member for The Wrekin (Mr Fowler) says that Parliament will listen when the demand for Assemblies comes from the regions of England. Our judgment is that this will not happen.

My hon. Friend the Member for Islington South and Finsbury (Mr Cunningham) argues that, because the regions of England do not want to move to a devolved system, as does Scotland, Scotland should not have a change. He says that this must be done at one time. If one part of the United Kingdom wants a change, it is foolish to say that it cannot have it until everywhere else falls into line. My hon. Friend is constitutionally conservative. For a man who is so radical about the procedures of the House of Commons, he has an in-built conservatism in his attitude.

Very few people have spoken in favour of the new clause. Very few have found merit in it. I do not know why the Conservative Party was foolish enough to pick this topic.

PART TWO

The Critique of
Thatcherism

INTRODUCTION

In 1983 John Smith became Shadow Secretary of State for Trade and Industry, ahead of his main rival from the left of the party, Robin Cook. Smith had Cabinet experience in the area, was seen as a safer pair of hands and balanced the front bench team in terms of the right/left balance. He set about campaigning for the Labour leadership's policy review within the party. For the first time he began to build a party base beyond his Scottish roots and, though he was seen as a representative of the right wing of the party, his critique of Thatcherism enabled him to transcend that reductive label. He became one of Labour's big hitters.

There were two elements to his critique of Thatcherism. The first, developed in a series of policy speeches and a relentless set of meetings with the party, voters, industry and the city – stepped up even more after he became Shadow Chancellor – was an intellectual critique of neo-liberalism and a reasoned presentation of the alternative. The second was an increasingly commanding presence in the House of Commons, most obviously in a brilliant performance during the Westland debates.

It was Smith who spotted the opening that the early droplets of information over Westland might be the harbinger of a political deluge and it was he who almost wrong footed the Prime Minister, Margaret Thatcher. Her economy with the truth to the House of the Commons about what she knew and when she knew it got her off the hook in the immediate political situation but the political damage was considerable and might have been fatal. The result was the establishment of Smith as an outstanding House of Commons figure: indeed commentators speculated that

Thatcher might not have survived if it had been Smith and not Kinnock leading for the opposition.

Westland plc

Hansard, 27 January 1986

On 13 January 1986, Smith was in full swing in the Westland affair. Such Parliamentary interventions are often at their best when they are short and to the point. The sting on this day was actually in the form of Michael Heseltine's famous and apparently innocuous question:

Mr Michael Heseltine: *May I ask my right hon. and learned Friend whether the Government have received any letters from British Aerospace giving its views of the meeting?*

To which Leon Brittan replied: 'I have not received any such letter.'

While this was factually true, the letter had gone to the PM, it was a clear attempt to mislead the House. Unfortunately it was Paddy Ashdown who followed in the debate and completely missed the point. Smith did not. His interventions during the day forced Brittan to return to the House in the evening to make a personal statement, which was again rather ambiguous. Smith turned the knife further into Brittan in his reply to this but he also lifted his sights a little towards the real target, Margaret Thatcher when he goaded the government benches: 'Throughout the whole of that performance this afternoon, the Prime Minster sat in silence. She had more knowledge than any other hon. Member because she was the recipient of that letter, and, no doubt, had read it before she came across to the House of Commons. In that circumstance, why did the Prime Minister not even lean across to the Secretary of State, who was within inches of her throughout the whole debate, and correct him if he was at some stage misleading the House?' Smith marshalled the case in this first speech and forced Brittan on to the backfoot. On 27 January, he coerced a humiliated Thatcher to return over and again to the dispatch box to say that she was telling the truth:

The word will be going out from those who conduct press affairs for the Government that matters have been answered and cleared up today, and that the House of Commons and the British public can put this matter safely behind them in the confident reassurance that, perhaps at long last, the Prime Minister has come clean with the House and with the public. Let us examine what the Prime Minister told us today. It was not a great deal. First of all, she told us that the first she discovered of the Secretary of State for Trade and Industry's behaviour in the matter was at the end of the inquiry. Secondly, she told us that some hours after the leak she was told in general terms of her office's involvement. Thirdly, she told us how the inquiry came to be instituted.

I cannot see how the addition of these small pieces of information, interesting though they are, changes the situation from last Thursday, when the Prime Minister was floundering in her inability to answer these questions. Now, suddenly, we are told that it has all been cleared up. It has not all been cleared up and the question that will be asked again and again is a very simple one. It is: before the Prime Minister decided to institute the bogus inquiry into the leak – bogus is what we now know it was – did she know about any of the involvement of her Ministers and her officials?

I have to concede that we have received a partial answer to one leg of that question, because she said that she did not know about the involvement of the Secretary of State for Trade and Industry. That is a little curious, because he says, and the Prime Minister said when she made a statement about this matter the other day, that he telephoned her or caused his officials to communicate with No. 10 on the basis that, subject to the agreement of No. 10, certain action was to be taken. It is odd that that was there and signalled from the beginning apparently, yet the Prime Minister says that she did not know of his involvement until after this laborious inquiry had been completed.

But let that matter stand. What we do not know is whether the right hon. Lady knew from her officials of their involvement in the leak before the setting up of the inquiry. That question simply has not been answered. It will be asked, and it will be asked, and it will be asked again until it is answered. The question is not an idle one. It is not one of a small matter of the mismanagement of government, an unfortunate leak, a slip, something that arose out of an unfortunate, but genuine, misunderstanding, as we are told.

Let me remind the House what the Solicitor-General wrote to the former Secretary of State for Defence in the letter which has become available only today, having been declassified and put in the Library before the debate started. In the penultimate paragraph, the Solicitor-General, writing to the former Secretary of State for Defence the day after the leak occurred, said:

On a different aspect of this matter, I want to express my dismay that a letter containing confidential legal advice from a Law Officer to one of his colleagues should have been leaked, and apparently leaked moreover in a highly selective way. Quite apart from the breach of confidentiality that is involved, the rule is very clearly established that even the fact that the Law Officers have tendered advice in a particular case may not be disclosed without their consent, let alone the content of such advice. It is plain that in this instance this important rule was immediately and flagrantly violated.

So let us get to the situation. On 7 January, when the Solicitor General knows that a flagrant violation has occurred, this is the time when the Prime Minister has been told in general terms of her office's involvement. She certainly must have known that there was a leak. It was on the front page of *The Times*, the *Sun*, the *Daily Mail* and I think that it got into the London *Standard* on that very day. In lurid headlines, the *Daily Mail* says: 'The great Cabinet shambles. Open war as Ministers attack Heseltine'.

The Times said: 'Heseltine told by law chief: Stick to the facts'.

The article goes on in that vein. The *Sun*, true to form, had a simple headline:'You liar'. That was all happening on 7 January.

The Solicitor General tells us that it is quite clear that a flagrant violation has occurred. I assume that the Prime Minister knew of the rule about Law Officers. But what was her reaction to that? Did she have people in and say, 'A flagrant violation has occurred. I am not putting up with it in this Government which I run and I want to find out what went on.'?

Nothing happened from the Prime Minister until the Attorney General stirred himself, realising that a flagrant violation had occurred. He did not go to the Prime Minister apparently, which is very strange, but to the head of the Civil Service. Perhaps he thought that he would get a more sympathetic response there than going to the Prime Minister, and be able to get his complaint out before he received his letter of dismissal perhaps. However, he goes to the head of the Civil Service and within minutes the Prime Minister – three days later – on 10 January says, 'I readily admit that I gave my authority for an inquiry to commence.' The question must be: why did it take the Attorney General and the head of the Civil Service to remind the Prime Minister of her constitutional responsibility? Why did she remain inactive? That is charge number one.

Charge number two is: is it really true that the Prime Minister knew nothing about the activities of her civil servants in No. 10? In that regard, Mr Speaker, let me remind you of something that happened this very afternoon. My hon. friend the Member for Linlithgow (Mr Dalyell) rose in his place and put a question to the Prime Minister. He referred to a question at column 455 of *Hansard* of 23 January put by the chairman of the 1922 Committee, the hon. Member for Woking, (Mr Onslow), to the Prime Minister. I hope that the House will forgive me if I quote the question and answer, because it is of profound importance.

The hon. Gentleman said:

My right hon. Friend will be aware that many right hon. and hon. Members on the Opposition Benches, like the right hon. Member for Plymouth, Devonport (Dr Owen), are not really interested in listening to the facts of the full account given by my right hon. Friend. What view does my right hon. Friend think that the House might have taken of any Minister in any Government placed in such an invidious situation by the action of a colleague who had failed in his duty to ensure that correct information was made public as soon as possible?

That is clearly referring to the conveying of the information suggesting that it was necessary for a Minister to make sure that that information was communicated. There can hardly be any doubt about that. Nor was there any doubt apparently in the Prime Minister's mind as to the meaning of the question, because she replied:

Yes, Mr Speaker, it would have been much easier, as the facts were commercially sensitive, if the relevant letters had been cleared as mine was with the Solicitor General. It was vital to have accurate information in the pubic domain because we knew that judgments might be founded upon that and that the Government could be liable if wrong judgments were made as a result of misleading information. It was to get that accurate information to the public domain that I gave my consent.

Why did the Prime Minister tell us last Thursday that she gave her consent to the leaking of the letter into the public domain?

[*Hon. Members*: Answer]

The Prime Minister: I shall gladly reply to the right hon. and learned Gentleman. I was quite content that I had given a whole account in the statement, cleared in every single detail, and the account in the statement was absolutely accurate.

Mr Smith: I know that the Prime Minister's statement was gone over with a toothcomb. The one she read out here is full of all the weasel words such as 'it became accepted as a matter of duty' and 'cover' instead of 'authority' – all those curious words that have been fashioned and honed after many hours of consultation to get them right.

The Prime Minister was OK when she was on the statement, but the question took her slightly out with the range of the statement. The question could not have been clearer and she said, 'I gave my consent.' Today, when she was asked about it by my hon. Friend the Member for Linlithgow, we all heard her say: 'When I said consent, I meant consent to the inquiry.' I must say that I felt something had gone wrong there, and I immediately checked in *Hansard*. It is obvious for everyone to see that the Prime Minister did not mean that. So she either gave us the wrong answer then or a wrong answer today. Which one was it? On the record in *Hansard* the Prime Minister admits that she gave her consent to the leaking of the information. Until she publicly corrects that account and answers the particular allegation that I have made, the question will remain unanswered.

The Prime Minister: I did not give my consent to the leaking of the information. May I make that quite, quite clear?

Mr Smith: If we are to accept the Prime Minister's statement that she did not give her consent, she was remarkably foolish to say so when she answered the question in the House. It takes me back to my days in the criminal courts. When some people gave unfortunate answers when required to do so about their activities they did not always get such an understanding response. 'I made a mistake,' said the Prime Minister. Did the Prime Minister make a mistake? That is one of the unanswered questions, and there are more.

What is worrying people who care about good government in

Britain is that this is typical of this Administration. I am sorry to say that there is no surprise throughout Britain at the evasions, denials and all the wrong goings-on of recent weeks and months. There is no surprise that things should happen in this way, because the standards of good government in Britain have been steadily deteriorating under the Prime Minister and her Ministers. That is why it appears to be enough to come to the House of Commons and get cheers from the ruling party for saying that matters should have been handled in a different way. Handled? Why cannot the Prime Minister say: 'It was wrong. It should not have happened and I am taking steps to make sure that it does not happen again.' No, it is all a matter of handling. It is a matter of manipulation and presentation.

I hope that the time will come soon in this House of Commons when Ministers, including the Prime Minister, when asked straight questions will give honest answers; when we will have a Government in whose competence, as well as in whose integrity, we can have confidence.

The problem is this: if we accept the explanation that has been given to us, it is a sorry tale of woeful incompetence. If we cannot accept it, the whole integrity this Administration is suspect.

This matter, I am sorry to tell the Government, simply will not go away, despite the attempts by Conservative Members, carefully planned throughout this day and carefully planned in advance, to disrupt the speech of my right hon. Friend the Leader of the Opposition. The Conservative party's tenacious defence of power is ruthless and absolute. Unfortunately for them, they have been found out and are being found out daily by the public.

An Industrial Strategy for Britain

Sussex University, 10 February 1986

*The extent to which the political economy of old Labour was different from the
political economy of new can be gauged from any number of speeches made by Smith
in the 1980s. That difference should not, however, obscure the extent to which Smith
was also working out a social democratic response to the convolutions in the world
economy that had produced Thatcherism in the first place. His speeches therefore tried
to combine an overtly collectivist critique of the political economy of Thatcherism with a
clear modernising sensibility. These two elements are well illustrated in this speech
made at the Science Policy Research Unit of Sussex University on Monday 10
February 1986 and his Mactintosh lecture.*

*While the moderniser in Smith deserves to be properly recognised, so does the
older traditional he represented. He did not believe in the sale of the motor industry to
the highest bidder because he did believe that the state could 'buck' the market. He did
not believe that the state was better at running the economy than business, but he did
believe that the state had a role and a responsibility to intervene when necessary and
to plan. In this he was swimming in the mainstream of much European social
democracy but his language was always more moderate and his delivery more measured
than the hard edge of the meaning of his words actually now convey.*

The impact of the Thatcher Government on economic policy
has been immense. The break up of the post-1945 economic
consensus with its commitments to full employment and the
mixed economy has had the most profound impact for the nation.
Monetarism has been, in the words of Chancellor Lawson 'a political
experiment'. An experiment that has not worked.

It is within this context that we must set my particular concern, the
concern with industrial policy. The Conservative vision has been one of
rolling back the State, allowing a greater role for the market, for a year
or two claiming to invest in high-tech 'sunrise' industries while refusing

to spend large amounts on the so-called 'sunset' sectors. In reality the picture has been more confused than a clear pattern of support for 'sunrise' industries, combined with an abandonment of the smoke-stacks. In the earlier years there was an apparent commitment to the high tech industries. That has now been abandoned, while all the while the other industries have been neglected. The result is that the Conservative Party under its present leadership appears to have no viable industrial strategy, largely because they have misunderstood the whole nature of the economic changes which confront us as a nation.

In terms of the overall spending on industrial policy through the Department of Trade and Industry the Government has cut back enormously from £3.2 billion 1981–2 to an estimated £1.502 billion in 1984–5. Support to specific industries, regional aid and support for new technology have all been cut and its overall implications have amounted to a willful neglect of manufacturing industry in the face of one of the worst international economic recessions we have ever seen.

The Conservatives have failed to see that we should not be talking about 'sunrise' and 'sunset' industries. Certainly we should be backing new technology to the hilt but new technology is significant precisely because it can be applied to established industries like steel, textiles and motor cars, not simply to obvious high technology products like computers. The question is not whether an industry is 'sunrise' or 'sunset' but whether it can be renewed or not.

Unfortunately, the results of the Conservatives' lack of a coherent industrial policy are all around us; between three and four million people unemployed, massive regional divisions and previously prosperous industrial areas sent into a vicious circle of decline. In September of last year two of Britain's major economic institutions published their overviews of the UK's industrial performance. The news is not good. NEDO in its report British Industrial Performance still sees Britain showing little improvement compared with its main trading partners.

Our economy, on most measurements, is trailing other advanced societies.

The TUC's *Economic Review 1985* is even more blunt about it. It says that the continued decline in manufacturing will produce a 'low productivity, low growth economy with an even more deeply divided labour market'. This decline was 'not inevitable, but a direct conse-quence of government policy', a policy which has, therefore, produced the loss of some 1.7 million jobs in UK manufacturing over the last six years. Manufacturing output is still 7% below what it was in 1979 when Labour left office and our balance of trade in manufactured goods was deficit of £4 billion last year, a deficit for the third year running.

Perhaps most damning of all was the Report of the House of Lords' Select Committee on Trade, not least of all because of the 'knee jerk' response with which its publication was received by Government. It is astonishing that a document which presented the serious problem of our decline in exports in manufactured goods in the context of the projected downturn in North Sea oil output as we approach the 1990's should have met with such a response. The Report concluded that on the basis of the figures presented to the Committee by the Treasury and the Department of Energy that:

So far as trade balances are concerned Britain may have no oil surplus by 1990; indeed by the end of the century we may be in deficit in oil once again.

But what is clear from these three reports is that the Government's 'cold shower' treatment of British industry has not worked, bankrupt-cies continue at record levels and the much vaunted growth in productivity that Tory propaganda is so fond of talking about seems to be evaporating. In fact the average growth rate since the Conservatives came to power has been well under half the average rate of growth between 1950 and 1974.

The situation is now so serious that many economic commentators and industrialists are talking of the country facing an economic crisis, and they are not using the term lightly. In a recent speech Sir Edwin Nixon, the Chairman and Chief Executive of IBM in Britain declared:

... we had better get used to continuing decline – and in its wake social and political decay and perhaps even democracy itself struggling for survival.

I believe that the people who make such statements are not scare-mongering, they are pointing out a grim reality which must be confronted. The whole economic position of the UK over the last six years has been dependent on North Sea oil, because our industrial manufacturing base has been so disastrously weakened. If you like you could say that North Sea oil has funded Mrs Thatcher's 'political experiment'. Our collapse in manufacturing has been masked by the contribution that North Sea oil revenues have made to our national wealth. There appears to be an intellectual argument to the effect that the collapse of our manufacturing does not matter while we have North Sea oil and that 'automatic' adjustments in the economy will compensate for its decline anyway. Indeed this is precisely what the Treasury does in its evidence to the House of Lords Select Committee. But North Sea oil is a finite resource and forecasts already suggest that it has passed its peak of production. This particular item will gradually disappear from the UK's balance of payments, and Britain will return to its historic position of depending on manufactures.

But as we have seen the manufacturing capacity on which Britain will depend when that moment comes has been devastated, The consequences of the UK's failure to match the levels of investment, the technological standards and the design skills of our competitors is that our capacity to re-enter the world of technology-based manufacturing has, on present course, been seriously eroded.

If we look at Research and Development, a key factor in any industry's ability to adopt new technologies, the level of R&D spending in the UK fell between 1981 and 1983, in real terms, to a level only slightly higher than in the late 1960s. Our ability to innovate is an important determinant of our economic performance. In a very real sense, the free market policies of this Government have failed. The assumption that, given a free rein, companies would pour profits into spending on Research and Development and product innovation has been proved false. Instead, profits have gone into increased dividends and short term gains on the Stock Exchange which either finance takeovers or fend them off.

The present fashion for takeovers cannot be seen as a solution to the problems of British industry, nor as a substitute for a British industrial policy. We must establish criteria which consider the consequences in terms of the future for employees and the advantages for the development of the industry itself. With the current free-for-all, the battle between the sector barons makes money for the advertising agencies and the City finance houses who rival each other with increased profits won through the game of 'Who Dares Merge.' It should be clear from what I have already said that I believe the central failure of the Thatcher governments has been a failure to confront the long-term strategic problems which face the British economy. We must therefore develop and get our industrial strategy right. The Labour Party sees the way forward as involving active demand management to raise the overall level of activity and investment, combined with an active supply side strategy involving a co-ordinated use of industrial and trade policy to address the regeneration of manufacturing industry which is now rightly regarded as central to the long term recovery of the UK economy.

The UK's manufacturing tradeable capacity must be restored in such a way as to allow a resumption of economic growth at socially acceptable levels of unemployment and output. The first problem is therefore how to raise the volume and quality of investment that producers are willing to undertake. The second is how to ensure that sufficient financial, human and other resources of the right amount and quality are available for the programme of investment and innovative activity required.

The first and overriding requirement in raising the volume of private sector investment is to raise the level of effective demand for domestic manufactured output. Although the public sector may itself embark upon a programme, for example, of public works projects, it is the private sector which must provide the bulk of the investment effort required. Tinkering via investment subsidies or other means to alter the relationship between the cost of capital and the rate of return on investment, has noticeably failed to alter the UK's chronic low investment performance. Private sector investment will not be forthcoming without the prospect of a period of sustained buoyant demand. Ensuring a high and sustained level of demand by raising capacity utilization (and as a consequence raising profit margins) is therefore a necessary requirement for industrial investment revival.

This will require the adoption of a trade and exchange rate policy to handle the transitional period before a regeneration programme can have such effect on the competitiveness of the UK economy. In this connection two points are worth emphasising. First, although it must be the case that in the last resort the UK should be prepared to go it alone and adopt whatever individual trade policies are required to sustain expansion, it is infinitely preferable that UK recovery should be part of a co-ordinated programme involving the European economies. The promotion of such an expansion should be a priority for UK international economic policy. Second, in the context of the vital policy for expansion and recovery of manufacturing, the extra degree of freedom offered by the existence of substantial stocks of assets overseas as a result of North Sea oil revenues being invested there cannot be ignored. The phased repatriation of overseas assets, with institutional tax privileges being made conditional on meeting specified asset portfolio or net investment flow guidelines could provide a significant proportion of the resources we need. Policies which limit overseas portfolio investment are nothing new. They have been pursued in Japan, France and the US, as well as many other industrialised economies for many years. Restriction on overseas investment stocks and flows have of course featured in the policies of Japan, the US and other industrial economies.

Necessary though demand expansion is, it cannot by itself be sufficient. For, although it is obvious that there is much to be gained in terms of raising the level of investment by a reversal of the macro-economic policies of the recent past, the efficiency with which that investment is allocated and used is also of great importance.

It is in this connection that an active industrial policy as part of a planned domestic reflation can make a contribution. It can do so in two main ways, First, by helping to ensure the efficient allocation of scarce investment resources. Second, by helping to raise the efficiency of each investment project through the promotion of innovative schemes for product and process development, the reorganisation of the production process and the transfer and diffusion of technology between defence and civilian uses, academia and the commercial world, and between the firms in individual sectors. Planning can help meet both these objectives by improving the flow of information upon which investment decisions in the public and private sector are based, and by the co-ordination of policies designed to make investment effective. I believe we can identify four principal planning functions.

Firstly, a central informational function to identify the capital requirements of the overall output and employment growth targets of the recovery programme, its manufacturing and industrial requirements, and within that to identify the key areas in which expansion should most effectively occur, and to indicate the broad types of investment required. We should be able to identify, as other advanced industrial economies have done, the opportunities and threats which face the various industrial sectors of our nation. We need to select priority areas in terms of potential comparative advantages, but also in terms of those areas where it is essential that the UK maintain industrial sectors to ensure that we have an industrial future at all.

The second main planning function would be by consultation and negotiation to discover the likely investment plans of public and large scale private sector enterprise in relation to the investment plan framework; and thus consider the main impediments, if any, to the scale and type of investment desired being undertaken. This will lead naturally to the third planning function, the provision of a framework for the negotiation and design of packages of support to encourage the private and public sector responses desired, for the evaluation of specific projects submitted for support and for the auditing and evaluation of the effectiveness of the support programmes. In this respect I think we have a lot to learn from the system of French planning contracts.

Fourthly, and finally, planning must also involve a framework for ensuring the provision of the sorts of resources required for the packages including provision where necessary for direct State funding or ownership stakes in enterprises and a coherent role for public procurement.

It is important to emphasize that the design of support packages and the provision of resources for them can go far beyond the usually emphasized need for financial resources in the form of subsidized loans, grants or the taking of equity, but could and should, where appropriate, extend to training and manpower requirements and the specification of standards or regulation for products. For instance any attempt to build up technological strength in advanced information technology, where the trade deficit increased ten fold between 1980 and 1984, must involve a collaborative effort in view of the scale, complexity and diverse location in the private and public sector of the resources and know-how required.

All of which will require specific co-ordination and monitoring, and the evaluation of individual projects. The Alvey programme is a step in this direction, although there is apparently no longer term commitment for state financial support beyond the initial five years, it is jointly financed by industry and the State.

The evolution of a framework to implement these planning functions requires a number of institutional developments. We already have NEDO, the forum around which Government, the unions and management formulate sector working policies and report to Government on their operation and effectiveness. A Labour Government would require a greatly strengthened planning organisation on the NEDO model to be the fulcrum of communication and implementation of industrial policy. Sector working groups in the present NEDO structure have done a great deal of valuable work but sadly they have been largely ignored by this Government. I strongly believe that the core of our industrial strategy depends on a strong working relationship between all sides of industry and the Government. This would not mean a return to the ideas of the nineteen sixties, nor a French-style 'Le Plan' but a new partnership to establish a firm basis for industrial recovery. Priorities will be set for investment and development within the NEDO sectors, whether it should be the motor industry, electronics or any other which needs urgent assistance. We have seen during the past week the results of the Government's neglect of the British motor industry, a nationalised industry which should be a central part of our manufacturing capacity and not a lottery ticket to be sold to the highest foreign bidder.

Ultimately the responsibility for the central planning function must reside with the Secretary of State for Trade and Industry, working

closely with the planning organisation. Although the overall policy
framework has to be formulated centrally and its implementation be
co-ordinated within centrally approved guidelines, the process of
formulation, the setting and revision of guidelines, and the detailed
negotiation, implementation and assessment of individual projects must
involve the use of decentralised institutions working at sectoral regional
and local level. A Labour Government will need local authorities to play
a major part in its new economic strategy and this will involve councils
in new regional planning bodies to ensure that public and private
investment decisions are made more accountable to the regions.

The Scottish and Welsh Development Agencies set up by the last
Labour Government have a proven record of intervention and investment
which has helped to alleviate some of the worst effects of the recession in
both these countries. We believe that new regional bodies for England
should have powers to invest in local industry through enterprise boards,
to invest in training programmes and to back local employment
campaigns and develop new technologies. These new agencies which
could cover, as a start, the key geographic areas of the North East, North
West, Midlands and Yorkshire, all areas which have suffered during the
past six years from the Government's lack of an industrial policy.

The public sector which has made a signal contribution to our
economic success in the past, has been greatly reduced in size and scale
by the ruthless privatisation policies of the Thatcher Government. The
Labour Party is giving careful consideration to the development of new
policies for an enhanced public sector which will be proposed to our
next Party Conference. I would like however, in the context of innovation and the consideration of industrial policy making, to draw
attention to one important policy initiative which is finding support,
not just within the formal ranks of the Labour Party, but also among a
wider audience. We need a new and flexible forum of state intervention
in the industrial economy.

The Industrial Re-organisation Corporation of the first Wilson Government, many of whose then young members now hold prominent positions at the head of British industries, pioneered the concept of creative intervention until it was foolishly destroyed in 1970. In later years the National Enterprise Board did valuable work although it was diverted from its principal functions by its absorption in the British Leyland rescue. The time has come, I believe, for the founding of a new organisation, perhaps named British Enterprise, organised and funded by Government, to be able to establish new industrial ventures on its own, to enter into joint ventures with the private sector and perhaps most importantly to act as a catalyst for innovation. There is so much that needs to be done that I believe that a powerful new organisation along these lines will prove to be essential. It is a form of public ownership and intervention which offers the possibility of flexible and direct action, with or without private sector co-operation, which could command wide support within industry as well as be an effective agent in the planning of our national industrial recovery.

An indication of the direction of the Labour Party's industrial and economic policy has been given in our Jobs and Industry Campaign. I would say that we have broadly approached things in the manner which I have outlined in this speech, that is we have considered things in a strategic sense. In three of our industrial strategy documents, on the motor industry, textiles and information technology, we have outlined a consultative approach to our industrial problems to begin a national debate between workforce, management and politicians about Britain's industrial future. It is my view that the recent crises over Westland and British Leyland have forced this debate fully into the public arena.

Long before the events of the last few days the Labour Party had given clear assurances that it was crucial that BL remains an independent full range manufacturer with the resources to maintain an internationally competitive model range and to collaborate with companies such as Honda on an equal basis. The developments within the Japanese industry of 'Just in time' manufacturing pose a significant challenge to our own industry. It is no longer just the 'hard' capital investment which is at stake, but a combination of forward planning with a new approach to the organisation of production. We can meet this challenge by promoting investment in key areas, by encouraging effective training and by boosting the research and development effort.

In the information technology industry similar threats confront us. Labour has four main objectives in this sector: 1. to sustain a strong British presence in IT and its applications; 2. to raise output and strengthen the UK IT industry through increased and better directed research, development, marketing and investment in production and process technologies; 3. to bring our IT trade back into a better balance; 4. and, above all, to help build a modern economy which can get Britain back to work.

I have sought to indicate some of the crucial elements in our approach to industrial policy. Each area of our actual and potential industrial effort needs particular consideration. Clearly some will need more attention than others. In areas where we are already successful, there is obviously less need for a Government to have to concern itself, apart from ensuring that the potential of our existing success is maximised. In other areas, there will clearly be the requirement to have proposals for reconstruction and redevelopment which can be formulated through the planning process.

But in every area we must sustain three engines of recovery. These are investment, research and development and training. I have already indicated some of our ideas on the first two but the third is probably the most crucial. As we have seen industrial training progressively being dismantled and as we have with horror observed our educational system diminishing at all its levels, it is clear that we have no hope of recovery unless we make a completely new and sustained commitment to education and training. Our aim – and it is a perfectly possible one – should be within, say, a ten year period, to attain the best trained and educated workforce and management in Western Europe. Our future success depends on our capacity to develop to the full the skills of our own people. It is not just a matter of offering new scope for individual development as an end in itself – desirable though that is.

Education is now a crucial element of a successful industrial policy. Far too many of our young people leave school at sixteen, poorly equipped for a world in which personal skills are the key to economic success and individual fulfilment. Far too many of our young people are unable to gain access to higher, further and continuing education which alone can offer them the opportunity to adapt and retrain in a world where change is swift and relentless.

I end on this note not just because I have had the privilege of developing these ideas in one of our excellent educational institutions but because it is a deeply held personal conviction. The Britain of the future, which the next Labour Government will help to shape, will, I hope, be one in which our success will be based on the fullest development of the skills and ambitions of our people. It could not have a more sure foundation.

The Eighth John Mackintoch Lecture

If the speech at Sussex stressed the continuity of John Smith's thought with the traditions of collectivism within Labour economic thinking, then his Mackintosh lecture on May Day 1987 at least hinted at the extent to which he recognised the need for the Labour Party to develop and argue for its own responses to the new economy.

It is a particular honour as well as a special pleasure to be invited to give the eighth John Mackintosh Memorial Lecture. I had the privilege of serving in the Commons with John for a good part of his Parliamentary career, and like most who came in contact with him, I owe him a debt of gratitude for the constant intellectual stimulus and infectious enthusiasm which he radiated and from which I and others derived incalculable benefit. I never had the pleasure of being one of his students, but being a history student at Glasgow University at a time when he was in the full vigour of his teaching years in this University, I had intimation of the massive inspirational effect he had on a generation of young people when I first met him at a joint reading party of the Honours history classes of the two Universities held at the Scottish Universities' residential establishment at the Burn in Angus. He was a specially gifted teacher as well as a distinguished Parliamentarian, and of course he combined his two talents and enthusiasms in his authoritative works on the machinery and practice of government which will I am sure, for many years to come, remain essential reading for succeeding generations of students.

The idea of having an annual lecture in his memory is particularly appropriate and one of which he would have approved, not least because of the obligation an invitation would put on the lecturer, particularly if he or she were a politician, to attempt the public articulation of their ideas or aspirations in something akin to an intellectual format. He would reason that whatever it did to the audience, it might do some good to the performer.

He was always insistent that political debate and discussion should centre on the broad sweep of events and ideas, rather than dissipate itself in the byways of specialism, and it is in that spirit that I have chosen my subject.

I wish to argue the case that prosperity, broadly defined as a steadily increasing standard of living in an efficient and productive economy, is not only consistent with a socially just and caring society, but that in an intelligently organised community, prosperity and social justice mutually reinforce each other.

For almost three decades after the Second World War – in what historians may describe as the Era of Full Employment – most Western democracies regarded the maintenance of full employment as not only the obligatory duty of civilised government, but as an indispensable part of a successful economic arrangement. The purchasing power of the employed, for example, was one of the essential mainsprings of demand in the economy. What was socially necessary was rightly also regarded as economically sound. In those times, if it had been predicted that in the late 1980s Britain would have well over three million unemployed and that the then right wing government would advertise its economy as successful, disbelief would have been profound.

The fact, of course, is that unhappily the Era of Full Employment came to an end somewhere about 1973 or 1974. Consequent upon that, the Right having acquired some different intellectual adornment and presenting itself as the New Right, seized an opportunity to argue that it was the burden of social justice, the size of the public sector, the amount of public expenditure, which caused the motor to unwind.

I believe that all along many of the conservative forces had secretly grudged the post-war concessions. Wisely perhaps, the Conservative Party, under the late Lord Butler's guiding hand, had conceded ground. Indeed, for a while they were prepared to compete in social provision. Witness the then Mr Harold Macmillan's well publicised drive to build one million council houses. They were most probably divided between those who regarded the concessions as desirable and others who conceded them only because there seemed no alternative in a society in which the Welfare State was manifestly popular.

But by the 1970s, when the post war expansion was petering out, the radical right were quick to pounce. In the United States and in

Britain, new theories were propounded and old theorists like Hayek were intellectually disinterred. In 1975, Mrs Thatcher captured the Conservative Party and subsequently the Government, and by 1980, Ronald Reagan had become President of the United States. The right were less bold in other parts of Western Europe where more scepticism existed – and still exists – about their nostrums. Essentially the argument was that events had proved the intervention of the State in the organisation of the economy to be harmful and in particular, the Welfare State created a major drag on the efficiency of the economy. Indeed, the greater the cost of welfare, the greater the loss of efficiency. The end of the Era of Full Employment came about, they said, because it could not be sustained. What was needed was the rolling back of the State and the reassertion of the influence of unrestrained market forces.

If they were correct in their proposition that economic efficiency and social justice had been proved to be mutually inconsistent, it was a powerful argument. By dint of shrewdly presented polemic and well financed publicity, the conservative forces pressed their argument home. Some powerful economic forces and some very well-heeled people had a strong vested interest in it being pursued.

I believe to the contrary that their analysis was fundamentally flawed, that the product of their theories had been disastrous, that at bottom, it was no more than a counter-attack by the forces of wealth and privilege to recapture the spoils which they felt they had been obliged to share for too long and that their theories offer no acceptable way forward.

In the first place, I do not believe that, as the right argue, growth faltered because of the burden of public expenditure, or labour bargaining power, or redistribution. I think a sounder analysis reveals that the causes were multiple and complex. The economic spending boom generated by the Second World War and the consequent imaginative reconstruction programmes, by European economic integration, by mass consumer spending and the automobile age, petered out. The process was accompanied by a disintegration of the world economic system as the Bretton Woods Agreement failed to stick. The OPEC price hike and the huge transfer of resources which it involved, came at a moment when the Western economies were in any case weak. The massive OPEC price increases were but one manifestation of a period of high commodity prices which have been replaced in the 1980's by a period of very low comodity prices, a factor which seems to me to have more to do with the comparatively lower rates of inflation than anything else. And, of course, greatly increased global competition took its toll as Japan and other Far Eastern countries captured, more of formerly captive markets. Saturated consumer spending on the demand side, and heightened competition on the supply side are far more likely causes of the economic stagnation than the theories of the new Right.

But even if the analysis were superficial, has the application of the new approach led to success? As J.K. Galbraith once noted, Britain was to become a laboratory and since 1979 we have seen the application to the British economy of these theories expounded and practised by Mrs Thatcher. She started, of course, with an enormous advantage not possessed by any previous British government – the abundance of North Sea oil and gas. The preceding Labour government did a very great deal, to ensure that by 1980 Britain was self-sufficient in oil production. This meant that the succeeding government was given an unprecedented freedom from balance of trade and balance of payments constraints which had so often in the past bedevilled successful economic management. While most of our industrial competitors had to wrestle, at least for a few years, with the high cost of imported oil, Britain had a breathing space and in addition received revenues from North Sea oil which were at their peak running at between £12 to £13 billion annually. The enormous advantage conferred on the Thatcher administration by this bounty has been sedulously underplayed by economic and political commentators favourable to the government and, of course, by her own highly effective publicity machine, but it is a fact which, for all the attempt to obscure, is of undeniable and cardinal importance. Indeed, I argue that the failure of the Right is the greater in that they started the experiment with a unique and unprecedented advantage.

Of course, it will be said that the price of oil did not stay high and that eventually it halved in value, although it is still worth £6 billion per annum. By this time, the Thatcher government had however discovered another technique for replenishing the national coffers – the asset stripping of publicly owned industries. In this way substantial sums are raised, and combined with some curiosities of public accounting, are very effective in tiding us over in the short term. Of course, the assets are no longer there, nor will the dividend and profit which they produce be available for the future, but as I will have occasion to observe later, in a slightly different context, there is little concern with the long term. Sufficient to say for this purpose that anyone can have an apparently successful sale (if speedy disposal is the objective) if he sells below value and the replacement of cash for assets does not add to the economic wealth or benefit the nation.

Despite the enormous benefit of North Sea oil and gas, and the temporary boost of asset sales, the record of economic management under Mrs Thatcher's administration can hardly be regarded as a convincing demonstration that we have found a new road to economic success. We have returned in the 1980s to the mass unemployment of the 1930s from which, for decades after the Second World War, we thought we had permanently escaped. Over £20 billion of scarce resources is diverted each year to pay the real cost of underwriting mass unemployment. The cost in human misery and lost personal opportunity is even greater. Since 1979, twenty per cent of our industrial capacity has disappeared, industrial output is still four per cent lower, and industrial investment – the essential seedcorn of the future – is still seventeen per cent lower. The North South divide – which Mrs Thatcher pretends not to exist – is the most acute it has ever been. It now divides Britain on a line between the Severn and the Wash. If two visitors from outer space were to land simultaneously, but in different parts of Britain, and to meet up a few weeks later to compare notes on what they had discovered, the report from South Shields would be so different from that from Surrey, that it would be concluded that they had not, in fact, been in the same country. The recent health survey, which fortunately was not suppressed as was intended, revealed from another standpoint the acute difference in services and opportunity which are tolerated in what we once thought was one nation. Perhaps the most alarming feature of our present economic situation is that in 1983, for the first time in modern history, we slipped into a balance of trade deficit in manufactured goods. From then, it has deteriorated so sharply that it was almost £6 billion in 1986 and it is predicted by the government itself to reach £8 billion by the end of 1987. Bearing in mind that manufacturing industry is our crucial wealth creator and an indispensable element in enabling Britain to pay its way in the world, the record of Mrs Thatcher's economic management is as dismal as it is alarming. That is the stark truth behind a temporary consumer spending boom fuelled by unrestricted credit which, however convenient politically in the short run in creating an atmosphere of synthetic prosperity, will rebound to our severe disbenefit, particularly in the acceleration of the imports of manufactured goods.

Even if they are, in fact, wrong in their historical analysis and can hardly point to a record of success in tackling the ills of our society or of our economy, the new Right have to be recognised as possessing a breathtaking sense of audacity and opportunism. Monetarism was for long the very ark of the temple. When finally its absurdities could no longer be ignored, it was quietly abandoned without even a word of apology for the grave damage it had done to British industry. A popular press, largely owned by beneficiaries of their policies, is, and no doubt will continue to be, an obliging megaphone for their propaganda. Nor are they restrained by notions of civility or tolerance. Mrs Thatcher does not want to defeat her opponents: in her arrogance, she aims to 'bury socialism'. Thus it behoves the Left to recognise the character of its opposition by arguing our case with a sense of robustness and determination. Not that we want to 'bury' opposing ideas or new proposals. That is not a language to be encouraged in a civilised democratic society. We must win by the open and honest argument appropriate to a free and tolerant democracy.

In that spirit, let me contest their two crucial propositions, namely that social justice achieved through community responsibility and spending is a drag on — or even incompatible with — economic efficiency, that the government should intervene only marginally, if at all, in the organisation of the economy, because market forces will lead to the best allocation of resources and to the creation of the only sustainable dynamic for the economy.

Let me deal first with the question of full employment which, on any view, must be a fundamental objective of a socially just society. There is no question that it has ceased to be, even if it ever was, an aspiration of the Thatcher administration. Year after year, even modest steps such as moderate public construction programmes, well within even the economic parameters set for itself by the government, have been ruthlessly eschewed. It is no longer credible for government apologists to claim, as they once did, that their opponents should give them at least the credit of caring about unemployment. No one who cared could have missed so many opportunities for remedial action. The truth is, is it not, that there is seen to be some advantage in a pool of unemployment: it keeps the workers in check, makes them less ambitious for better wages and conditions, keeps them demoralised, and, of course, it causes more problems for trade unions than all the restrictive laws rolled into one and doubled in intensity.

I hope I do not need to persuade many about the essential immorality of such a policy. Over forty years ago, Beveridge argued with clarity and conviction that full employment was the centrepiece of social citizenship. In rejecting the *laissez faire* idea that slack in the labour markets was a desirable condition he said that the labour market 'should always be a seller's market rather than a buyer's market. The reason is that difficulty in selling labour has consequences of a different order of harmfulness from those associated with difficulty in buying labour. A person who has difficulty in buying the labour that he needs suffers inconvenience or reduction of profits. A person who cannot sell his labour is, in effect, told that he is of no use. The first difficulty causes annoyance or less. The other is a personal catastrophe'.

He would be astonished if he were with us now to find that unemployment at its present level was tolerated, or that over £20 billion was drained from our public resources to finance it.

But leaving aside the moral question, what on earth is the economic advantage of unemployment viewed from the viewpoint of society as a whole? I see in the millions of unemployed, not just personal catastrophe, but unused and untapped energy and talent. I see every week in my own constituency the cost of unemployment in our welfare and social services, as well as in the lives of the good people I have the privilege to represent. But I also see a shocking economic waste, and I ask myself continuously what kind of economic theory is it that resolutely refuses to pay to put people into work, but pays them (albeit at low levels) not to work. It is not that there is not work to be done. In the Labour Party's programme 'New Jobs for Britain' we identify four areas of action. A package for economic enterprise through stimulating investment in manufacturing, particularly in the regions, and cutting National Insurance contributions on a regionally differentiated basis, can create 250,000 jobs, principally in the private sector. A capital investment plan designed to revive the housing programme, improve the transport infrastructure, and reverse the inner city rundown, can create 250,000 jobs in both public and private sectors. An expansion of our caring services, in health, personal social services, education, and other areas can create 300,000 jobs principally in the public sector.

Finally, a national training programme converting the current piecemeal schemes into a coherent strategy for returning skills, particularly to our young people, can produce 360,000 jobs and training places. All this is work which desperately needs to be done to meet real deficiencies in society. It will provide an impetus of demand in the supplying industries. It is clearly affordable. The net annual cost in each year of its two year course would be £6 billion, precisely the sum available to a Chancellor who chose instead to cut 2p off the basic rate of income tax and to reduce public sector borrowing to below 1% of GDP at a time when, because of the new sources of credit which finance the present consumer spending spree, private borrowing has reached 10 per cent of GDP. So let it not be said it cannot be done. It can be done in precisely the ways we have outlined, at the costs which we have calculated. And surely it makes sense in strictly economic terms, let alone in terms of moral aspiration or social balance or elementary justice, to tackle work which needs to be done by people who need to do it. Keynes was, of course, driven to distraction by the refusal of the inter-war governments to tackle unemployment on economic grounds. He said, 'Pyramid-building, earthquakes even wars may serve to increase wealth, if the education of our statesmen on the principles of classic economics stands in the way of something better'. In an attempt to find a wholly absurd human activity which drove home his point, he outlined his now celebrated scheme. 'If the Treasury were to fill old bottles with bank notes, bury them at suitable depths in disused coal mines which are then filled up, top the surface with town rubbish, and leave it to private enterprise on well tried principles of *laissez faire* to dig the notes up again (the right to do so being obtained, of course, by tendering for leases of the note-bearing territory) there need be no more unemployment and, with the help of the repercussions, the real income of the community and its capital wealth also, would probably become a good deal greater than it actually is. It would, indeed, be more sensible to build houses and the like: but if there are political and practical difficulties in the way of this, the above would be better than nothing.'

In our society there is work in abundance waiting to be done: what is lacking is the political will to authorise it. But let it not be said in this case that social justice does not complement and reinforce real economic benefit. Or take the National Health Service. Does it operate to our economic disadvantage? One would have thought that universal access to a good system of health care, irrespective of individual wealth or position, was not only the *sine qua non* of a civilised society, but a clearly demonstrable economic benefit. We know, of course, that it would not have happened had not a Labour Government created it. Although the Right are careful not to attack it too explicitly because it is so deeply rooted in the affections and interest of the vast majority of the population, they would never have created it. It is a sense of survival rather than of belief which forces Mrs Thatcher on to the political back foot to claim that the NHS is safe with her. Yet we know, do we not, that her belief is in a two-tier provision with an expanding private sector which will inevitably lead to different standards of health care apportioned according to the ability to purchase them. There are already clear enough signs of such a system developing. In the United States, whose arrangements in these matters Mrs Thatcher usually finds attractive, they hardly run a more efficient and more economically beneficial system. I read with astonishment, in a recent book by ex-President Nixon, two lines which told me how appallingly inefficient what he called socialised medicine was in Britain. The facts are as follows. In Britain where universal health cover is provided, we spend 6.2% of our GDP on health. In the United States where cover is far from universal (in Harlem for example there are 80 registered physicians for a population of more than a million) the proportion is 10.8%. On a very conservative OECD calculation of the relative costs of administration, in the UK these amount to 2.6% of total spend, while in the United States they are 5.3%. There is other evidence that they are higher, but even on a cautious basis the US private system, even when non-universal, costs twice as much to administer. In our private sector, the cost of administration for BUPA is 10% and a further 6% is spent on what are called administrative systems. So I do not think we need accept any arguments from those who would undermine our Health Service that they would create a more economically efficient way of providing a basic and essential provision. Health has to be paid for whether it is provided by one route or the other. The essential question is one of social and political, not economic choice. But in our case, it looks as if the economics are on the side of the Health Service as well.

I would argue that these are practical rebuttals of the new Right's case in two important areas. However, I want to deal directly with one of their most central – and in my opinion, most erroneous – propositions. It is the notion that inequality is necessary as a dynamic of economic activity. Without the lure of riches or the fear of poverty, economies, they say, do not progress. Albeit, it might be a fairly despairing conclusion for society, they say it is a fact of life and claim the support of human nature. George Gilder, one of the American apologists put it thus – 'the poor most of all need the spur of their own poverty'.

Now I doubt if I want an economic prosperity in which the supporting engine is driven by a haunting fear of poverty or a dread of illness, or by the amassing of large concentrations of wealth and consequent power. But I need not face the dilemma because none exists. This is not an economic theory: it is the re-articulation of political and social prejudices convenient to the rich and powerful and spread on their behalf by their apologists.

In the first place, they do not act upon the theory themselves. If it were true, why do they deny their succeeding generations the incentive and the spur of need by bequeathing fortunes which guarantee a life of comfort without effort? If it were remotely true, should they not be in the van of those urging the most swingeing of inheritance taxes?

Secondly, the rich are not, in fact, against welfare provision. They may be against public provision on a universal basis to the community. But they are strongly in favour of a private welfare state for themselves.

In the United States, and also increasingly in Britain, private health care systems, elaborate pension arrangements and private education are all provided, often through tax deductible systems involving what amounts to a public subsidy. Not for them the spur of insecurity. And if it is not needed to give incentive to the powerful and successful, how does its effect somehow become curiously remedial when applied to others!

The new Right, and Milton Friedman in particular, have even argued that the inequalities of *laissez faire* are truly more egalitarian because they will lead to more growth and greater prosperity for all. The sociologist, Philip Green described this aptly as 'the homage that vice self-confidently pays to virtue'. Or, as R.H. Tawney, who got most things right, put it 'the argument is that the wealth of the few is the indispensable safeguard for the modest comfort of the many, who, if they understood their own interests, would not harass the rich with surtaxes and death duties, but would cherish and protect them'.

But in Britain, in the last eight years when a major redistribution in favour of the rich has undoubtedly taken place, where is the evidence of its beneficial effects on the economy. It seems that a great deal of the money must have been invested in other economies: some of it has probably been spent in accumulating apparently desirable semi-royal jewellery; the bulk has probably gone in simply increasing the standard of living of the wealthy. With investment in industry still seventeen per cent below 1979, it is not obvious that conferring largesse on the rich leads to immediate practical investment where the nation requires it. And, of course, as we all know, the institutional investors who invest the pension contributions and savings of the wider community are a far more powerful motor of investment than all the rich could ever be.

The Swedes have shown the fallacy of the new Right argument that the non-rich must live in neurotic fear of failure to provide an incentive to effort. They provide positive evidence that social justice and economic efficiency can be achieved together. But in our own history is there not adequate negative evidence that their disjunction leads to failure. There are unhappy parallels between the 1980s and the 1920s and 1930s. What does the new Right now propose which was not tried then? The cruel society of the means test was not one of economic efficiency. Surely there was more to the great depression than the so-called failure of the unemployed to look for work. Surely the 1920s was more than just a decade of workers' misperceptions about job availability. And what was achieved by way of economic success by the cuts in the meagre support then offered to the casualties of their theories. So much of the new right is the old right once again – no more than 'cauld kale het up'. Bunk then, and bunk now. We need not, and should not, for one moment abandon our belief in the just and decent society because those who dislike it on political grounds fallaciously argue that it is economically beyond our reach.

So I reject the argument that this sort of inequality is a necessary condition of economic success. What I find revealing is that while we have to offer incentives to the better off, we are urged to place disincentives in the way of the poor. They face a marginal rate of loss on increases in income in our present shambolic system of social security which would make the rich quail. And I ask: if we are building an incentive society, what incentives there are in modern Britain for the unemployed if no amount of effort on their part can create jobs, or for the poor, if no amount of work will ease their poverty? In the belief that the beneficial economic effects of large tax reductions for the upper income groups could be proved to have an incentive effective, Chancellor Lawson commissioned Professor Brown to study the matter. The results were so inconclusive – and therefore non-supportive – that we hear no further reference to it.

So let us not accept for one moment the first proposition of the new Right that we require to tolerate injustice or inequality in the name of economic efficiency.

The second major thrust of the new Right is that economies prosper when the government takes a passive role in the wealth creation process and leaves the necessary dynamic to the supposed magic of unrestrained market forces.

After eight years of the Thatcher experiment, not only do we have the economic waste of unemployment, we have an industrial economy which is smaller, receives less investment, produces less output, and has the most adverse – and deteriorating – balance of trade in our modern economic history. Even worse, perhaps, the technological base of British industry is disturbingly weak. We simply are not developing the new products and processes which can alone pioneer new industries for the future and modernise existing industries in a way which will make them internationally competitive. But it is not in my opinion enough to point to the failure of Thatcherism. Democratic socialists today must put the achievement of the successful economy as high on their list of priorities as their other objectives. Indeed, it is my argument that it is the essential prerequisite and guarantor of the achievement and maintenance of the

society which is socially just and individual enhancing. When Tony
Crosland wrote *The Future of Socialism* in 1956, during the Era of full
employment, he assumed that growth was assured because of technological progress alone. He was regrettably profoundly wrong, although it is
fair to say he lived to recognise his error and he was not at that time
assailed by critics of either left or right who fastened on the faults in his
premiss. In those more confident times, it was more easily believed that
problems of economic management were subordinate to the issues of
political or social choice. Now we know better. What is more, I think we
can now see that so far as Britain's industry was concerned the 1950s and
1960s were decades of dangerous complacency. It was an illusion. It was
then that British industry comfortably enjoying markets not yet challenged by the other countries of Western Europe or the Far East failed to
modernise itself or prepare for the future. It was an error in which
management and trade unions and all political parties participated. The
demise of our motorcycle industry, through the appalling complacency of those who managed it, was not seen as the harbinger of
future events.

We know better now, not perhaps because we are more percipient,
but because the elephant is in our front garden. Our lack of competitiveness is abundantly demonstrated in our relentless relative decline.
The restoration of our industrial economy must be a key objective
because it so manifestly needs to be done and without that occurring all
our plans for social progress simply could not be sustained.

There is, however, another reason apart from sheer necessity. I
believe profoundly that the fairer distribution of wealth and income in
our community in which I passionately believe as the way to create a
more just and genuinely more free society, can only be successfully
achieved in a democratic society on a rising curve of economic progress
and prosperity. It may be theoretically possible to redistribute on a
declining curve or in a static state. My own political judgment, deeply

held, is that it is politically impossible in a democratic society. If evidence were needed of the fundamental truth of this proposition we need only look at the corrosive effects of the reverse redistribution which the Thatcher government has effected in our present circumstance.

I argue therefore that, if we truly wish the better society, we must on the Left give more attention than in the past to the business of growth, of efficiency, of economic progress. We must be prepared to be engaged in a positive sum game in which a greater cake is created, the more equitable division of which can be more effectively achieved. That is why the clear emphasis which the Labour Party has placed on the politics of production, and on our plans to rebuild Britain's industrial strength is manifestly correct. This generation of democratic socialists accepts the challenge to build the economy which is technologically advanced, which is based on high productivity which is internationally competitive, and which above all plans ahead.

How is that to be done? It is here that I join battle with enthusiasm with those on the Right who believe that the only way is through unrestricted market forces and that the role of the State is minor.

If there is one obvious characteristic of our present economic situation it is that reliance on these beliefs leads inevitably to an appalling concentration on short term action and results. Let us take two crucial areas of our industry, namely education and training and research and development. It cannot be denied that we have become woefully weak in both. Perhaps we have never had the best system of industrial training in Britain, but whatever it was, it has systematically been destroyed since 1979.

Sixteen out of twenty three industrial training boards dismembered, 29 skill centres closed down, and technical apprenticeships halved. The collapse of training particularly in engineering has been stunning in its speed and its extent. When our economy expands, it will imediately run into massive skill shortages in a potential labour force which has become de-skilled. Similarly, in research and development, we have taken appalling risks. Of the five leading industrial nations (USA, Britain, France, Germany and Japan) Britain devotes the smallest share of its GDP to civil research and development. Both public and private investment in civil research and development have actually diminished since 1981. I need not catalogue the mournful table of statistics: most objective observers would agree that, in recent years, Britain has an unbelievably bad record in these two vital areas.

The effect in terms of international competitiveness can best be demonstrated by comparing the output of the average British and German industrial worker. The German produces twice as much. That is not because he works harder or longer. Indeed, in the German engineering industry they have just agreed on the shortest working week in Europe. It is because the German worker has at his elbow twice the technological capability, and he is twice as well trained.

Why has this trend of recent years come about? I believe it can be shown to flow directly from the decision of the government to withdraw from responsibility in both these areas and to leave them to the caprice of voluntarism.

Some British companies, of course, do take their responsibilities seriously and realise the basic importance for their future of careful and intensive training and of new product development through research and development. The overall situation is regrettably not such. And if we examine the reasons, I think we can see why. Individual companies, particularly the smaller ones, worry that if they spend resources on training, the investment may be recouped not by themselves, but by competitors who poach their employees. Smaller companies worry about expenditure on research and development, the benefits of which are necessarily long term and the cost of which usually has to come out of current surplus, if the initial impact is to reduce the short term profit leading to a market judgment that the share price should fall and often open the door to the acquisitive predator. At the same time as the public expenditure on research and development through the universities, colleges, and research organisations is being reduced, there exists no fiscal incentive through the taxation system – and precious little direct government financial support for investment by companies themselves. So we see in dramatic form how the abandonment of government responsibility is not compensated by voluntarism or the market. Indeed, the latter often accentuates the deficiency.

The same process is, I believe, at work in the investment mechanism. Investment institutions which exist to provide retirement pensions should by their very nature be long term. After all, their purpose is surely to provide pensions thirty or forty years into the future. Yet they compete for market approval on the basis of a quarterly analysis of their performance, in which every incentive exists for them to secure short term gains which advertise the comparative skills of their managers. Thus the market forces the long term to become the short term.

The whole process is accentuated when the government withdraws from responsibility for the proper supervision and control of takeovers and mergers. Despite a wider range of statutory powers available to it the present government has imprisoned itself in its own decision to apply exclusively competition criteria. Thus it permits a merger mania to flourish despite the lack of evidence that larger conglomerates perform more efficiently, encourages a dangerous short term profit-making mentality in institutions and others, and fails lamentably to secure the application of proper criteria about the effect of take-overs on the shape and effectiveness of our industry, let alone the interests of employees. Notably our principal industrial competitors do not indulge in such irresponsibility.

So I argue that present evidence does not support the view that the withdrawal of government responsibility and abdication to the unrestrained forces of the market leads to the development of long-term and secure investment in industry, to adequate research and development, or even elementary education and training. It is sobering to reflect that seventy five per cent of Britain's industrial workforce receives no proper training at all.

That is why we argue with force and conviction the counter case: that our industry and our wealth creating capacity can only recover if the government accepts responsibility for that recovery. That is why we propose three engines of growth – a new approach to investment, a new commitment to research and development, and a new start for education and training.

We propose to establish the British Investment Bank to provide a new source of finance for industry. Britain is almost unique among Western industrialised countries in having no state bank charged with the responsibility of supplying capital to industry. The Japanese established one in 1902. In Germany, the Kreditanstalt fur Wiederaufbau (KfW) has played a vital role in providing finance to assist structural adjustment, encouraging the export of capital goods and in assisting specific financing problems of small and medium sized firms. France has the Crédit National which, although not state owned, works closely with the French government which subsidises its loans. The KfW and the Crédit National each financed investment valued at more than £1 billion in 1986. As a crucial part of the process of rebuilding a competitive industry in Britain, the British Investment Bank will be charged with the responsibility of providing capital on favourable terms designed to suit the long term needs of industry and targeted in the pursuit of the strategic goals of industrial policy. We hope to start at long last a tradition of industrial banking in Britain in which the private sector banks and financial institutions can also play a positive part.

We intend a profound and long lasting commitment to research and development with particular emphasis on new product development. As a nation, we simply have no alternative choice. Manufactured imports into Britain have grown fastest in the high research intensity and high value added sectors of industry. These now account for 45% of our imports and the level of import penetration, in the high research intensity sectors, has almost doubled in the last few years. To correct this ominous trend, we need a commitment of public expenditure through our public institutions and positive incentives to industry which the present stance of fiscal neutrality in corporate taxation policy prohibits. Not a day goes by without evidence of more prominent scientists leaving our shores. Indeed Sir John Harvey-Jones, the recently retired Chairman of ICI, foresaw the possibility of ICI moving essential parts of its high technology operations out of the UK because of the present failure of policy. A brain drain of our scientists and engineers was predicted by the Right if high taxation policies were pursued: it is in fact occurring because of low levels of public expenditure. Our high class scientists do not in any event earn the salaries which would propel them into the highest tax brackets: that is the privilege of the financiers and the new wealthy of the City. Most of our scientists leave because they are discouraged or prevented from carrying out the research which is the motivating factor in their lives. Sometime soon, Britain must harness our great inventiveness as a nation and our success in pioneering brilliant new scientific advances in the pursuit of our industrial recovery. As part of that process, and to help take Britain forward in high technology sectors and in the industrial application of research, we intend to create British Enterprise, a new state company which will have the capacity to initiate new ventures either on its own or through joint ventures or by facilitating company development. Neither Celltech, our leading biotechnology company, nor Inmos, our only and mainly innovative, silicon chip producer, would exist but for an initiative by the now dismembered NEB. We intend to use British Enterprise flexibly and creatively to lead or to support, as the case may be, but always to take British industry forward.

We ought also, as a matter of urgency, to form the ambition to create the best educated and trained workforce in Western Europe, defining workforce properly as everyone from the process worker to the managing director. The industrial economies of the 1990s and even more so in the next century will compete with each other essentially on the skills of their people. Above all, that is why education and training must be a central responsibility of any intelligent government and why it simply cannot be abandoned to some notion of voluntarism or the market.

These forces for growth require to be co-ordinated in an industrial strategy for Britain. We intend to formulate that strategy through a partnership of government, management and trade unions in a revivified National Economic Development Organisation in which those who work in our industry will, on the basis of their experience and commitment, help set the goals and achieve the targets. We do not believe that government itself can find all the answers, nor that it should seek to attempt to do so. It can, however, provide the leadership to help the active participants in our industry to undertake the task. With their help, we can identify the areas of vital strategic importance where Britain must develop its strength and then set about the task of building that strength. I take, as one illustrative example, the information technology industries. In this so called sunrise sector, we are already in serious deficit in our balance of trade and our expansion is relatively slower than our competitors to a dangerous extent. Professor Ashworth, the Principal of Salford University, and an ex-Chief Scientific Adviser to the Cabinet Office, chaired in one of the Little Neddies a group of businessmen, experts, academics, and trade unionists who produced a plan for recovery in information technology. The Ashworth Report is today gathering dust on a shelf in the DTI because the government do not think it is their business to intervene. But surely the Government has an unavoidable responsibility to lead the devising of an industrial strategy for our nation. That is why in implementing the national strategy we intend to establish, through a greatly strengthened Department of Trade and Industry, a powerhouse force for the real economy which will give leadership and accept responsibility for action.

Since an efficient industrial policy requires the mobilisation of all our resources, an effective regional policy must be a key component of the strategy. Under this government, regional industrial policy has been effectively abandoned and we have seen how market forces have accentuated and deepened the North/South divide. What is left of regional policy is seen as an instrument of social policy, a half-hearted palliative for the effects of decline. We intend, through the DTI and the Scottish and Welsh Offices, to initiate a new policy for the regions and nations of Britain which enables them to rebuild their indigenous strength, not just to secure local prosperity, but as an indispensable part of the national recovery. The emphasis will be on regional and national initiative using a range of incentives to ensure that the engines of growth operate effectively throughout the country. John Mackintosh would certainly have approved of the positive role we plan for the contribution by the Scottish Assembly.

We believe that if we do not plan for success, we shall not succeed. But it is crucial that the planning is strategic and selective. The role of government in all the areas I have described is essentially developmental in the context of a mixed economy in which public and private sectors pull together in a positive sum game. There is abundant room for individual initiative and effort. Indeed I believe more room can be created for its effective expression and success. The small engineering company, for example, prepared to go to the limits of high technology to win for itself and for Britain, has everything to gain from our vision of the future. At each stage, whether it is in investment or research and development or education and training, it has the potential of active and supportive assistance from a government which shares its ambitions for success in a competitive world. Too often at present it is denied not only essential support and encouragement at home and abroad, but faces the threat of a hostile acquisition if it dares to go beyond the short term limits of the present system.

The fundamental weakness of the unrestrained market system is, I believe, that it chronically fails to secure the long term. Whatever else Adam Smith's hidden hand can achieve there is precious little evidence that it is enough on its own to chart a successful future for our country. There has to be a gathering together of the potentially dynamic forces in a strategic way if our essential industrial renaissance is to be achieved and that involves the acceptance of responsibility for leadership in that task by the government which we elect. In the same sense, we will not achieve social justice and opportunity for all our people if we stand aside from the responsibility and expect it to happen by some fortuitous circumstance. There are crucial interconnections achieved when a government is prepared to accept the challenge of achieving both prosperity and justice. Good education and training available to all who can benefit from them is not only a life enhancing opportunity for personal development and achievement, but in a modern age an indispensable element in an intelligent economic policy. Tawney once eloquently observed that the task was to enable ordinary people to achieve their extraordinary potential.

I well understand that it all requires great effort and even greater skill: that all aspirations are more easily articulated than achieved: that there will, in the future as in the past, be many obstacles in apathy, in emnity, in lack of imagination.

But I believe, as I know John Mackintosh did, in democratic optimism, in our capacity as a nation to set our own objectives for the society in which we live, and to set about achieving them in a spirit of resolute determination. Neither our democracy, nor our aspirations for all its citizens need be thwarted by the power of the forces ranged against us nor by the implausible arguments to which they resort.

We are in the Labour Movement, guided by the high and ennobling principles of democratic socialism. Each generation must find its own way in the circumstances of its own time to give them practical effect. I believe that the challenge to us is to create the society which is productive and prosperous, but which shares its wealth with a sense of justice in the knowledge that that is not only a better way, but a more secure foundation. It is a challenge which can be met with confidence and with optimism.

The Market is Not Enough

Hansard, 5 November 1987, Opposition Day

Much of the critique of Thatcherism that John Smith developed in these years seemed to be vindicated in the crash and slump which followed the Lawson boom. On 19 October 1987 the Stock Market crashed on what became known as Black Monday. Following a sustained attack on Lawson's Autumn statement on 3 November 1987, Smith returned to the attack on 5 November 1987. His technique was to move from the particular to the general, especially to argue for further cuts in interest rates and an international response to an international crisis. Lawson rated Smith much higher than Hattersley but on this occasion only comments in his memoirs that Smith, like almost everyone else, was overreacting to the events of Black Monday.

I beg to move: 'That this House, recognising that the stock market collapse results from failures in international economic cooperation and the excessive priority given to finance at the expense of the real economy, and that the collapse has serious implications for the level of economic activity in the United States and for investment and employment at home, notes that the United Kingdom still has close to three million unemployed, that manufacturing output has only just returned to the levels of 1979, and that Her Majesty's Government admits that there will be a downturn in the growth rate, an increase in inflation and a record deficit of £9 billion on manufactured trade in 1988; and urges Government to initiate action among the leading industrial countries in order to concert adjustment of economic imbalances on a planned basis including expansion in the economies of Western Europe, to significantly cut interest rates, to target increases in public expenditure in order to prevent an economic downturn, and to adopt an industrial stategy aimed at systematically developing the strength of industry, technology and skills throughout the whole of the nation.'

This is a timely debate. Following the crash in the financial markets, and with the threat of an economic crisis looming, the House should concentrate its mind on the lessons to be learnt from the turbulent events of recent weeks with one overriding objective the urgent steps that need to be taken to ward off the threat of economic downturn, with the painful consequences for jobs, the standard of living and the national economic strength that would come in train of that.

We know from the Chancellor's Autumn Statement that there are difficulties ahead. The statement was portrayed in euphoric terms by parts of the British press, with its close identity with the interests of the Conservative party. However, it is sometimes useful to see what the foreign press says. The *Wall Street Journal* reported the Chancellor's Autumn Statement. Its headline read:

'Lawson Warns of Hurdles Facing Britain's Economy', It continued:'Chancellor of the Exchequer Nigel Lawson painted a picture of Britain's economy next year, warning that the nation faces slower growth, higher inflation and a mounting balance of payments deficit.'

Let us be in no doubt that we face difficult times. Major change has occurred and markets have collapsed all over the world, particularly in London. Many people sense that we are at the crossroads in the economic development of the country and that if the wrong decisions are taken now they will have consequences for many years ahead. There is a tendency to blame all that on the markets. It is said that they had over-valued and were correcting. The Chancellor offered that as one of the explanations in his Mansion House speech last night.

The Chancellor's initial reaction in the early days of crash was more outspoken. He said that it was a grotesque aberration and a grotesque over-reaction. He talked about the markets behaving with a herd instinct. The epithets came cascading from the Chancellor as he laid about the markets which at other times he had revered, or possibly worshipped. Last night at the Mansion House the right hon. Gentleman stood in his white tie and tails, the principal guest at the Lord Mayor's banquet for bankers and merchants of the City of London, I thought that he should put his thoughts rather differently. He said:

I would like to salute the City for the way in which it has comported itself throughout almost three weeks of a financial blizzard which blew in across the Atlantic.

There was no crude references to grotesque over-reaction, the herd instinct or absurdity. If nothing else, it shows how singing for one's supper can modify one's approach to events.

The Chancellor's case on the cause of the collapse was simple. He said that it was all down to the Americans. The billing and cooing of the Thatcher Government towards the United States' Administration has apparently been replaced by tones of harsh and unforgiving rebuke.

That is the line from the Chancellor. However, as we know, a message has gone from the Prime Minister to the President of the United States, the contents of which have not been revealed. It may say, 'Do not take Lawson too seriously. He is rude by nature and cannot help it. I am still your friend. Maggie.'

The Chancellor's main point was that it all happened because of a lack of political will in the United States; a lack of will to tackle the budget deficit. When things go wrong the Chancellor and the Government, notably the Head of the Government, always find someone else to blame. This time it is the naughty Americans. Basically, the Chancellor, said that they should be put in the dunce's corner until they had sorted out their problems and that no international action should be taken to deal with an international crisis until the Americans had sorted themselves out.

The Americans have a responsibility for the events that have occurred. They were running twin deficits – the budget and the balance of payments – which could not be sustained. The budget deficit is not the only factor. After all the Japanese have a large budget deficit, which is not cause for concern. The reason is that the Japanese, by their own savings, can fund the deficit. Apart from anything else, they tend to buy Japanese and they save. The United States was, and is, relying on the rest of the world to finance its deficit.

I believe that the Chancellor and others may have concentrated excessively on the budget deficit. It is the trade deficit that affects the nation more directly. Both deficits may have to be reduced, but it is crucial that we appreciate that it should be done on a gradual basis that will not cause a major disturbance to world trade and to recession. It is a one-eyed view of the world simply to blame the Americans. The imbalance is at the heart of the matter. The United States has a large deficit while others, notably Germany and Japan, are in surplus.

I fear that the truth is that for many years the major industrial countries have put the tackling of the imbalance well down their order of priority. Perhaps that was nowhere more compellingly illustrated than at the Venice summit held earlier this year during the general election. I hope that those, including our Government, who took part in that self-congratulatory and vacuous occasion now feel ashamed at the irresponsibility that they showed in not tackling the issue then. We recollect that the United States Secretary for the Treasury asked the Organisation for Economic Co-operation and Development countries to set targets for expansion so that they could help the United States in the gradual reduction of its deficit. However, he got no assistance from the other countries.

Why was there a failure of international economic co-ordination? Why was there a failure to act in a situation that all the countries must have known would end in tears? Far too many of them believed that, just as in their own countries. free markets were the regulators of the economy, so international economic relations could be left to the free forces of the market. They could not have been more wrong.

In 1985 some effort started to be made to deal with the dollar and exchange rate instability, through the Plaza agreement of 1985 and the Louvre accord of 1987. In his speech to the International Monetary Fund the Chancellor advocated a new move away from total reliance on market forces and floating exchange rates with his hybrid concept of managed floating. Those faltering attempts at international co-ordination are to be welcomed. It is particularly beneficial for politicians such as the Chancellor to have to realise that their free market nostrums do not work in the real world in which they operate.

There are some differences in attitude displayed by the Chancellor between 1980 and 1987. On 3 July 1980 the Chancellor answered a written question. He was asked: 'what mechanisms exist for medium or long term alteration of the exchange rate?'.

The hon. Mernber who asked the question was given a short and snappy answer. The Chancellor said: 'Market forces'.

The Chancellor reinforced that in a written answer on 3 November 1980, when he said: 'The exchange rate is determined by market forces, not by the Government.' In a written answer on the following day he said: 'The effect on the exchange rate of a reduction of United Kingdorn interest rates relative to the United States rates, if any, would depend upon the circumstances of the time.'

This is the important part: 'There is no stable or reliable relationship between interest rates and the exchange rate.' On 7 October 1987 the Chancellor was quoted in the *Guardian* as saying:

I believe . . . that we can and should use the experience we have gained to build a more permanent regime of managed floating. I do not see the past two years simply as a temporary phase. Our objectives should be clear: to maintain the maximum stability of key exchange rates and to manage any changes that may be necessary in an orderly way.

The *Sunday Times* on 11 October 1987 said:

Elaborating on these proposals, Lawson explained that monetary policy – the determination of short-term interest rates – should be pursued in a way consistent with exchange rate stability.

In other words, interest rates would be adjusted to keep the exchange rate stable. So much for there being no stable or reliable relationship between interest rates and exchange rates. Of course, we welcome the progress of the Chancellor's education, but it has been an expensive education for Britain, just as the experiments in monetarism have been disastrous for British industry . . . [*Intervention*] . . . Opposition members welcome the progress in the Chancellor's education. It is now vital that there should be an international response involving Governments. The fact is that the shattered markets are looking to

Governments to play their indispensable role in the regulation of world economies. A gradual but steady reduction in the United States deficits – particularly the trade deficit – must take place in concert with expansion in Western Europe and Japan. It is not good enough to wait until the Americans do something, hint at action on interest rates and seek to reinstate the Louvre accord. That response by the British Government does not rise remotely to the level of events. The British Government should now take the lead in urging a meeting of the G7 countries with the purpose of working out a new international accord, not just not just to put the United States in the dock, but to engineer – I suppose that the Chancellor would say 'manage' – joint action to save us all from disaster.

The accord should concern itself with interest rates, but it should also contain agreement on one crucial factor: if United States deficits are to decline, Western Europe and Japan must expand to meet the situation. We need an accord related to economic policies as well as financial matters. That is at the heart of the matter. Although the Chancellor has spoken at length about the arrangements since 1985, the fact is that they have broken down. We need a new approach, a sense of urgency and a recognition that internationally interconnected economies cannot be dealt with by policies followed by countries with regard to only their own interests. [*Interventions*] The truth is that the British Government have no policy response at international level. We are constantly told that Britain has achieved a new and semi-miraculous status in the world, that some new respect has been acquired, so why is that not used to give a lead towards a new international accord? [*Interventions*] I do not know whether the Government's inaction is due to a lack of appreciation of the dangers or to an incapacity to respond. Increasingly, the Chancellor reminds me of the Emperor Nero, to whom he bears a passing facial resemblance. The difference is that Nero knew when Rome was burning. The link between the international scene and the British economy is direct, so there is a threat of recession in Britain regardless of what happens in the United States. If America succeeds in reducing both its deficits, but especially its trade deficit, there will be less room for British exports in American markets. If it fails to reduce the deficits and interest rates have to rise, that will push the American economy into recession and there will be consequences for Britain. Therefore, it is vital that we do not wait for the Americans to find a solution before we adopt a strategy for our country.

We need a programme of public investment to provide better facilities, better communications, progress in our inner cities and some hope to our declining regions. That would be worthwhile in itself, but with the possibility of a recession it becomes economically imperative. After all, the Government tell us that our finances are sound. What better base from which to start a new public investment programme? Other countries are doing that. It may not have escaped the notice of those who follow these matters that a fiscal package introduced by the Government of Japan earlier this year amounting to 6 trillion yen – about £25 billion – included a public works component of £1 billion. If it makes sense for the Japanese to invest in their infrastructure, why does it not make sense for Britain to do the same? Doing so would provide new jobs, improve the functioning of the economy and help us to avoid recession.

There may be a reason why the Government do not want to embark on that – perhaps because they are saving that money for tax cuts in the next Budget. In Britain's current economic position, nothing would be more irresponsible than to embark on a programme of tax cuts that would inevitably suck in imports and add to a balance of trade deficit in manufactured goods that is heading towards £8 billion. If the public expenditure programmes were planned with care, concentrating on the regions and the inner cities – where people are out of work, where there is slack in the economy and where, goodness knows, so much desperately needs to be done – we could achieve social and economic results with a low risk of any inflationary consequence. That would be an effective short-term strategy, leading to real benefits in the medium and long terms.

However, we need to do more. We need to improve the long-term competitiveness and strength of the British economy, especially British industry. We are, perhaps, approaching the end of the period during which North sea oil has been a major prop to the British economy. Time after time the Government have been rescued from the consequences of their folly by the reservoir of North Sea oil and the huge funds that it has made available to them.

It has given them protection against balance of trade and balance of payments problems. Yet this still-oil-rich country is heading towards a balance of payments deficit of £3–5 billion.

We know that investment in industry is still 7 per cent below its level in 1979 – far lower than that of our competitors. We know also that since 1980 Britain has been the only country of the five major Western industrialised nations to reduce spending on research and development as a proportion of gross domestic product. There is a complete failure to realise that technology is the driving force of the modern economy. We need a new approach to education and training so that our people can acquire the skills necessary to become the best educated and trained workforce in Western Europe.

The Chancellor used to say that there was no need for the Government to spend money on research and development, and on education and training, because the Government would make industry profitable, and industry would then spend money on research and development and on education and training. Industry has become more profitable, but I am sorry to say that there has not been the promised increase in spending on research and development, and on education and training.

We argue the need for an international response. We also argue for a national strategy as well as an international accord. There should be a reduction in interest rates throughout the countries in Western Europe with which we are closely associated. We need a fiscal response and the public investment programme that I have advocated. We need to build long-term strengths so that this country will have an industry that can sustain us in the 1990s. The trouble is that we have a Chancellor who is compromised by having to get out of the monetarist position that he adopted previously. His policies and recommendations do not fit the time in which we live. Unless the Government alter their course in the way recommended in the motion, not only will they fail, but this country will suffer.

Everybody Needs Good Neighbours

Hansard, 7 June 1989

Smith had been a major presence in the key debates during the Westland crisis, and he was again the Opposition's most effective speaker during another crisis in Thatcher's government. It was Smith who first called Alan Walters the 'unelected Chancellor.' Walters, an obscure academic, had advised Margaret Thatcher between 1981–83 and then effectively traded on this connection to became a celebrated new right economist on both sides of the Atlantic. He returned to Thatcher's side in 1989 when she and her Chancellor were increasingly in disagreement over a number of core economic issues, most importantly British membership of the European Exchange Rate Mechanism. Smith's speech laid bare the divisions at the very heart of the government and was a resounding parliamentary triumph.

I beg to move, 'That this House deplores the confusion and disarray of the Government's economic policy, the record balance of payments deficit, the rising rate of inflation and the damaging level of interest rates; notes with concern the continuing neglect of the real economy and the failures to invest adequately in education and training, research and development, and the regions, which undermine Britain's prospects of success in the single market of the European Community after 1992; and calls upon the Government to give urgent priority to such supply side investment in order to reduce the balance of payments deficit and begin to create a strong, balanced and competitive economy for the 1990s.'

When he presented his Budget in March 1988, the Chancellor of the Exchequer exhibited a sublime degree of self-confidence. His Budget gained fulsome praise from the Prime Minister, who said that it was 'brilliant'. She was not in any way inhibited by the fact that she had sabotaged his exchange rate policy a few days before. The House will recall the Chancellor's confident boast, given in his wind-up to the debate on the Budget resolutions, that Britain was: 'experiencing an economic miracle, comparable in significance to that previously enjoyed by West Germany and still enjoyed by Japan.' In presenting his Budget, the right hon. Gentleman said: 'the present upswing, unlike almost all its predecessors, has not led to any resurgence of inflation

The Chancellor, warming to his task, said in the wind-up to the Budget debate: 'we are now talking about getting it down from something between 3 and 4%'

As for the balance of payments, there would be 'no difficulty in financing a temporary current account deficit of this scale'. But the self-confidence and the self-congratulation proved to be short-lived, because it was based on blissful ignorance, the sort of ignorance demonstrated by a man on the top of a ladder who does not know he is about to fall off. The so-called temporary current account deficit soared to more than £14 billion and has been sliding relentlessly further into the red ever since.

Inflation, described by the Chancellor in a phrase that will haunt him as 'a temporary blip', has doubled to 8% So, today, far from talking about temporary blips, the Chancellor prefers to warn us, as he said in his OECD speech of last week, 'against people who are impatient for quick results'. That was his message to the OECD Ministers in Paris.

But, as interest rates blip higher and higher for longer and longer, is it any wonder that people are losing confidence in Conservative economic policy? With interest rates moving to 14% perhaps higher, with soaring borrowing costs threatening investment in industry and risking overkill and recession, is it surprising that people are becoming impatient for some results? But whose expectations was the Chancellor really trying to calm?

On the day the right hon. Gentleman announced the latest increase in interest rates he was addressing the Tory Women's Conference. He was reported in the *Independent* as having opened his speech to the Tory women by saying as follows about the timing of the interest rates:

'I had two conflicting thoughts. I thought it was a rather tactless time in the middle of the Women's Conference. Then I thought – where else could I look for such mature, intelligent, responsible support?'

They heckled him. I think the Chancellor has a problem with Tory women – [*Interruption.*] – because there is another place, not too far from where he lives where there is not much in the way of mature, intelligent and responsible support for him. The Prime Minister, in an extremely revealing interview in the *Glasgow Herald* told us about the nature of her relationship with her Chancellor of the Exchequer. She said : 'Nigel is a very good neighbour of mine, and a very good Chancellor. Geoffrey is a very good Foreign Secretary. I am not going any further. You know I have to do reshuffles from time to time. I hate them. Why? – because I have a very good Cabinet. But I know that there are young people who have to have an opportunity, as others had it. I hate them.'

I think she must mean the reshuffles. 'I have to work myself up because I know that I have to do them. I hate them.' And then, ominously: 'So will they.'

Good neighbourliness is highly relevant to the confusion and disarray which lies at the heart of Government policy and, on that subject, my sympathies are, to some extent, with the Chancellor of the Exchequer. After all, when he picks up the telephone and wants to get through to No. 10, it must be rather disconcerting to be told, 'Walters here. Would you like to speak to Griffiths?' It is not clear who the real Chancellor of the Exchequer is. We have here the nominal Chancellor of the Exchequer.

Although he and the Prime Minister are neighbours, he should take account, as many of us who are aficionados do, of the theme song of the *Neighbours* programme which we hear twice a day on BBC television. The song goes:

Neighbours – everybody needs good neighbours.
Just a friendly wave each morning helps to make a better day.
Neighbours need to get to know each other.
Next door is only a footstep away.

Neighbours – everybody needs good neighbours.
With a little understanding, you can find a perfect blend.
Neighbours should be there for one another.
That's when good neighbours become good friends.

The Chancellor of the Exchequer may be a good neighbour, but Walters and Griffiths are the good friends. Time after time, in the management of his policy, he has been up-ended by the Prime Minister's own intervention.

The Prime Minister wants some quick results, as Britain's inflation rate soars to 8% and the ludicrous target of zero inflation looks ever more absurd. To avoid the verdict of the judge and jury, the Chancellor has resorted to the lame excuse of the international trend, his flimsy international alibi. At the Organisation for Economic Co-operation and Development he talked about G7 inflation. What on earth is that?

The phrase is intended to give the impression that inflation is a national contagion that no one can avoid, the mere fact that one is alive means that one will catch it and that it does not have much to do with the Chancellor. It is instructive to look at the inflation rates of the other G7 countries. Japan has 1.2%, the Federal Republic has 2.7%, France has 3.4%, the United States of America has 5%, Canada has 4.6%, and Italy has 6%. The average is 4.4%, while Britain has 8%.

There is no such thing as G7 inflation, but there is British inflation, which is not externally caused. Neither oil nor other key commodities have risen spectacularly in this decade, as they did in the 1970s. The resurgence of inflation is domestically driven and caused by the Government's mismanagement of demand, their foolish credit boom, their own utility price increases and the Tories' inflationary 'own goals,' to borrow a phrase favoured by the Confederation of British Industry.

The mismanagement of demand has made worse the most serious problem of all: Britain's worsening balance of payments deficit. The 1988 Budget combined foolish and unfair tax cuts with an unsustainable credit boom and dramatically aggravated Britain's emerging external deficit. Sadly, that deficit is no mere temporary blip. Since 1982, Britain's non-oil current account has been in deficit and has grown worse every year except 1985. That long-running trend of deterioration, concealed for a while by North Sea oil, is at the heart of Britain's balance of payments deficit. However, the Chancellor refuses to acknowledge the problem. He has seriously and consistently under-estimated its scale. Absurdly, Treasury Ministers claim that the deficit is a sign of success. The Chief Secretary to the Treasury does so regularly. By implication, the growing surpluses of Germany and Japan are evidence of economic failure, and their expanding role as the world's foremost creditor nations must be a lamentable national humiliation for them. Alternatively, the Treasury likes to present the deficit as yet another temporary event: a short-term result of excessive demand and a temporary misalignment of demand and supply in the economy. But the deficit is a long-term structural problem that will not be cured merely by the easing of domestic demand.

Since the Chancellor fails to understand the cause of the deficit it is not surprising that he cannot accurately forecast it. In 1988, we were told that it would be £4 billion and it was £14 billion. This year, the Chancellor says that it will be about the same, £14 billion, but so far this year we are heading for a new record deficit of more than £17 billion. When he replies, will the Chancellor explain why the European Commission, the International Monetary Fund and the OECD have all forecast a further record slide into the red this year? The OECD's latest forecast, available to the Chancellor in Paris last week, reportedly predicted that Britain would run record deficits this year and next.

What is the explanation for that discrepancy, given that the OECD forecast must be agreed with the Treasury? I trust that the Chancellor, this afternoon, will tell us the Treasury's revised forecast for the balance of payments this year. Clearly the figures that he gave the House in his Budget statement not so long ago are no longer credible in the House, at the OECD or in the financial markets.

The forecasts are important because they reveal how long high interest rates will be needed to attract the hot money flows which the Chancellor wants in order to finance the balance of payments deficit. High interest rates are not merely a device to curb inflation, but the price we must pay for living beyond our means. We are having to pay the Lawson risk premium, the speculator's ransom, required to attract capital into sterling and finance the balance of payments deficit. That price is rising, as the market's confidence in the Government's economic policy falls.

The Government have failed to tackle the weakness of Britain's economic fundamentals: the burgeoning balance of payments deficit and the resurgence of inflation. Those are facts which no amount of hype about Thatcher miracles can conceal from the currency markets or the electorate. The Government's dependence on higher and higher interest rates is more and more a sign of policy weakness and evidence of confusion and disarray, rather than a firm policy resolve.

A good example of that confusion and disarray arose at Prime Minister's Question Time on 23 May, when the Prime Minister, in answer to a question from my right hon. Friend the Leader of the Opposition, clearly implied that, at 13%, interest rates were adequate to curb domestic demand. The evidence of a slowdown in the credit boom is growing, if not yet fully conclusive.

However, 13%. was not enough to satisfy the currency speculators and failed to buy off their anxieties about the British economy. Here revealed is the self-inflicted contradiction of the Government's economic policy. The Chancellor has chosen to rely on high interest rates as a universal economic panacea, but interest rates are a double-edged sword. They are a weapon that cuts both ways: raising the exchange rate and curbing demand. Those two objectives can conflict, and that is precisely what is starting to happen in the British economy. As demand begins to fall away, high interest rates threaten overkill and recession. However, the Chancellor still needs to attract that hot money to finance his external deficit. [*Intervention*] I shall give way to the Chancellor if he will tell me what he thinks the appropriate rate should be. Not only is this House interested in whether he thinks they should be higher; even more importantly, does the Prime Minister think that they should be higher? The markets never know whether the Chancellor, the Prime Minister or Sir Alan Walters speaks for the Government.

The confusion between the Prime Minister and the Chancellor over interest rates and monetary policy merely exacerbates the inherent conflict within the Government's foundering economic strategy. No. 10 is returning to monetarism and wants to avoid any further rise in interest rates. The City catches wild rumours that the Chancellor has resigned, but the Treasury line remains that interest rates will stay as high as necessary for as long as necessary. Is that still the Government's policy?

The Chancellor of the Exchequer (Mr Nigel Lawson): Yes.

Mr Smith: In that case, they had better get a grip on some of the advisers in No. 10 who tell the press that another Government policy is to be followed. In all this confusion and disarray one searches in vain for the medium-term financial strategy, that wonder of modern economics in which the Chancellor would repudiate day-to-day management of the economy, disparaging it as flying by the seat of one's pants, in favour of medium-term targets. But the medium-term financial strategy has turned out to be just another temporary blip in the history of modern economics. The medium-term financial strategy has been aimlessly drifting in ever decreasing circles until it has finally disappeared up the Chancellor's own monetary targets.

Recently, the Chief Secretary to the Treasury bravely attempted to resuscitate the medium-term financial strategy when speaking to a conference of small businesses, called 'Small Businesses: The Quiet Revolution'. He told the conference – I quote from his Treasury handout:

Government policy now operates in a medium-term framework which gives individuals and firms the confidence to plan ahead.

He was speaking on Wednesday 24 May, the same day on which interest rates rose to 14% jump, the tenth such jump in borrowing costs since last summer. That is the medium-term plan to give small businesses confidence with which to plan.

I shall tell the Chancellor, who seems sceptical, what the small businesses said about his 14% interest rates. The National Federation of Self Employed and Small Businesses received the news with dismay, commenting that each percentage point increases the cost to industry by an extra £250 million. The federation complained that small businesses will be hit hardest, and went on to say that they were the pawns in the Government's move to defend the pound. So much for the medium-term financial strategy and the confidence it engenders.

I asked the National Federation of Self Employed and Small Businesses to give me an example of what it meant, which it did, calling it 'Real Example No. 1'. It concerns a company in Gwent, a supplier of equipment to the heating and plumbing industry. Its owner borrowed £25,000. His repayments on 19 May, when he first took out the loan, totalled £343 a month. This year, on 18 May 1989, his bank statement showed that the repayments had gone up to £552.44. He is also suffering from bad debts on the part of his creditors, because they, too, are being squeezed. If interest rates rise to 15%, as the federation says seems likely, his repayments on the loan will have doubled. So much for the medium-term financial strategy and for encouraging small businesses.

The truth is that higher interest rates are a costly and ultimately futile attempt to restore confidence in the Government's failed economic policy. They will hurt British industry and British families, and especially home owners, whose mortgage misery is caused by a tax this year on home ownership – the price of the Chancellor's earlier mistakes.

The market's judgment of the Government's economic policy and the resulting fragility of sterling cannot be reversed by high interest rates alone. Such rates are a recipe for further industrial decline, as soaring borrowing costs become an intolerable burden on British industry. Real confidence will be restored only when the Government start to tackle the fundamental problems of the British economy and stop indulging in what the *Daily Telegraph* recently called 'rhetorical self-indulgence abroad accompanied by an ever-burgeoning culture of economic self-gratification at home' – something with which we have grown familiar over the weary 10 years of this Government.

Real confidence will return, as those on all sides of industry know, only when we in Britain invest in the supply side of the economy with the same relentless determination as West Germany does. If we are to boost our industrial capacity and trading performance we must invest, as our motion states, 'in training, research and development, and the regions', and especially in manufacturing industry. Only investment can build the strong and competitive economy that Britain needs to meet the challenge in Europe after 1992.

Despite the Government's receipt of £78 billion in North Sea oil revenues – one statistic that the Government seek to smother: we never hear the apologists in No. 10 drawing our attention to the existence of North sea oil revenues – we have massively under-invested, especially in the manufacturing tradeable sector of our economy. Investment in the manufacturing sector has only just crawled back to the level achieved by the last Labour Government, and the cumulative loss over 10 years amounts to about £18 billion of investment forgone. We have squandered North Sea oil and have failed to invest, while our major rivals without that unprecedented windfall have raced ahead. In that excess of self-indulgence which characterised his 1988 Budget speeches, the

Chancellor arrogantly compared Britain's so-called economic miracle with that of West Germany. He was so disparaging as to refer to the West German economic miracle in the past tense. We have heard that the West German economy is sclerotic, arthritic and hidebound and somehow much less efficient intrinsically than the bounding, vigorous economy that characterises the United Kingdom.

Let us look at our feeble performance compared with West Germany's investment record in manufacturing, research and development and training. The share of GDP invested in manufacturing in West Germany in the eight years from 1980 to 1987 is more than 50% higher than for the same period in the United Kingdom. Is it any wonder that West Germany's share of world trade since 1980 has gone up from 19.9% to 21.5% while that of Britain has fallen from 9.7 to 8.1%? Is it surprising that our deficit in manufactures with West Germany has grown from the £2 billion that the Government inherited to the £8.5 billion that it is now?

I looked through a list of figures comparing British investment with that in West Germany, and I shall select a few. West Germany spends £432 per employed person on research and development compared with only £265 in the United Kingdom. Over 70% of engineers in West Germany have recognised qualifications compared with 40% in the United Kingdom. The figure that I find the most shaming of all is that only 30%. of our workforce have recognised qualifications equivalent to at least one O-level, compared with 70% in West Germany.

Let us look at West Germany's investment in machine tools. In 1987, it spent £3 billion on machine tools, compared with £670 million in the United Kingdom. West Germany now installs as many new robots every year as the total number of robots in place in Britain. Overall, machine tool purchases have increased by 100% in West Germany against a rise of only 10% in the United Kingdom. That is what is happening in West Germany. What is happening here? I hope that the

House will not feel that it has to rely on any kind of biased statistic on a matter as serious as this. That is why I shall quote what the Engineering Employers Federation said two days ago in the *Financial Times*. It said:

The federation predicts the negative trade balance in all engineering products will worsen by 30% from a deficit of £8.9bn in 1988 to £11.6bn this year.

It says:

Aerospace products will be the only significant UK metal-using manufacturing sector to remain in the black in international trade this year. Mechanical engineering, for the first time in recent years, will slip into the red, moving from a positive balance of £166m last year to a deficit of £1.6bn this year, the federation estimates.

The engineering industry last had a positive trade balance, of £2.8 billion, in 1982. Last year the deficit more than doubled from £4.2 billion in 1987.

That is the sad tale of what is happening in a crucial part of our manufacturing sector. No wonder our balance of trade and our consequent balance of payments deficit are frightening.

Instead of following the example of successful competitors the Government continue the decade-long neglect of our manufacturing industry, the internationally tradable sector of our economy. That is the fundamental fault in the British economy and the fundamental flaw in the Government's policy. They compound this error, which is right at the heart of the matter, with confusion and disarray in the day-to-day management of the economy, especially on the demand front.

Before March 1988 the Chancellor was shadowing the Deutschmark at the level of DM 3 to the pound. That was until the Prime Minister brutally overruled him, as she pointedly reminded him recently. More recently, the Chancellor has been assuring markets of his firm intention to raise interest rates as high as is necessary for as long as is necessary. No doubt he will seek to make that clear again today and the markets will ask, as they ask every time he says it, whether the Prime Minister agrees with him. Two weeks ago in an answer at Prime Minister's Question Time the right hon. Lady cut the feet from under him and precipitated a currency fall which in turn brought another increase in interest rates. Hardly a day goes by when we do not have a further indication of dissent and confusion in that border zone between No. 11 and No. 10 Downing street.

On the No. 10 side of that zone there are some influential lodgers. There is Sir Alan Walters, the real Chancellor of the Exchequer, and the monetarist guru Professor Brian Griffiths. They are there to torment the Chancellor, and as he gets through and speaks to them, he no doubt remonstrates with them for conspiring against his policies. I do not envy the Chancellor in his difficulty in seeking to make some sense of the policy to which he is committed. He ought to get support from the Prime Minister once the Government have decided upon their economic policy. This country cannot have its economy managed by constant warfare between Nos. 10 and 11 and all the consequences that have flowed from that in recent months. [*Intervention*]

I thought that I had been making clear almost to the point of repetitive boredom the Opposition's commitment to tackling the fundamental problem of Britain's economy, which is the supply side problem. I am making clear not only our disagreement about the incompetent demand management that is practised by the Government but our disagreement about their excessive reliance on interest rates as the only weapon. Can we get that clear?

I should like all Conservative Members to deal with the policy. I should like them to start explaining why we invest less than West Germany. I should like them to tell us why they do not speak up for small businesses, which complain so vociferously about the effect of higher interest rates. [*Interruption*] What we are debating here today is the confusion and disarray in the Government's economic policy. [*Interruption*] Conservative Members find it entertaining if someone disagrees with his Front Bench. I say one thing back to them – Old Bexley and Sidcup to you. The fact is that there is confusion and disarray in the Government's economic policy. A child could see that. Their short-term tactics are as muddled as their strategy is inadequate. That is why today, on behalf of a troubled nation, we call them to account.

European Monetary Union

Hansard, 2 November 1989

Following the departure of Lawson and Howe, John Major was appointed Chancellor and Britain was in its brief membership of the EMS. The Labour Party's frequent changes of mind and policy on membership of the European Community and later Union had never presented a problem for John Smith because he did not alter his views. He was consistently in favour of British co-operation with the EEC and supported the moves that created the European Union. He also supported John Major's decision that Britain should enter the Exchange Rate Mechanism of the European Monetary System. It is a decision that has been much attacked but it was not the wrong decision in principle. The problem was that Major took Britain at far too high a rate of DM3.95. The high rate meant that the membership of the ERM was a constant problem for the British currency, a lower rate and the political fate of the long Conservative government and John Major himself might have been very different. Smith and the Labour opposition did not oppose the decision to enter the EMS. In part this was because the party was fast modernising its antediluvian stance on membership and extent of engagement with the European Union and in part this was because Smith believed that membership was in the long term economic interest of Britain. Making speeches while in opposition that are an endorsement of government policy are never easy and Smith's forensic skill, so in evidence during Westland and in

the critique of Lawson's reckless Chancellorship, could not be deployed. However, the
EMS dispute had seen the deepest split in the Cabinet of the Thatcher years and the
political necessity was to expose the weakness of the government while agreeing with
the final outcome. This was a different sort of Parliamentary and political occasion and
it demanded a different sort of speech.

I agree with the Chancellor of the Exchequer that today's debate is timely and important. That is because it is, I think, the first time that the House has been able to debate in full the issues of economic and monetary union and the report prepared under the chairmanship of Jacques Delors, the President of the European Commission. The House will be assisted in its task by the excellent report on the subject published in June by the Select Committee on the Treasury and Civil Service. That report and the evidence provided by the Governor of the Bank of England and the right hon. Member for Blaby (Mr Lawson), the former Chancellor, also provide useful background information for the debate. It is noteworthy that the Select Committee report felt it was necessary to warn against and even anticipate the lack of clarity and the deliberate ambiguities in the Government's policy on European economic issues. Hon. Members will recall that the Select Committee complained that at the European Council in Hanover in June 1988 the Government had 'accepted far-reaching language too lightly' when they endorsed the idea of economic and monetary union. The report recommended: 'It is important that the Government should make its position absolutely clear at the Madrid summit and should not again go along with language whose full implication it does not accept.' The Select Committee concluded: 'It is obviously dangerous for the Government to go on paying lip service to ideas to which in reality it is fundamentally opposed.' Those were prophetic words. That is precisely what the Government have done and continue to do. In Madrid, they endorsed stage 1 of Delors while they were still internally divided over whether to join the exchange rate mechanism. As they had completely ignored the Select Committee's prescient advice, is it any wonder that the ship of state hit such troubled and turbulent waters, and that the Cabinet has been wrecked upon such 'a singularly ill-concealed iceberg'? Recent events have revealed all too clearly that the Madrid formula was a fudge – lip service designed to conceal the confusion and disarray in Government policy – and it has now been totally blown apart. The gulf between the former Chancellor and the Prime Minister could not be more clear. The House, our European partners or the electorate would not find credible the argument that the former Chancellor's support for United Kingdom entry into the exchange rate mechanism – I quote his latest formulation-at the 'earliest practicable time' – can be squared with the Prime Minister's sceptical and reluctant attitude towards what she calls a 'higgledy piggledy system'.

The events after Madrid convinced the right hon. Member for Blaby (Mr Lawson) that he could not persuade the Prime Minister on the issue of the exchange rate mechanism. He knew that advisers advise, and the Prime Minister decides. On the basis of Sir Alan Walters' advice, the Prime Minister has decided to postpone indefinitely United Kingdom entry into the exchange rate mechanism. Having struck his iceberg, the Chancellor resigned and, with his resignation, the credibility of the Madrid formula, which is highly relevant to what we are discussing today, has collapsed.

It will not do for Conservative Members to try to obliterate the events of the past two weeks from their memory. We will not allow them to obliterate their memory of the events. I invite Conservative Members to turn on the television on Sunday, when they will find the right hon. Member for Blaby going over some of the issues again.

The attempts by the right hon. Member for Huntingdon (Mr Major), the new Chancellor of the Exchequer, to square the circle and recover a commitment in good faith to join the EMS will fail to convince, because the credibility of the Government's commitment to stage 1 of the Delors report is clearly questionable. One might almost say that it has been undermined. The House will recall that Delors stage 1 envisages that all member states should participate in the exchange rate mechanism, and stage 1 will begin as from 1 July next year. It is plain from the Prime Minister's Walden interview and from her infinitely expanded preconditions that the Prime Minister has no intention of accepting United Kingdom entry into the Exchange Rate Mechanism before the next election. Perhaps it is no coincidence that Professor Patrick Minford, a monetarist colleague of Sir Alan Walters, believes that the issue of the EMS is 'effectively dead'. I suspect that the issue will not be laid to rest so easily, even if the Prime Minister and many Conservative Members wish it to be so.

At the Strasbourg summit next month, decisions will be taken on the convening of an intergovernmental conference due to be held in the autumn of next year to consider the consequent stages 2 and 3 of the Delors report. The current and future presidencies of the Community show no sign of wanting to delay the decision-making process. In fact, they appear to want to speed the process up. It is also apparent that the proposed intergovernmental conference may, on majority voting, proceed to draft an entirely new treaty, rather than amending the existing treaty, which would require a unanimous decision of all the member states. There is no guarantee that Britain can veto proposals that we do not believe to be in Britain's best interests. There is a clear risk that vital decisions can be made about the future of European economic convergence that would leave Britain on the sidelines. Given the Prime Minister's attitude, that may well be the legacy of a decade of Thatcherism.

During the Prime Minister's Walden interview, it became evident that the conditions now attached to United Kingdom entry require the whole of Europe to embrace Thatcherism, but despite all the hype about Thatcherism being exported, it has not happened over the past 10 years; nor will it happen in the decade ahead. Let us take, for example, the Government's isolated position on the Social Charter, which the Prime Minister has described as Marxist. [*Hon. Members*: Oh!] Tory Members may not think that the social charter is relevant to the future of the European Community but we think that it is highly relevant. They have no right to determine unilaterally the terms of debate.

The extent of the Government's isolation on the social charter reveals how out of touch they remain on other key issues of economic co-operation and convergence. Our approach is to accept stage 1 of the Delors report and to negotiate entry into the exchange rate mechanism on reasonable and prudent conditions. These conditions, as I explained to the House on Tuesday, include entry at an effective rate, adequate central bank swap arrangements to tackle speculative flows, increased support for regional policy and agreement on a co-operative growth strategy. These conditions are important and not unreasonable.

Two weeks ago, my hon. Friend the Member for Dunfermline, East (Gordon Brown) and I visited Paris, Brussels and Bonn, to discuss these concerns with the relevant authorities. It was encouraging to find on many of these issues a common basis of understanding and shared concerns with our partners in Europe. In key respects, the points that we have raised are already under discussion and are being addressed as the debate provoked by the Delors report unfolds. We find common acceptance of the need to tackle the growing payments imbalances within the Community, the importance of collective action by the central banks to tackle speculative attacks against currencies within the EMS and the crucial importance of regional policy, which features prominently in the Delors report, to ensure that growth and development are balanced and evenly spread throughout the Community as the single market unfolds after 1992.

These are not impossible conditions. They are practical concerns already on the agenda for Europe in the decade ahead. The Labour party is ready to shape that agenda. Only last week, the European Parliament voted for a resolution that embodies the Labour party's proposals, and is concerned primarily with stage 1 of the Delors report. It urged: 'The pound should participate in the EMS as soon as possible'. It called for 'active industrial policy coupled with extensive regional policies, control of speculative movements and the elimination of the largest inter-Community deficits and surpluses.'

This resolution, which includes all Labour's conditions for entry into the Exchange Rate Mechanism, will be presented to the Strasbourg summit as a decision of the European Parliament. I am delighted that the Parliament has embraced so much from the Labour party's agenda for Europe in the decade ahead. I have heard hon. Members say that that is what makes them suspicious, but let me give them some further information. I was surprised, although not disappointed, when I heard that the Conservative group in the European Parliament not merely voted for the resolution that I have just quoted but also supported some key amendments proposed by Labour Members of the European Parliament. Indeed, a Conservative Member of the European Parliament, Mr Bryan Cassidy, the Conservative group's economic spokesman, attributed the key amendment to 'the influence of the 45 strong British Labour group which now dominates and controls the Socialist group as a whole.'

We are delighted that some Conservative MEPs understand and even welcome the wisdom of the Labour party's approach. The fact that they are taking our lead and following the Labour party's team in Europe speaks volumes for the style of leadership and the quality of teamwork that they have seen operating within the Conservative party in the United Kingdom. Unlike Conservative Members, they have recently had an encounter with the electorate. That concentrates the mind wonderfully. At the ballot box in June they saw all too painfully the result of the Prime Minister's attitude to Europe and her bungled

European election campaign (Labour gained 10 seats from the Conservatives at the European elections of June 1989). In recent years, the British people have become increasingly concerned at the growing gap in terms of economic success, standard of living and social provisions between Britain and other leading Community countries. They perceive – I believe that this was reflected in their votes in the European parliament election – that it is harmful to the Community as well as to the Government to resist in a niggardly negative manner the moves to raise social standards and provide a floor of rights for employees. They understand that that is bad for Britain generally. We are not leading Europe; we are falling behind. The Government's obsessional insistence on unrestricted market economics, the removal of social protections and a minimalist role for Government, in opposition to the widely held views of the rest of the Community, prevents progress and harms Britain's political interests. It shows that Britain is being unreasonably unwilling to compromise and co-operate with our European partners.

I fear that Ministers are as partisan abroad as they are at home. Whenever their narrow ideological obsessions collide with the idea of greater European co-operation, it is the European concept which is sacrificed. The coming clash on the social charter at Strasbourg is wholly unnecessary. The Government are wrong. They will once again isolate themselves within a Community which is becoming increasingly less tolerant of the Prime Minister's Don Quixote-like charges at European windmills.

The plain truth is that Europe will always be politically diverse. It is as unlikely as it would be illiberal to expect or to demand the entire Community to embrace one economic or political set of values, let alone the absurdities of Thatcherism.

The social, economic and environmental issues of the 1990s will not be resolved by the universal panacea of *laissez faire*. The EMS has spent the past 10 years curbing the excesses of the currency markets, but in other important policy areas more than the price mechanism will be required to sustain growth and improve the quality of life. Such realism about the limits of market forces will dominate the agenda of the 1990s and influence the evolving trend of economic convergence in Europe. It is vital that in the decade ahead Britain has a Government who are capable of combining that realism with the commitment to deal constructively with our partners in Europe.

For the reasons that I have given, it is important that Britain participates in good faith in the debate on the Delors report. The Labour party has indicated its willingness to consider these issues. We are prepared to accept stage 1 of the Delors plan and are ready to negotiate the conditions under which the United Kingdom should enter the exchange rate mechanism.

What will follow stage 1 of the Delors report remains to be seen. The agenda for the proposed intergovernmental conference has yet to be agreed. The proposals set out by the Delors committee for stages two and three of economic and monetary union are very far-reaching, and represent only one among a number of possible proposals to achieve greater monetary co-operation and economic convergence. There has been cogent criticism of the Delors report. In many ways, it is far too schematic in tone. It makes assumptions which are neither argued nor justified, and it is on the whole dangerously insensitive to the political dimension of economic decision taking and the need for democratic accountability. Perhaps it suffers from being the product of a committee dominated by central bankers.

The Delors report may be a useful starting point for debate and discussion, but it could never be regarded as a blueprint for the future of Europe. I hope that that answers the question that the hon. Member for Berwick-upon-Tweed (Mr Beith) addressed to me. I mention two major reservations that we have about stages two and three. Let me make it clear that we would not be willing to accept any system of central banks which would be independent of political control, just as we strongly oppose an independent status for the Bank of England such as the former Chancellor, the right hon. Member for Blaby appears to have been considering a year ago and which was only tantalisingly revealed in his post-resignation comments this week. I do not know whether the present Chancellor will pick up that idea and seek to persuade the rest of his colleagues.

Mr Major indicated dissent.

Mr Smith: Almost undoubtedly, the Chancellor looked as if he was saying no, but I am not sure. We are firmly against such a concept for the EC and we do not accept that binding rules for budgetary or fiscal policy are a necessary condition for the achievement of monetary union. I remind the House that that is one of the central parts of stages 2 and 3.

In the proposed system of independent central banks there is no democratic accountability at all. The whole point of having an independent banking system, Bundesbank-style, is that it is insulated from politics. That was somehow regarded as a desirable feature. There is no form of democratic accountability either from Ministers or from any kind of parliamentary mechanism. That is a fundamental objection to the proposal, and, as my hon. Friend reminds me, that will be the unanimous view of my right hon. and hon. Friends.

The binding rules are not a necessary condition for the achievement of monetary union in any event. The Chancellor of the Exchequer drew attention to the Select Committee's conclusion that 'The power of the House of Commons over the centuries has depended fundamentally on the control of money, both taxation and expenditure. This would be jeopardised by the form of monetary union proposed by the Delors Report which would involve central undemocratic direction from within Europe of domestic budgetary policies.'

I am happy to accept that enthusiastically, and I am sure that all Opposition Members accept it too.

Mr Taylor: I thank the Minister for his excellent recent remarks. We have had some fun, but he has made some excellent recent remarks. He seems to agree with my right hon. Friend the Chancellor that stages 2 and 3 of the Delors report are completely unacceptable as a blueprint for the future. Would he honestly say – I mean this sincerely, John – whether there is anything at all in the three conditions laid down by the Government and the Chancellor for joining the ERM with which the Labour party would disagree – apart from its own reservations? If we could agree, we could send a unanimous message to Strasbourg. Is there anything in our three conditions – freedom of movement of trade, freedom of financial stability and the right exchange rate – with which he would disagree? If not, we can for the first time for many years send a unanimous message to Strasbourg.

Mr Smith: I am tempted to say, 'Well, Teddy, I can't remember when I last heard you speaking like that, whether it was in Cathcart or at Glasgow university.' The hon. Gentleman referred to me as the Minister. I must ask him to exercise just a little patience in that respect. In two years' time I shall be happy to accept his words. But I shall do him the courtesy of answering his question. The conditions that have been attached to stage 1, not stages 2 and 3, by the Government are not the appropriate conditions, and the ones that the Labour party has proposed are.

For example, I do not know to what level inflation has to be brought down before the Government are satisfied. I suspect that that might be a moving goalpost. If the Government really mean what they say about these conditions, they would define the level of inflation that

THE CRITIQUE OF THATCHERISM

would be regarded as desirable. That might be a useful line of inquiry for the hon. Gentleman to pursue when he is asking questions of Ministers who are responsible for formulating policy now and for conducting the negotiations in the EC.

Mr Benn: What my right hon. and learned Friend said about the retention of the Bank of England under the Bank of England Act 1946 is important and welcome. He will know that under that Act, the Treasury has the power to give directives to the Bank of England, the Bank of England has the power to give directives to any other bank and the Treasury has the power to define what a bank is. Therefore, enormous powers will fall to him as Chancellor and I hope that he will follow that through by saying that, if necessary, he intends to use all of them.

Mr Smith: The constitutional position of the Bank of England in relation to the Government is satisfactory at the moment. I see no reason why that should be changed. A wide range of powers is available to the Chancellor of the Exchequer and no Chancellor should willingly give them up. He certainly should not contemplate handing over power over key economic monetary issues to bankers who are not accountable to the British people. As I think my right hon. Friend has gathered, that conditions our view of the proposals contained in the Delors report for a system of central banks and it is consistent with the view that we take at home. I was shocked and astonished to discover that the former Chancellor was contemplating handing over the power to decide some of those matters to the present Governor of the Bank of England. I am sure that most hon. Members would basically agree with that proposition, although the fact that the former Chancellor revealed that view makes one wonder whether there are not some in the Conservative party who might take a different view. The Chancellor has revealed a new plan today. He has produced the plan for competing currencies – to give it a shorthand title. It formed an important part of the Chancellor's speech. I am tempted to say that it is one of the matters that should be referred to the Select Committee, since the right hon. Member for Worthing is the Chairman. I am rather torn on whether this wheeze of competing currencies should trouble the Select Committee. I would enjoy the prospect of the Chancellor explaining it to my hon. Friend the Member for Hackney, South and Shoreditch (Mr Sedgemore), but I am sure that there are many more useful matters that could occupy the Select Committee's expert attention.

It is clear that the Treasury's plan for competing currencies would have pleased Heath Robinson. It is yet another example of the Conservative's addiction to unfettered market forces. It is envisaged that currencies in Europe would engage in a Darwinian struggle for supremacy within the single market after 1992. It is an idea which, as the Chancellor knows well, received a cool reception – to put it as politely as I can – from the other European Finance Ministers when it was informally floated at the regular council meeting at Antibes in September. No other member state in the Community supported the scheme and, typically, even the Conservative Finance Ministers of Europe found the idea more than a little bizarre.

A multi-currency scheme would lower the efficiency of the single market. Not for the first time, the application of free market ideology would damage the very market that it seeks to advance. Transaction costs would soar dramatically with the complexity of making payments in numerous different currencies. It is much more likely that a multi-currency system would quickly degenerate into a single currency system. The laws of the currency jungle would guarantee the supremacy of the Deutschmark, and to adapt a well-known sentence from Thomas Hobbes, life for the pound would be 'nasty, brutish and short.'

It is hard to imagine a scheme that would more rapidly hand British monetary sovereignty to the German authorities in the Bundesbank. If ever there were a 'half-baked scheme', this is it. It does not reach even the minimum level of plausibility. It is hard to escape the conclusion that the plan for competing currencies is nothing but a diversion, a further attempt to conceal the Government's divisions over the EMS. As the editors of the latest edition of the *Oxford Review of Economic Policy* conclude:

The idea seems so risible that we can only believe that it is not a serious suggestion but a delaying tactic to confuse the debate over economic and monetary union.

I thought that it might be the last joke by the Chancellor of the Exchequer, left as a little surprise for whoever might be his successor. I am astonished to discover that his successor takes it seriously enough to present it unvarnished and unamended to the House.

The other 11 member states of the Community show no sign of wishing to indulge the Government's enthusiasm for competing currencies. Still less do they accept the patronising tone of the Prime Minister when she demands that they catch up with Thatcherism. Far from Europe catching up with us, it is high time that the Government concentrated on catching up with our Community partners and competitors. Economically and socially, over the past 10 years Britain has fallen behind. We have failed to match the level of investment in education and training, in research and development, in the regions and in manufacturing industry, which has been achieved, for example, by West Germany. The result is our massive trade deficit with the Federal Republic. Despite all the hype about economic miracles and arrogant assumptions that we have now surpassed the German miracle, there is still a lot of catching up to do.

Why are the Government prepared to stand back while social provision in this country falls behind the best practice in Europe? When will the Government conceive the ambition to catch up with European levels of pensions, with European standards of protection for the low paid and with the best levels of European child care provision? Those are the key elements of the social dimension to Europe which the Conservative party opposes, cannot understand and does not even want to discuss today. That is why it has tried to block the social charter, even though it is clearly supported by the majority of British people.

The social charter and the legislative action programme that will flow from it are indispensable to the successful conclusion of the single market. Without adequate minimum standards, the social and political cohesion of the Community will be seriously weakened. Without the social charter, it will be harder to build the strong economy and fairer society that Europe and Britain will need in the years to come. Labour Members know that there can be no lasting economic convergence and monetary co-operation without a strong commitment to a social Europe, which is why Britain needs a Labour Government to build a Europe that is not only a market for business but a community for people.

PART THREE

Shadowing the Major Government

INTRODUCTION

*After the Party conference in 1988 Smith suffered a heart attack. He reflected on
the experience and on his recovery in an article for the Evening Standard:*

My heart attack was a complete surprise. I suppose I had
known that in middle age overweight persons living hectic
lives were more at risk than others. But to know something
and to believe it for oneself are two different things. I suffered the fond
illusion shared, I fear, by many – that I was invulnerable. Whatever else,
it could not happen to me. I know better now. My first thoughts as I lay
in a hospital bed and realised that I would probably survive were about
how fortunate I had been. I had had the attack in the casualty department of the Edinburgh Royal Infirmary – one of the best hospitals in
the world. Within minutes I was whisked into a specialised coronary
care unit and received superbly expert attention and care. I had got to
the hospital because of two people – my wife and a neighbour who is a
doctor. Although I did not have the classic symptoms of an approaching
heart attack, my wife knew something was wrong and stopped me from
taking the shuttle plane to London as I had planned to do. She also got
our neighbour to have a look at me. It was he who – providentially for
me – took me to the hospital for a check up. I still shudder to think
what would have happened if they had not saved me from myself. Left
to my own devices, I know that I would probably have collapsed in a
plane, in mid-air somewhere between Edinburgh and London. I might
have survived but I am far from certain about that.

I do not know whether it was the result of medication or a psychological surge of relief but when I was able to take stock of my situation I felt strangely euphoric. I know I talked endlessly – and probably foolishly – to my wife and daughters. I am glad to be back in Westminster. The joys of relaxation were beginning to pall just a little and an urge to get back into the fray began to assert itself just before Christmas. I am now, I think, a little wiser. I have cause to be very grateful for wonderful health care and to a supporting family. I have a positive policy to keep actively healthy and I am planning leisure as well as work. But it should not have required a heart attack to teach me such obvious common sense.

Though he returned to mainstream politics and delivered some of the heaviest hits of all during the last days of Thatcher, he became the predominant opposition politician during John Major's years in office. Thus Margaret Thatcher's fall and the election of John Major as Prime Minister coincided with the most important era of John Smith's period as Shadow Chancellor, the run-up to and the fighting of the 1992 general election.

The course of exercise that Smith embarked on after his heart attack included walking the Monroes. It was a powerful demonstration effect to his political rivals and opponents that he was back and fully fit. He needed to be. The first years of the 1990s, the end of the Thatcher era and the beginning of a period of political drift and flux under John Major, were ones in which John Smith was one of the half dozen key politicians in the country. Major's strategic inaptitude and political myopia, especially with respect to the critical issue which required a lead, Britain's relationship with the European Union, could not have been in more marked contrast to the settled consistency of Smith's political vision. The irony is that it was the strident, perhaps over strident articulation of that vision in the 1992 General Election, especially in the shadow budget, that allowed Major to win the most remarkable general election victory of the postwar era. Though this perhaps saved Major's reputation from being consigned with rapidity to the dustbin of history, the structural flaws in his approach to politics and the running of the country remained. Smith was to face him head to head in the last years of the by then Labour leader's life. But in 1990 the key political questions were Europe and the state of the economy.

The Dog Days of Thatcherism

Hansard, 23 January 1990

The contest between Major and Smith began while Major was still Chancellor of the Exchequer. The economy was in deep recession and showed little sign of recovery, despite the best efforts of Major to talk things up. The heady days of the Lawson boom were by now a distant memory. Smith had been making essentially the same speech for a decade and occasionally the weariness of opposition politics and his inability to be actually making the decisions came through in his speeches.

I beg to move: 'to leave out from 'House' to the end of the Question and to add instead thereof: 'declines to approve the Autumn Statement, deplores the continuation of economic policies which have caused a record balance of payments deficit, high inflation and the highest interest rates of the leading industrial nations; and calls for a strategy to promote investment in manufacturing industry and the public services in order to strengthen the economy, improve the efficiency of industry, and enhance the quality of life and opportunities for all citizens in the decade ahead.'.

This is the first economic debate in the House in the new decade. Perhaps it is not inappropriate to seek to take stock – as the Chancellor did to some extent – of where we stand in economic terms at the end of the 1980s and to look ahead to the prospects for the 1990s. Today we had a modified version of the hype, exaggeration, self-congratulation, casuistry and complacency that have, over the decade, characterised the

Government's presentation of economic policy. Unfortunately, for apologists such as the Chancellor, they have been blown apart by three stark economic facts which no Government apologists or media *apparatchik* can gainsay and which, significantly, the Chancellor did not mention in his speech. The first fact is that we have the highest balance of payments deficit in our economic history. Is it not remarkable that the Chancellor can come to the House with the knowledge of such a fact, yet not manage even to mention it in the first economic debate of the decade? The second stark and unavoidable fact is that Britain's rate of inflation is the highest of the major countries in the European Community. Why should we be lectured about the perils of inflation by this Chancellor when we have a worse record than our principal competitors in the Community?

Another stark fact that the Chancellor hardly mentioned is that interest rates, at 15% they have increased 11 consecutive times in the past 18 months, are the highest among the leading industrial nations. What a verdict that is on the so-called successful economic policies followed during the 1980s. Because reading previous speeches of Conservative Ministers is as instructive as reading their current ones, I referred back to the corresponding debate last year, when the former Chancellor said that inflation would

edge up a little over the next few months but then, just as it did in 1985, it will start coming down again. Let there be no doubt about that whatever.

I remind the House that Conservative Ministers are good at the reassuring game. Whenever any awkward matter comes up, they assure us that things will be all right for the future. I will tell the House what the rate of inflation has been in the subsequent months. In January 1989, when the former Chancellor gave us that confident prediction, it was 7.5%; in February, it was 7.8%; in March, 7.9%; in April, 8%; in May, 8.3%; in June, 8.3%; in July, 8.2%; in August, 7.3%; in September, 7.6%;

in October, 7.3%; in November, 7.7%; and in December the last available figures 7.7%.

Anyone can work out that those figures are steadily high [*Interruption*] I am reminded by Conservative Members that the former Chancellor may have been predicting that in the careful words that he used. That will not wash. He said that it would come down, but in only two of the 11 months since has it been marginally below; in nine months it has been higher. The underlying rate of inflation that the Government prefer as a criterion – they hope to exclude the mortgage interest effect from the calculation, as though millions of people did not have to suffer the burden of extra mortgage payments – was 5.5% when the former Chancellor made that optimistic statement. For the past three months the figure has been 6.1% the highest that it has been for almost seven years. We end the decade with not much success on the one front to which the Government appear willing to sacrifice all other economic objectives.

I do not think that I am the only hon. Member to sense that feeling of a decade ending and a new one beginning. During the Christmas recess, I was looking at an interesting speech by the Lord President of the Council [Geoffrey Howe] who, since he has been relieved of some of the cares of his former onerous offices, has taken to giving his observations on the British political and economic scene. In his New Year's message to the East Surrey Conservative Association, the Lord President of the Council – whom I think has the habit of giving such communications to the East Surrey Conservatives from time to time – addresses some of those questions. He tells the good folk in the East Surrey Conservative Association that the re-conquest of inflation is a vital condition for progress. It was the word 're-conquest' that attracted my attention. If we have successfully vanquished the dragon of inflation during the 1980s, why do we need to reconquer it? The right hon. and learned Gentleman is very careful with his words.

He went on to give some of his thoughts on how Britain stood in relation to competitor countries, and said:

Britain enjoys no automatic pilot to prosperity. Much, much more, remains to be done if we are to match the living standards of West Germany, the public facilities of the French.

I was not quite sure what he meant by 'public facilities'; if I thought that the right hon. and learned Gentleman was intending to be witty, I would give him the benefit of the doubt, but I rather doubt that there is a hidden message there, so let us loosely interpret the phrase as meaning public services 'or the can do entrepreneurial culture of the United States let alone the low crime rates of Japan.'

I think that there are some other features of Japanese society that we might aspire to as well as the low crime rates.

That was an interesting example of how the right hon. and learned Gentleman was beginning to understand that we were falling behind others; that is the coded message there. He has been thinking about his period as Foreign Secretary. He has plenty of time to think about it now and he has been pondering these matters.

Warming to his theme, the right hon. and learned Gentleman then tackled the question of manufacturing industry. It is almost incredible that he of all people should say this, but he said to the people of East Surrey: 'We need equally to conquer the tendency of regarding manu-facturing as almost a residual element, a left-over in our economy.'

Who on earth created this tendency but the right hon. and learned Gentleman when he was Chancellor of the Exchequer, from 1979 to 1983? I feel that the right hon. and learned Gentleman was the most militant of the monetarists, who started this process of the decline of British manufacturing industry.

Then he turned his attention to public services. He said:

Litter and scruffiness in our public places, and in far too many of our public services, are the breeding ground for delinquency. Poor standards of service are far too widely tolerated. Shoddy bus stations or dirty trains or noisy hospitals or cold waiting rooms are unworthy of the nation we aspire to become.

It is very interesting that after these 10 years of marvellous progress these debilitating signs should be all around us, but there we are.

He then went on to reflect further on it, and this will astound the House as well. He said: 'Putting an end to this scruffiness will require public money, of course'

There is something going on in the brain of the right hon. and learned Gentleman. But behind all this persiflage, this circumlocution, this coded language, what is the message which some of the East Surrey Conservatives may or may not have been able to detect? I will put it simply to them and help any members of the East Surrey Conservative Association who still remain puzzled. What he is saying is very simply this. First, the battle against inflation has been lost; secondly, other countries which we were supposed to have surpassed are doing better than we are; thirdly, manufacturing industry is, after all, very important; and, fourthly, our public services are in a shocking and disgraceful condition. [*Intervention*] One is entitled to mock even people as great as the Lord President of the Council, particularly when they are giving us such useful messages. I am trying to help the House, as I am trying to help the people of East Surrey, to decipher the true meaning behind the somewhat Delphic statements, because these indicate a very important change.

An attempt is now being made to rewrite history. We heard the Chancellor of the Exchequer have a stab at it in his speech today. 'Not everything is perfect,' is now the line; 'there have been some mistakes along the way.' I think that there is a tendency to seek to bury the last Chancellor's with him. I noticed that first when the new Chancellor was asked whether inflation would be his judge and jury. He said, 'These are not my words.' It was almost a case of 'Don't watch my lips as far as this is concerned'. It is now said that mistakes were made, but hon. Members will notice that most mistakes fall within the period of office of the departed Chancellor. I do not think that will do, however, because the present Chancellor of the Exchequer was an enthusiastic participant, as Chief Secretary to the Treasury, in the development of a great many of these policies. He was as guilty as any of the hype, the exaggeration, the gross inflation of the Government's alleged achievements.

Perhaps the best example came during that period of intense excitement which convulsed the Conservative party at about the time of the March 1988 Budget. Then they were telling us that Britain's economic miracle had become the outstanding reality of the decade, if not of the century. The right hon. Gentleman, opening the debate on 26 April 1988 on the Finance (No. 2) Bill, said that the Government's strategy had 'without doubt transformed the British economy.'

[*Hon. Members*: Hear hear.] I am glad that I take the House with me, but I wonder if I shall get as ready assent for the next proposition to which the present Chancellor of the Exchequer drew attention. He said:

During the 1960s we praised and envied the German economic miracle. In the 1980s the position has been precisely reversed.

I notice that there is not quite so much baying from Government Members and that is an extremely wise position for them to adopt, because they may have noticed it was reported in the financial news in the *Guardian* today the report by Herr Haussmann, the German economics Minister, on the state of the West German industry: 3% growth predicted next year, 2.5% inflation, 7% rise in personal disposable income, 6.5% rise in consumer spending and, perhaps most important of all, a huge trade surplus last year of 148 billion Deutschmarks, which in sterling terms is just over £50 billion.

What on earth do hon. Gentlemen mean when they talk about our having somehow surpassed the German economic miracle? The previous Chancellor did it as well. He said that Japan still had an economic miracle, but Germany's was in the past. Here we have facts that cannot be gainsaid and the present Chancellor, like the former Chancellor, should apologise for ever having dreamt of such fantastic ways of expressing the Government's policies, because the facts do not fit the hype. For decades, the West Germans have been following consistently policies that have given long-term support to their manufacturing sector and have built up good public services. They have been following that path consistently, and the key to it has been investment. If we have a lesson to learn from West Germany, it is the crucial importance of that factor.

The Chief Secretary to the Treasury (Mr Norman Lamont): Does the right hon. and learned Gentleman consider it to be entirely without significance that the British economy, whether measured from 1980 or 1979, has grown faster than that of Germany, whereas in the 1970s it grew more slowly? Does he regard that as a point of interest?

Mr Smith: During one part of the decade we had a spurt for growth which is coming to a halt, and we shall have a repeat of the stop-go policies. If there has been a successful decade and if we have been better than the West Germans – that is the burden of what the Chief Secretary and his colleagues have been saying – why do we have a record balance of payments deficit of well over £20 billion while they have a trade surplus of £50 billion?

The Government cannot wriggle out of that. They made an absurd and ridiculous claim and, now that the facts are revealed, they will not even admit that they made such a claim. The hype and over-exaggeration has come back to haunt them, and so it should because they should never have attempted to mislead the public in that way.

In the early part of the decade, our share of world trade, by volume or value, dropped. It may have stabilised in recent years, and I am not certain where it is headed [Interruption.] and it may be at a lower level than when the Conservatives came to power. But I get the feeling, which I am sure others will have got, that a desperate attempt is being made by Conservative Members to clutch at a few straws that are about. But the major facts are there and cannot be gainsaid.

A major reason why the Federal Republic of West Germany has had consistent success is the importance that that country gives to investment in manufacturing and to public services, particularly education and training. The West Germans have by far and away the best record in the European Community on education and training, and that has stood them in excellent stead. We failed to invest in education and training in the 1980s, and we have inadequate ambitions for the 1990s.

Perhaps the crucial difference between Germany and Britain is that the attitude of the Government there is different both to education and industry, and they encourage both to work together to improve the quality of the staff employed in West German industry. Concern is being expressed by British industry about the level of investment. The CBI felt moved to submit a memorandum to the National Economic Development Council about what it saw as the real problem of investment now. I remind Conservative Members that this is at the end of this so-called fabulous decade. The CBI says:

it is no exaggeration to state that the United Kingdom economy is at a crossroads. The twin problems of price inflation and a serious deficit on the current account of the balance of payments must be tackled, without tipping the economy into recession and against the background of a pitifully low level of personal savings, which account for no more than 4%of personal disposable income, down from 13% in 1980.

One gets the feeling that the CBI does not believe that it has been the most fabulous decade of the century. It goes on: 'If the objectives of reducing inflation and the current account deficit are clear' – and the Chancellor said nothing about an ambition of eliminating the current account deficit; indeed, I do not think he even mentioned it – 'so is the economic priority for 1990. It can be summed up in one word: investment.'

The CBI goes on to express its concern:

Yet all the indicators suggest that business investment, particularly in plant and machinery, is set to level off in the two years ahead and is in danger of falling back. It is investment in new plant, in training and in new products and services which is the key, not just to economic growth but to growth without inflation.

The CBI draws attention to what it calls 'a worrying investment gap' between Britain and our principal competitors, and points out that fixed investment in 1988, the boom year, in Japan was £3,699 a head; in the United States, £3,234; in France, £3,190; in West Germany, £2,946; and in the United Kingdom, £2,318, the bottom of the league for fixed investment in the best year that one could take for the Government. The CBI says: 'The threat to investment is, therefore, the most significant feature of the current economic situation.' The Chancellor claims that the Government have a successful record of investment. The Government always define it as business investment. They constantly say, as the Chancellor just said, 'Do not worry about it; we have a good record.' One wonders why the CBI does not think that. I drew attention previously to an important article by Mr Andrew Glyn in the

Financial Times on 8 November of last year. That was recently picked up by Mr Edward Streator, President of the American Chamber of Commerce (United Kingdom), who, many hon. Members will recall, was a former distinguished Minister at the United States Embassy in London and a former United States Ambassador to OECD. He, too, noticed the importance of that article and the difference between business and manufacturing investment. Ambassador Streator said:

I would refer to the work done by Andrew Glyn of Oxford, who pointed out recently the stark contrast between material production where investment was still below the level of 1979 in 1988 and the services sector where the level of investment has practically doubled. In terms of business investment, gross fixed capital stock for agriculture and industry

and most of it is for industry

actually declined 8.4% between 1979 and 1988, while it increased 93.1% in the same period for services.

He endorsed Mr Glyn's conclusion:

It would be a fantasy to believe that finance and business services can take over from manufacturing and generate the foreign exchange necessary to pay the import bill.

I hope that we all agree with that. That is the distinction. Manufacturing investment has languished, although overall business investment may have increased. I will put that in starker terms for the benefit of the Chancellor, because he counts as business expenditure even expenditure on a car park outside a leisure centre or a metro shopping centre which has been built on the former site of a manufacturing enterprise. That is going on all over the country. Most of my hon. Friends have constituencies in which once there were productive engineering companies, but they have been knocked down, the sites have been cleared, and now leisure centres or large shopping complexes are being built. The Government say that such investment is as good as or perhaps even better than the previous investment. The crucial difference is that, when we had a bigger manufacturing sector, we made goods and sold them abroad. Now we have shops that import the goods that other people make, and we buy them.

We know what the Government could do about investment. I must tell the House about the Autumn Statements, not only this one, but the public expenditure programme of the past decade. In the period 1978–88, in real terms, industrial research and development was cut by 30%, regional development by 72% and export promotion by 81% How can a country with a massive trade and balance of payments deficit cut export promotion support for British exporters? The result is that as export markets open up in the Soviet Union and throughout eastern Europe, British companies could not be worse placed in relation to their competitors in the European Community. Year after year, the Government have cut back their support, especially for smaller businesses which have difficulty in maintaining an export service and an export initiative. Once again, the result is that, in the new trade routes which will open up in eastern Europe, Britain will be left at the back of the queue because of the activities of this Government.

Most bizarre of all in this Autumn Statement is the fact that expenditure on training is to be cut for the year to come by £110 million. If that was not enough, it is to be cut for the next year by £220 million. One of the Chancellor's elusive devices is to talk about priority areas in public expenditure. He selects some items of expenditure as priorities and he says that, although he is prudent about public expenditure, we can see how much more he is spending in the priority areas. If there are priority areas, it follows, as night follows day, that there are non-priority areas. Training is clearly a major non-priority area for the Government.

We have a crisis in training which does not seem to have penetrated the Chancellor's mind; he scarcely mentioned it once in his speech today. In case it is thought that I am seized by a sense of exaggeration to criticise the Conservative party, I shall quote from objective commentators on these matters. Perhaps I should not say 'objective commentators', because I shall quote from the proceedings at a conference of the Institute for Economic Affairs. I do not claim that the conference was objective, but it is interesting to consider what was said, as described in the *Financial Times* on 15 January 1990. The article said:

Mr David Lomax, group economic adviser for the National Westminster Bank, spoke for many at last week's IEA conference in describing the standard of vocational training and education up to school-leaving age in the UK as 'appalling' and the Government's performance on education and training as 'execrable'.

Another speaker, Mr Walter Eltis, director general of the National Economic Development Office, pointed out that 90% of 16 and 17-year-olds in Japan and the US are in full-time education. In Britain this applies to less than 50% of 16-year-olds and only about 30% of 17-year-olds'.

I hope that the Government will take account of the fact that he also cited research showing that 'an upgrading of 1% of the labour force from unskilled to skilled can boost productivity by about 2%'

The work of Professor Sig Prais for the National Institute of Economic and Social Research is possibly even more interesting. He went through a number of issues of industrial importance and looked at the training record of parts of British industry. In an article on 11 January, he pointed out:

The essential difference between Britain and Germany lies in the proportions with intermediate qualifications, such as apprenticeships, City and Guilds certificates, or secretarial qualifications. He pointed out that 60% of the German workforce had such qualifications, compared with only 30% in the UK.

He then went through various areas in which we are losing out. He mentioned kitchen furniture in which, as we all know, British industry is losing out. He mentioned clothing manufacture, and I hope that the Chancellor will pay a little attention to this. The professor found that in clothing manufacture 80% of German machinists had completed two or three year examined courses. In the United Kingdom plants, the survey did not come across a single machinist with such a qualification. If we do not train our people, and especially our young people, what chance do we have of competing against the country with the best education and training record in the European Community, if not the world?

The case for training is unassailable. When we cause people to be trained effectively, we do not create only an important economic asset. The difference between a successful and an unsuccessful economy is the investment in human resources in training our people – so that they can beat the competition. The Chancellor might also reflect and this aspect is mentioned far too little that an intelligent anti-inflationary policy would release labour bottlenecks by training people, reskilling them and upgrading their skills so that unnecessary inflationary impulses did not come from that sector.

Perhaps most importantly, the case for training is one of personal opportunity and of giving our young people the opportunity that young people in other countries already have. I know that the Government always say that we should look at the increase in jobs over a particular period. However, many of those jobs are part time and low skilled; what the former Chancellor of the Exchequer once called 'low-tech, no-tech' jobs, which he thought were quite suitable for our young people. Young people in other countries are having their minds stretched, their ambitions enlarged, their skills developed and their personal happiness increased at the same time as their economy is being strengthened while our Government do nothing.

It is no wonder that we heard on the radio this morning from the chief inspector of education in Bedfordshire about the shambles in which the schools in his area find themselves. We can go right through the infrastructure and find examples of the Government's neglect. In the past decade, they have persistently been indifferent to the manufacturing sector and have persistently neglected the public services.

Most disturbing of all, as we consider the development of our economy at the end of the decade, is the feeling that we are adrift and that the Government do not seem to have any policy or strategy in crucial areas of economic interest. What is the Government's exchange rate policy? Has fighting finally ceased between No. 10 and No. 11? Is it true, as the former Chancellor told us, that the Conservative party would never be a party of devaluation, or is it true that the rather more surreptitious policy of the present Chancellor is to allow the pound to slide gently downwards?

What is the Government's strategy on inflation? How can they have a sensible counter-inflationary strategy when they have interest rate increases which provoke mortgage increases and are bound to be reflected in wage claims? They have also let loose a series of Government-caused price increases in the economy from electricity, transport and water through to other areas. What is their strategy to promote investment and to deal with the investment gap to which the CBI rightly draws attention? Is there still a medium-term financial strategy? Those who study the history of the Conservative party must have been curious about the fact that medium-term financial strategy, which was the rock on which Conservative economic policy was based, was not even mentioned in the Chancellor's speech. I suspect that we no longer have an MTFS a medium-term financial strategy but an STES a short-term electoral strategy.

What the Chancellor hopes to do is somehow to get by until the next election, stagger through the months ahead, in the hope that when she blows the whistle for the next election – and he hopes desperately that this will be the case – the economy will not appear in too unfavourable a light. That is what Government economic policy is all about. What the Chancellor said in his evidence to the Select Committee was very revealing; the Select Committee which once again gave us such an interesting report. Sometimes it is in the evidence rather than in the conclusions of our colleagues who sit on the Committee that one finds the interesting nuggets of information. The most interesting to me was when the Chancellor described – and he volunteered this he was not led into it – managing the British economy as 'surfboarding on a fairly heavy sea'.

It is revealing that the Chancellor sees himself as a surfboarder. All Chancellors have some sort of image of themselves. The lately departed Chancellor, although a former naval person, seemed to think from time to time that he was an aviator: we were treated to his notions of soft and hard landings. Unfortunately, he took some advice from the Opposition and left the plane rather hurriedly. His predecessor had a slightly different image. One sometimes wondered whether he knew if he was the shepherd or a member of the flock alive or dead but his image was much less dynamic.

Now we have a surfboarding Chancellor. In his mind's eye he is a sort of bronzed figure in Bermuda shorts, riding the waves, practising to take on all comers at the next Commonwealth Finance Ministers' conference. But is not the reality also revealed by that imagery? Surfboarders are not much in control of the essential elements; they are at the mercy of winds, waves and hidden currents. That is what is happening now. The Chancellor is moving from wave to wave, not sure if he is heading for the beach or the rocks and in perpetual danger of suffering what surfboarders call a 'wipeout'. In his case, I suppose I might say and I ask the forgiveness of the House in advance, it is a major wipeout.

That is no way to run an economy, either in imagination or in reality. We end the 1980s disorganised, uncertain, confused, not knowing what the Government's policy is and I speak for the nation because it is a worried, perplexed and disturbed nation. That is one of the things from which Ministers seem, at their peril, to be happily insulated. They believe that variations in public opinion are merely temporary and that all will come right, as it did did it not? in 1985: inflation came down and they went on to win the election, and it will all happen again. Ministers are in for a very rude awakening because the people are beginning to realise that things have gone badly wrong in the British economy, and that we are slipping behind our principal competitors, particularly as we face the challenges of 1992. They know, despite the hype, that the Government have been responsible for some major mistakes in the 1980s, and they know that those who made the mistakes should not be given the responsibility for guiding our affairs in the 1990s.

The Economy and Recession

Hansard, 5 December 1991

By the end of 1991 the economy was in a deep recession. Major had appointed his campaign manager Norman Lamont as Chancellor and the two were still trying hard to talk up a recovery. Smith exposed their position with a direct use of their own words back at them, one of his favourite and most effective techniques. He also stressed, as he had done throughout his career – one of his first parliamentary questions had been to ask if consideration would be given to the volume of male employment generated by the opening of new factory in Scotland – the central economic and social significance of

manufacturing. In this speech he links the general failure of Thatcherism to the partic-
ular failures of the Chancellors he has faced across the floor of the House in his time as
Shadow Chancellor.

I beg to move, 'That this House deplores the Government's economic policies, which have caused the severe and continuing recession and which are damaging all parts of the economy and all areas of the nation; and calls upon the Government to initiate without delay an investment based recovery including financial incentives for investment in manufacturing, tax credits for the enhancement of technology, assistance for regional economic development and a major programme of education and training to tackle Britain's continuing skills crisis.'

I happen for my sins to have been shadow Chancellor since the last election in 1987, during which period there have been three Chancellors of the Exchequer. The first was the right hon. Member for Blaby (Mr Lawson), who is not remembered with exactly ecstatic affection by Conservative Members. Despite being described by the right hon. Member for Finchley (Mrs Thatcher), then Prime Minister, as both 'unassailable' and 'brilliant, brilliant, brilliant', he is given a much lower rating by contemporary Conservative opinion. Whenever they gather in private, he is berated for the economic mess in which their political fortunes are floundering, although in public, as hon. Members know only too well, the fiction is resolutely maintained that Conservative economic policy has been a continuing success. The right hon. Member for Blaby will be remembered as the Chancellor who dismissed rising inflation as a temporary blip and who, having put up interest rates to 15%, nonetheless assured us that the economy would have, to use his phrase, a soft landing. The right hon. Gentleman may personally have achieved a rather soft landing, but sadly that was not true for the economy of which he was in charge.

There followed the present Prime Minister who spent about a year in the job – a year in which the British economy went steadily downward into a deep and savage recession, parallelled only by the recession in the early part of the decade which was presided over by that other Tory Chancellor, the right hon. and learned Member for Surrey, East (Sir Geoffrey Howe).

The present Prime Minister assured us that there would not be a recession at all. Speaking to the Association of British Chambers of Commerce on 6 December 1989 he said: 'I do not myself think a recession is either likely or necessary.' Even 11 months later, in presenting his autumn statement to the House, he refused to use the word 'recession' throughout and forecast: 'the British economy is coming back on track'.

To be fair to the right hon. Gentleman, he did appear to have a revealing glimpse of self-doubt in his own assessment when he told the *Financial Times* in an interview on 27 October 1990: 'It will take some time. It always does to change the economy. It's like turning the Titanic round as you know.'

Well, we do not know; we do not think that that was the Titanic's problem.

I believe that there is a unifying characteristic about the three most recent Tory Chancellors – a stunning inability to predict even with vague accuracy what is about to happen to the economy, coupled with the disreputable technique of bogus reassurance which would put Arthur Daley to shame. In the latter respect, the present Chancellor is the undisputed champion. Shortly after he became Chancellor, he told the Treasury and Civil Service Select Committee on 5 December 1990 that the recession would be 'short lived and shallow.' As the economy went into a nose dive, the right hon. Gentleman was soon proved to be absurdly wrong. Perhaps chastened by that experience, he seems to have decided by the time of the Budget that he would be more realistic in his forecasts for recovery. In his wind-up speech in the Budget debate on 25 March 1991 he told us: 'I am not in the business of publishing forecasts that are more optimistic than I think is the case, as that leads us nowhere. It is better to put the facts before Parliament and the country.' He went on to predict:

There is every reason to expect that growth will start again towards the middle of the year.

He repeated that forecast a month later when speaking at a press conference of the International Monetary Fund in Washington on 29 April. According to *The Times*, the *Financial Times* and the *Independent*, the Chancellor said – and I quote from the *Independent's* copy: 'The recession would be over somewhere around the end of the second quarter' that is, the second quarter of this year.

Therefore, the Chancellor, who was by that time careful not to be over-optimistic, predicted that recovery would begin in July of this year. By June of this year he was beginning to moderate that forecast somewhat. He told David Frost on TV-am on 2 June this year: 'In my Budget speech I said that from the middle of the year the recovery would begin, it may be slow at first. It will begin in certain sectors, probably in the housing market . . . there are vague stirrings, but the signs are there.'

I have on previous occasions reminded the House of the outraged reaction of the building industry to the Chancellor's statement, but one person at least appears to have been persuaded – and that is the Prime Minister himself.

In an interview in the *Daily Telegraph* on 19 June this year, under the banner headline 'Recovery coming in weeks' – this way back in June – the Prime Minister was asked about the faint stirrings that the Chancellor had detected in the housing market. The interviewer said:

'The Chancellor did speak of vague stirrings in his recent television interview.'

The Prime Minister replied: 'I think you can look anecdotally at what is happening.'

I am not sure how one does that, but I am quoting exactly what the Prime Minister said, and it must be right because it is in the *Daily Telegraph*. He went on:'Anecdotally you look around you, you find lots of those For Sale boards now have Sold stickers on them.'

To help the comprehension of the readers of the *Daily Telegraph*, there are photographs of signs with 'Sold' stickers on some of them. [*Intervention*] Some 850,000 people have been put out of work in the past 18 months and that is the figure about which the hon. Gentleman should think. If we are conquering the unemployment problem, why do vacancies keep falling? Vacancies have fallen again from 106,000 to 103,000. There are now 24 claimants chasing every notified vacancy and the number of vacancies in Greater London has almost halved, leaving a remarkable 84 claimants for each vacancy. Anyone who thinks that that is a satisfactory state of affairs has a lack of ambition for our economic success.

I return to the Prime Minister and the 'Sold' signs all over the area at which he looks anecdotally. At this point one wonders what world the Prime Minister lives in, as repossessions mount to a record level, projected to be 100,000 in this year alone, and as the housing market remains wholly depressed.

No doubt encouraged by the Prime Minister's reassuring anecdotal ventures, the Chancellor continued into the early autumn promising recovery around the corner. He told the *Financial Times* in an interview on 16 September:

'Britain is coming out of recession. The statistics are highly encouraging and pointing very much in the right direction.' A month later, at the Conservative party conference in Blackpool, the Chancellor told the Tory faithful: 'the green shoots of economic spring are appearing once again'. I must bring the House rapidly up to date.

Interviewed by Mr Walden last Sunday, the Chancellor appeared to be sadly bereft of statistics or even of anecdotal sightings of recovery. Rather lamely, he claimed: 'I have never changed my view about how I saw the path of the recovery, so far things have turned out very much as I expected'. In what I find an astonishing backtrack, he then told Mr Walden: 'We are not assuming, in our view of the future, that there will be a great and sudden revival necessarily of the housing market we are not assuming that housing is leading the economy out of the recession on this occasion'.

The words 'on this occasion' should be translated as 'in this interview'. It was precisely the housing market in which the Chancellor claimed to detect the 'vague' and faint 'stirrings' which led the Prime Minister off on his anecdotal trail.

Will the Chancellor now admit that what he said in June on TV-am about 'vague stirrings' in the housing market and what the Prime Minister told us about 'Sold' signs everywhere was rubbish then, as it is rubbish now? What is most revealing is that if we accept that Ministers believed what they said at the time, they were woefully ignorant of the catastrophic effect that their policies were having on the housing market and on the construction industry generally.

Ministers appear to have no concept of the mortgage misery and the consequent alarming surge in repossessions and lost homes, which are the direct result of their economic mismanagement. The collapse in the construction industry simply cannot be talked away. I noticed an article by Mr Andrew Taylor in today's *Financial Times* which said: 'Bad news continues to pour out of the sector with no sign of the recession loosening its grip on residential and commercial property markets.'

The article quotes Sir Clifford Chetwood, chairman of Wimpey, Britain's second largest housebuilder, as saying: 'I have been in the industry 42 years. These are the worst conditions I have experienced.'

The article goes on: 'Tarmac, the country's biggest housebuilder, said this week that trading conditions had deteriorated substantially during the last two months.'

That is, the 'last two months' in which recovery is supposed to be happening before our very eyes. Where are the encouraging statistics which are pointing very much in the right direction?

In his Mansion House speech given this year at the Guildhall, the Chancellor told us that the good news was that 'In Britain we are now on the road to recovery. Retail sales are on an upward trend.'

The Chancellor felt so strongly about that matter that he waxed indignant in our previous debate. Indeed, he challenged me to withdraw my sceptical remarks about his statistical justification. Unfortunately for the Chancellor, since that debate the release of the latest figures for October shows a 0.5% fall in retail sales for the month, a 0.3% fall for the August–October quarter over the previous quarter, and even a 0.3% fall compared with the equivalent period a year ago. On 19 November, the *Financial Times* reported: 'The Treasury agreed that sales had been flat for the last three months.' It quoted a Treasury spokesman as saying: 'On the face of it the figures are a bit of a disappointment.' We cannot look for recovery in that quarter – certainly if the Treasury assures us that it is not happening.

Construction is a disaster and retail sales are poor. What about industry? The Government claim that we should be encouraged by a 0.3% rise in GDP in the third quarter, a rise which has occurred exclusively, as they well know, because of the full resumption of North Sea oil production after a period of interruption. However, in the onshore economy, non-oil GDP continued to contract by 0.3%, with manufacturing flat and services falling. Over the past three months – sad to say – both the value and volume of exports have declined, and manufacturing output, which constitutes about a quarter of our GDP, has barely moved since April. Car production in October fell by 27% and sales of new cars plunged by 22.5% in the same month.

Perhaps the most worrying feature of all is the alarming growth in liquidations and the rise in unemployment. The Association of British Chambers of Commerce revealed last week that companies are going out of business at a faster rate than at any time in the past five years. Dun and Bradstreet tell us that, in the first nine months of this year, business failures are running at a rate of 930 per week – a 70% increase over the previous year and the largest increase for 11 years. Other alarming figures, from the real economy in which our constituents live, are that, in the past 18 months, unemployment has soared by 850,000 and 100,000 homes are being repossessed this year alone. Against that tragic background, is it any wonder that consumer confidence has been slipping in successive months ever downwards – September down on August, October down on September, and November down on October? I agree, nonetheless, with the Chancellor on one point. In his Budget wind-up speech, he said:

'It is better to put the facts before Parliament and the country.' In the absence of candour from the Government, that is just what this debate is about.

I ask the Chancellor how he can conceivably justify his claim earlier this year that the recession would be over 'somewhere around the end of the second quarter.' That is to say in the middle of this year. There is no doubt that he claimed that, and there is no doubt that that has not happened. Here we are, approaching the end of the fourth quarter, and the very best that one can say is that we are bumping along the bottom of a deep and damaging recession. That is all too clearly understood by those at the sharp end in industry, commerce and finance, as well as by our constituents.

The repeated claims of recovery around the corner, which are not fulfilled and which have been the Chancellor's stock-in-trade month after month, have fatally damaged his credibility and that of the Government as a whole. Indeed, the Chancellor's efforts are now regarded as risible as well as incredible. At the recent Royal Variety Performance, Mr David Frost, who was compering the proceedings, told the company that the Chancellor could at last give a completely firm forecast of when the recovery would occur – he said that it would happen definitely in the fifth quarter of the year. That statement has some aptness, because Mr David Frost elicited the 'vague' and 'faint' stirrings that the Chancellor detected in the housing market.

What is deeply disturbing for Parliament and for the country is the 'wait and see' attitude, which is the Government's substitute for a policy for recovery from recession. They hope for a consumer-led recovery. Indeed, on 4 June, the Chancellor told the OECD conference in Paris:

'Consumer spending led us into recession and I expect it to lead us out.'

Many people might think that high interest rates led us into the recession, but I let that point pass for the moment. In the Walden interview, the Chancellor even seemed to lose confidence in that hoped-for salvation. On the retreat once again, he said :

'We are looking for part of the recovery to come from consumer demand, but by no means all. It does take time' – we have heard that before – 'what we need is what Disraeli once called the alchemy of time.' Intrigued by that reference to alchemy, which I did not think was all that honourable an occupation, I consulted *Collins English Dictionary*, which I have in the office. According to that dictionary, alchemy – alchemy of time is what we are relying on – is 'the pseudo-scientific predecessor of chemistry that sought a method of transmuting base metals into gold: an elixir to prolong life indefinitely: a panacea' – it is hardly believable – 'or universal remedy.' The Chancellor was being even more percipient than he realised. The truth is that, after 12 years in power and with an election fast approaching, the Government are merely hoping that something will turn up. In no sense is that an economic policy for this country. What we need surely is an invest-ment-led recovery which recognises the fast-approaching challenge in the form of the single market after 1992 and which seeks to rebuild the industrial capacity on which this country depends. Over the Conservative years, we have seen the persistent reduction in the capacity of our manufacturing sector, which, after all – we repeat it endlessly, but it is a fundamental truth about our economy which should be appreciated by the Conservative party – is our fundamental wealth creator and the indispensable internationally tradeable part of our economy. For a country which has a tendency both to inflation and a balance of payments deficit, the overriding objective of policy must be to enlarge our capacity to produce the goods that customers wish to buy, both at home and abroad. That is exactly what is not happening now.

To show that that is not just a view that is held uniquely by the Opposition, I shall quote from the *National Institute Economic Review* of May 1991, which argued – in my view, persuasively – that:

The loss of manufacturing capacity in the early nineteen eighties must be partly to blame for the overheating of the economy at the end of the decade and the consequential problem of inflation and payments imbalance. It's only too likely that the present recession will create the conditions for just the same kind of overheating to occur again sometime in the nineteen nineties if nothing is done to compensate.

So what is being done to compensate? Seemingly nothing. Let us take the projections for investment, the very life blood of economic development. After a dramatic fall this year in gross fixed investment, which the Chancellor conceded in his autumn statement to be almost 11%, the consensus of economic forecasts, which was helpfully compiled by the Treasury, shows an even further fall in gross fixed investment next year. According to the International Monetary Fund, the United Kingdom will be bottom of the investment league of the G7 countries next year and, according to the Confederation of British Industry, manufacturing investment, which is already falling this year by around 15%, is expected to fall again next year by almost 4.5%.

However, in this situation, the Government do not propose any action to bridge the investment gap. We appeal to them, before even more damage is done, to reconsider their rejection of the case for fiscal incentives to encourage company investment in manufacturing by increasing capital allowances and by introducing tax credits for research annd development expenditure to stimulate the adoption of new technologies in British industry. Those proposals are backed by a wide consensus in industry. The excellent House of Lords report, 'Innovation in Manufacturing Industry' of January this year, argued strongly for the principle of such fiscal incentives. It is also supported, as the Chancellor well knows, in Budget submission after Budget submission by the Engineering Employers Federation, the CBI and the Trades Union Congress. I have no doubt that, in anticipation of next year's Budget, the representations will be resumed with even more urgency than before as our industrial situation deteriorates even further. I hope that the Chancellor does not, on this occasion, turn a deaf ear.

What is galling for our industry is that, allegedly in the name of creating a level playing field, the present Government have created a situation in which, in the context of international competition, our industry has to play uphill in both halves against competitors whose Governments specifically encourage industrial investment. I make no apology for once again urging the compelling case for a new approach to education and training. In *Training Statistics 1991* the Chancellor seems to find this amusing, but the skills shortage is the most serious problem that this country faces and should not be a subject for amusement. *Training Statistics 1991*, issued recently by the Department of

Employment, again reveals the astonishing prevalence of serious skills shortages even at a time of severe recession and high unemployment. It takes a bit of believing, but in the past 12 months, according to the Department of Employment, 24% of all enterprises reported skills shortages. The figure rose to 41% in high technology sectors, such as mechanical engineering.

The amount of training that employers are planning to provide has fallen dramatically. The balance of large manufacturing firms plans has become negative, falling by a staggering 67% between October 1989 and July 1991, with a balance of 20% of those firms planning to decrease training in the next 12 months. That is further evidence of the baleful effect of savage recession on industrial companies which are forced to cut essential investment and essential training simply to survive. According to the Government's own report, fewer than half the participants in employment training complete the course; 55% go straight back into unemployment; and only 23% find a full-time job at the end of it. That is no doubt why the Treasury quarrelled with the Department of Employment about giving it more money for schemes that achieve such poor results.

Perhaps most damning of all are the international comparisons. Our weakness in developing intermediate skills is starkly revealed in a paper by the National Institute of Economic and Social Research, which was published in January this year. It shows that, in Britain, 31% of technical workers in manufacturing had no vocational qualifications. In Germany, the figure was only 8%. At higher levels of qualification, only 14% of British technicians were qualified, while in Germany the figure was 36% It is absolutely clear that to compete, against Germany and others, in the single market after 1992 and in the world of constant technological change, those investment and training gaps must be closed. The Government can no longer shuffle off responsibility for training on to companies, particularly companies that have been debilitated by the recession. The Labour Party believes that it is in the necessary marriage of technology and training and in the continuous enhancement of investment, particularly in manufacturing, that we can find the way forward to the competitive and productive economy that alone can guarantee our economic progress and support our standard of living.

As is often said, it is quite true that we need a recovery of confidence before we will see an end to recession. The Opposition believe that such confidence can be secured and maintained only by an investment-led recovery. Once this country starts investing in enlarging its industrial capacity, in enhancing its technological capability, and in developing the skills of our people, there will be a sound basis for self-confidence in our economic future. There is no sign whatsoever that this Government and this Chancellor comprehend those realities. That is why, after 12 years of failure, they will soon be relieved of the responsibilities of government.

European Community

Hansard, 21 November 1991

The Intergovernmental Conference of the EC devised a new treaty for a European Union at a series of meetings which culminated in the summit at Maastricht. Prior to this famous meeting the British Parliament debated the recommendations of the IGC which were to be ratified at the summit. The long and bitter debates on the Maastricht Treaty quickly became more about the politics of the Conservative Party than about the politics of the European Union. Smith kept up a running commentary on the internal fight and the 'opt-out' which Major forced through on the social chapter to save the unity of his government. In this opening shot all the themes are present and presented in Smith's characteristic style.

Over the two days of this important debate, hon. Members have explored almost every nook and cranny, to use a contemporary expression, of the implications for this country and for Europe of the treaty amendments which may emerge from the European Council meeting at Maastricht, itself the culmination of two intergovernmental conferences which have been proceeding throughout the year. There have been echoes of previous debates – the long, sometimes weary saga of the consideration of Britain's place and role in Europe.

It is worth remembering that it is 20 years since the House took the decision to join the European Community. A very great deal has changed since then, although that has perhaps not always been recognised by the regular participants in our national sovereignty debate. We have today and yesterday been back over the referendum ground. Yesterday, the right hon. Member for Finchley (Mrs Thatcher) aced the Prime Minister with her demand for a referendum. She was not dissuaded by the fact that the Prime Minister had apparently firmly rejected a referendum in a reply to an intervention by my right hon. Friend the Member for Chesterfield (Mr Benn). Later, the Prime Minister appeared, to use one of the right hon. Lady's phrases about the Foreign Secretary, to 'go a bit wobbly'.

Late last night, the Financial Secretary to the Treasury, who wound up for the Government, repeated the wobble by saying that we could not now decide whether there would be a possible referendum in 1996. I gather today that prime ministerial sources are trying to roll back to the position that the Prime Minister had before the right hon. Lady sprang her initiative upon him. That is hardly an example of clear, firm government. In its own way, it is a very revealing insight into the influences upon this Administration.

Hon. Members have, as is quite proper and according to their point of view, sought to draw lessons from the history of our relations with the other states of Europe. For my own part, I believe that, in the 1950s, successive British Governments made an incorrect assessment of the strength of the movement to found the European Community. It was believed, first of all, that it would not happen and that, if it did, it would not amount to very much. However, with the perspective of history, we can now see how wrong such a judgment was. One might also note a similar error in judging the potential success of the establishment of the European monetary system in the late 1970s.

I seek to draw the conclusion from those experiences that in this country we have a tendency to underrate the forces behind European integration. We should have learnt that one of the penalties of standing back is lack of influence on the design and development of European institutions which eventually we feel obliged to join. Far from diminishing, the forces behind what we might call ever-closer union are increasing. Within the existing Community we are seeing the establishment of the single market after 1992.

I have little doubt that two of the major reasons why economic and monetary union is more likely to become a reality this time round is that a single market is being established and that nearly all the member states of the European Community are now members of the Exchange Rate Mechanism. Having regard to some of the right hon. Lady's observations yesterday, some might consider it ironic that she was the Prime Minister when the crucial decisions in both those matters were made.

There are other factors of great importance to the debate. Capital movements have been almost entirely liberated over the whole OECD area, creating an entirely new situation from that in which Governments operated exchange controls and restraints on capital movement. In trade and in finance, we live in an increasingly interdependent world, and most certainly in a much more integrated Europe. In those circumstances, it seems to be essential that we are prepared to recognise the limits of theoretical national economic sovereignty which the real world that we live in imposes. There are limits to theoretical economic national sovereignty, which are imposed by the realities of the world in which we live. What is more, we ought to be prepared to help to create a system that restores, at least in part, the influence that Governments should be able to have over economic and monetary policy. That is why Labour favours progress towards economic and monetary union – provided that the United Kingdom economy is made strong enough to gain rather than to lose from that experience, and that there is an adequate framework of accountability.

No one in the whole Community is proposing an immediate move towards a single currency. The draft treaty provides that in 1996, or by the end of 1996 at the latest, the Commission will prepare a report to the Council of Economic and Finance Ministers, and thereafter to the European Council. The final decision then is postponed. The final decision – this is the assumption on which those engaged in the debate are operating – will be made in 1996 or 1998 – perhaps later, for all I know. The declaration that I saw made mention of a fast transition towards a single currency, which is not terribly consistent with the notion of real economic convergence. A single currency – it is surprising that the Prime Minister and other Government Members made little reference to this – would offer Britain some advantages, and I will describe what they could be.

We could achieve a low rate of inflation, low interest rates, and a strong and stable currency – but only if we took steps to achieve real economic convergence, which would mean adopting economic policies that stimulated investment, promoted innovation and new technology, strengthened our regions, and built a world-class work force through a relentless commitment to education and training of the kind for which Labour constantly argues. Those policies are vital for our economic success in the 1990s whatever decisions are taken on economic and monetary union. It is absolutely clear that a country with a strong economy has little to fear from a single currency. In addition to the vital requirement of real economic convergence, it is equally important to secure a proper framework of accountability for economic and monetary union if it occurs. We have heard nothing from the Government about their participation in the discussions in the economic intergovernmental conference about the accountability of the proposed European central bank and the allocation of responsibilities for economic and monetary policy between the Economic and Finance Ministers and the proposed central bank.

The Labour Party has argued consistently for the bank to operate in a stronger framework of political accountability than the present draft treaty proposes. Like the French Government, we believe that ECOFIN – the Council of Economic and Finance Ministers – should play a crucial role in determining overall economic and monetary policy. We believe that it is important, for example, that the setting of the external exchange rate for a single currency should be a matter for ECOFIN.

On those and other matters, we simply do not know what the British Government have argued for or against, because Ministers have not reported back to the House on those issues. It would be appropriate tonight for the Chancellor to set out clearly the Government's position on the framework of accountability, which is one of the main areas of discussion at the intergovernmental conference. To my knowledge, we have not yet heard from Ministers about how the central bank should be controlled or about the role of the Finance Ministers in the proposed new system. Instead, when they last reported to the House in our debates on economic and monetary union in January, the Government told us that the main thrust of their policy was to advance the cause of the hard ecu.

Let us remind the House briefly of the history of the Government's approach to such matters. The Government's early response to the Delors report was totally dismissive. However, once it became clear that there was real impetus behind the initiative, the former Prime Minister, the right hon. Member for Finchley, announced at the Madrid summit in 1989 that there would be a British alternative to the Delors plan. The then Chancellor, the right hon. Member for Blaby (Mr Lawson), was not present at the Madrid summit, which might help to explain why the Treasury was taken totally by surprise by the Prime Minister's initiative.

On 18 September 1989, writing in the *Financial Times* , that distinguished commentator, Mr Samuel Brittan, observed: 'One very senior British official first heard of Mrs Thatcher's promise, after the Madrid summit, to table alternative ways of achieving monetary union to that of the Delors Committee on his car radio.'

Mr Brittan then said that the official, whom I am reliably informed is now permanent secretary to the Treasury, 'was so astonished that he nearly drove his car into a tree.' That was the genesis of the plan for competing currencies. It did not have a long life. It is, as I recall it, the so – called 'market solution', in which currencies would engage in a Darwinian-type struggle for survival. Our Community partners soon put the hems on that one. There was no seconder to the motion.

In the following year, the Government tried again. The then Chancellor, the present Prime Minister, launched the so-called 'hard ecu plan'. It was first revealed at a lunch meeting when he spoke to the German Industry Forum on 20 June 1990. The idea was that a 12th currency, a common currency, would be established, which could never be devalued, and which might develop into a single currency – or so some thought.

Whatever else could be said about the hard ecu – about its merits or demerits as an instrument of economic policy – it had its political uses for the Conservative Party. It enabled the then Prime Minister to claim that it could not develop into a single currency. It enabled the then Chancellor, the present Prime Minister, to say that, if peoples and Governments so chose, it could develop into a single currency. It even enabled the Financial Secretary to the Treasury to argue before an astonished House of Lords Select Committee: 'a single currency could actually happen more quickly going down this path.'

In the January debate, the Chancellor warmed to the theme of the hard ecu. It was his initiative to be taken in the intergovernmental conferences. In that same month, he published detailed proposals, which were available at about the time of the debate. They were called 'Economic and Monetary Union: Beyond Stage One.' In the months thereafter, the Chancellor told us that there was growing support in the Community for his plan. One country after another was said to be treating with increasing respect this deft and ingenious British plan. How strange it was, therefore, that yesterday the Prime Minister, the veritable architect of the hard ecu, no longer sang its praises. Indeed, nothing has been heard of it since May this year.

In the *Financial Times* of 13 May, there was a headline: 'Hard ecu plan to be reviewed'. The story read:

'Britain may back down in its hard ecu plan. The proposal will be reviewed by senior UK officials in the next few weeks as a goodwill gesture to Britain's partners.'

That story was undoubtedly read with pleasure and relief in the capitals of the Community, but the Chancellor was not pleased at the briefing activities of his Treasury officials – his increasingly desperate Treasury officials. Speaking at a conference at the Grosvenor House hotel on 30 May, the Chancellor struck back. He said:

'I am happy to rebut suggestions that we are abandoning the hard ecu. On the contrary, the ideas which led us to put forward our proposals are making some headway with our partners. We are often condemned for maintaining our position in the face of widespread disagreement, but we are certainly not so perverse as to throw away a good idea just because our partners agree with us!'

He put an exclamation mark after it. With regret I have to tell the

House that that last reference by the Chancellor was, I fear, the last known sighting of the hard ecu. In recounting these events, I am reminded of the story of the hunting of the snark, in which that mythical animal was destroyed. Something similar happened to the hard ecu. So I must ask the Chancellor the pertinent questions. Did it die? When did it die? Who killed it? Where is it buried? I hope that the Chancellor can give us a full report on the sad demise of the hard ecu.

It is abundantly clear from the draft treaty that it contains no hard ecu, and no common or 12th currency proposal. There was not even an agreement to harden the existing basket ecu mechanism. For example, the proposal in article 109E of the draft is that the currency composition of the ecu basket will be frozen at the start of stage 2.

The ineluctable conclusion to which one is driven is that the hard ecu was never more than a device to paper over the cracks in the Conservative Party. It achieved precisely nothing for Britain's interests in the negotiations. That is a theme which sadly continued to be dominant in the Government's approach to these matters. In the absence of the crack-covering hard ecu, what do the Government propose by way of amendments, if any, to the current Dutch treaty text? Did they make any proposal on how the central bank should be governed? Are they content with what is proposed? Do they wish to strengthen the role of Economic and Finance Ministers, as I believe would be right? If so, what proposals do they intend to make in the remaining weeks of negotiation?

We believe that ECOFIN should be responsible for setting the Community's overall economic policy. In order to do so, its secretariat needs to be strengthened greatly, with a permanent staff so that it is capable of carrying out the task of surveillance and economic co-ordination. It already has that role, but it could play a greater role in future.

There is one matter on which I agree with what the Prime Minister said yesterday. That is the important question of budget deficits. He said that negotiations were still proceeding on that matter and that there had been no acceptance of a binding element in stages 2 or 3. As presently drafted, the treaty is far too rigid. The 3% figure in the protocol seems arbitrary and surely, at the very least, there must be some common definition of what a deficit is considered to be when member states have different Government accounting practices.

Since I am agreeing, in principle, with the line that the Government took on that matter, I hope that the Chancellor can enlighten us further on what the Government propose.

Since we are delving into such matters, I took the trouble to inquire about another aspect of our relationship with Europe today – the Conservative party's application to join the European People's Party Parliamentary Group as an allied member. I have here a letter from the chairman of the Conservative Party to Mr Wilfried Martens, the president of the European People's Party. He says: 'I would like to take this opportunity to state once again that this application' – that is the application by the Tories to be allowed to tie up with someone; they have never managed it in all the history of the European Parliament, but they are feeling a bit lonely – 'enjoys my full support and that of the Prime Minister as Leader of the Conservative Party.' I was intrigued by the fact that a letter sent on behalf of Conservative Members of the European Parliament says the following: 'I should like to emphasize that my colleagues fully support, *inter alia*: 'the institutional development of the community into a European Union of a federal type'.

I think that the chairman of the Conservative party would be better employed sorting out a few of those matters before he comes back to the House. I apologise for raising such matters in detail, but it is the duty of the House to do so [*Interruption*] I shall no doubt be corrected and hon. Members can always intervene, but I have it here in writing, and it would be surprising if it were wrong. I have mentioned our views on the development of economic and monetary union, but one matter that we have not touched on sufficiently in the debate is the curious view the Conservative Party have on the Social Chapter and social action programme.

In the remarkable speech by the right hon. Member for Bexley and Sidcup (Mr Heath) this afternoon, it was as unusual as it was refreshing to hear a Conservative voice talking of the need for equity and social justice within the European Community. The right hon. Gentlemen recognised, as we do, that it is hardly consistent to argue for qualified majority voting to create the single market if one opposes it on the social action programme, which gives rights for employees. It is staggering that the Government will apparently take the negotiations at Maastricht to the brink of failure because of their obstinate, dogmatic insistence that they will have nothing to do with competence in the social field or with majority voting in that area.

The Government could change their policy on that precise matter without great difficulty. If they are worried about whether it is the right thing to do, I remind them of an article the Secretary of State for the Environment [Michael Heseltine] wrote in *The Times* on 29 November 1989, in which he said:

We paid a heavy price when others designed the common agricultural policy. It would be unforgivable to repeat that mistake in industrial and financial policies. The same argument applies to the Social Chapter.

That was well said by the Secretary of State for the Environment. I hope that he will speak to the Prime Minister and the Chancellor of the Exchequer and help them to come to a wiser view.

In the course of this debate, we have understood that the real priorities for Europe in the years that lie ahead are for the Community to become wider, more cohesive and more democratic. Those are certainly the Labour Party's objectives. We have aims and objectives-the same cannot be said of the Conservative Party. In the same Lobby tonight will be those who want a referendum and those who do not, and those who want a single currency and those who do not. Most remarkable of all, walking through the same Lobby will be the right hon. Member for Old Bexley and Sidcup and the right hon. Member for Finchley, thus demonstrating the organised hypocritical disunity that passes for a Conservative Party. That is why it will be not only a duty but a pleasure to vote against the Government tonight.

A Scottish Parliament Now

Fountain Hotel, Glasgow, 10 January 1992

As we saw in his reply to Eric Heffer back in 1978, John Smith changed his mind about the issue of devolution. This was part of a deeper change of heart on the centrality of constitutional reform to Labour's package of modernisation. It is hard to escape the conclusion that this was in part simply a conversion born of regular defeat. If the constitutional structure of Britain had continued to make Labour the natural party of government then the demands for altering that system would have remained much more muted and much more isolated in Liberal and Nationalist ranks. However, there had always been an element in the Labour Party that was interested in the modernisa- tion of the constitution and the first real experience of legislating this sort of change, aside from Northern Ireland, had been the devolution bills of the 1974–79 government. Smith was thus converted by necessity as much as by experience and once he had mastered the complex brief, he became a convert to the possibilities such reforms had for promoting and extending the politics of democratic optimism in which he believed. Just as the Tories launched their Labour Tax bombshell campaign at the beginning of 1992, so Smith was in Scotland pushing Labour's constitutional reform programme.

The Scottish Parliament which will be established by the next Labour Government must have substantial economic and financial powers. That need is clear. The Scottish economy has suffered greatly under this government. Scotland has become poorer relative to the rest of the United Kingdom during the years of Conservative misrule. Scottish GDP as a proportion of UK GDP fell from 8.7 per cent in 1980 to 8.2 per cent in 1990. GDP per head fell from 94.4 per cent of the UK figure to 92.6 per cent over the same period.

Since this Government came to power more than a third of manufacturing jobs in Scotland have been lost. Unemployment has risen by over 60 per cent and now stands at more than 226,000. Homelessness has risen by more than 75 per cent and the proportion of Scottish children dependent on Income Support has risen from less than one in twelve to more than one in five.

Despite Government claims, the current recession has hit Scotland hard. There have been major job losses in banking, in defence, in electronics. Just this week *Scottish Business Insider* magazine's survey of Scotland's top 200 companies reported that profits in Scotland have fallen by two per cent compared with last year's rise of 14 per cent, employment is falling and the amount taken in tax is down 42 per cent, reflecting major losses among Scottish companies.

It is against this depressing background that Labour launched its two campaigns this week, first setting out our strategy for industrial, modernisation and regeneration, then yesterday in Scotland, launching our campaign for a Scottish Parliament now.

Ever since the 1970s the great constitutional dilemma of Scotland's relationship within the United Kingdom has been unresolved, and increasingly under this Government that, has led to disputes, disagreement and tension. Whilst the rest of our Community partners have been adapting their systems of government to the new economic and political realities, Britain has endured constitutional paralysis. Labour's plans for Scotland have always been about achieving the better government of the United Kingdom. Labour has always seen that constitutional reform must have a stable financial base.

Over the years in the United Kingdom the distribution of public expenditure has reflected the fact that in some parts of the country there are areas of greater need, or where sparseness of population needs to be taken into account, as well as factors such as the state of housing, levels of poverty and unemployment. The existing pattern of equalisation has resulted in identifiable public expenditure levels in Scotland, Wales and Northern Ireland which are higher per head of population than the UK average. This system of pooling resources centrally and distributing public expenditure on the basis of need has been operated by successive Labour and Conservative Governments. The financial systems of all advanced nations are underpinned by two fundamental principles – progressive taxation on the one hand and the equalisation or pooling of resources on the other. The flagship of the Conservatives' third term was an attempt to destroy progressive taxation through the poll tax, and unjustified handouts to the rich. The question they must now answer is whether their objective for a fourth term would be to destroy equalisation.

Statements from Government Ministers and Conservative Party spokesmen repeatedly threaten that the price for the establishment of a Scottish Parliament must be the break-up of the UK system of public expenditure. On the 11th of December in the House of Commons, Ian Lang said that the current distribution of public expenditure 'would be jeopardised by any change in the constitutional arrangements'. Earlier last year Home Office Minister, John Patten said that, if current public expenditure patterns continued after a Scottish Parliament had been set up, 'immense strain could be put on the Union'.

Sadly Mr Lang has made no contribution whatever to the debate on the future of Scotland. I imagine that is because he has no contribution to make. He limits himself to negative comments on our positive proposals, but even if he is not willing to say anything positive he and his Government colleagues must face up to the consequences of the veiled threats they have issued on public expenditure. Are they really saying that if a Scottish Parliament is established there should be a revenge raid on public expenditure in Scotland?

Is Mr Lang saying that devolution cancels out the need for any form of needs assessment? Is he proposing this to reduce public expenditure in the less well-off regions of England as well and to increase it in the richer regions?

Labour believes this is an absurd and needlessly destructive proposal. As the Shadow Chancellor, I want to make it clear that the next Labour Government will continue to pool resources and to distribute public expenditure according to need.

We see no need to destroy the public finance system because of devolution. The reality is that the Conservatives are making common cause with the separatists. It is ironic to see a party, allegedly so committed to the United Kingdom, taking a line so damaging to its existence. We are not creating a new bureaucracy. The Scottish Office administrative structures already exist. The Scottish Office will spend more than £12.5 billion in the next financial year.

What is lacking is proper democratic scrutiny of how that budget is spent and what policies are pursued. The Parliament building is ready and waiting. There are many ways in which a Scottish Parliament would save money through avoiding the sort of wasteful mistakes like the poll tax fiasco and the bureaucratic and unwanted NHS reforms. Labour will create a sensible, stable and flexible system of public finance for a Scottish Parliament. The principle of equalisation will continue through the payment of a block grant from the Treasury to the Scottish Parliament. The foundation of the Parliament's finances will come from the assignation to the Scottish Parliament of income tax and VAT paid in Scotland. The Parliament will also have the power to vary the basic rate of income tax up or down by a small amount within a band defined in advance by the legislation. The advantages of Labour's financial package is that it is straightforward, will not delay the establishment of a Scottish Parliament and will ensure stability in the crucial early years.

These measures will provide the Scottish Parliament with the flexibility necessary to respond to the wishes of the electorate while maintaining the coherence of UK economic policy. If the Scottish people elect an administration in Edinburgh committed to tax reduction, the power to reduce income tax will be there. If, on the other hand, there is a demand for more expenditure on, say, education, that power will also be there.

Like the UK Government, the Scottish Parliament will have to bear in mind that a successful economy is the basis for public expenditure. It will not be able to spend more than resources allow and expansion of services will be dependent upon economic growth. It is insulting to argue that Scots cannot be trusted with powers which are seen as an essential discipline by every other tier of government.

The Parliament will be able to use its substantial powers and will be answerable for its actions at the ballot box. By definition, the extension of democracy means trusting the people and their representatives to take responsible decisions and to answer for the consequences of those decisions. The aim should be for a Parliament which has the power to act on its own and which fits into an overall UK economic policy-making framework.

That is what Labour intends to create. Labour is the only party which can say with confidence to the Scottish people that, if they vote for us, a Scottish Parliament can be legislated for within the next year and be operating within two years. That is Labour's pledge. The others are either opposed to change or cannot realistically hope to deliver it in the near future. It is a tribute to the work of the Scottish Constitutional Convention that the attacks on its financial proposals, like so much else, have been founded on dishonesty. They have been as predictable as they are unconvincing. Scotland must never again be subjected to the sort of unpopular policies it had to put up with during the Tory years. Labour will deliver lasting change in the Government of Scotland to ensure the policies implemented in Scotland are those supported by the Scottish people.

Running for the Leadership

Tuesday 14 April 1992

The combination of policy review and skilful campaigning was not enough to prevent a record number of Conservative voters, 14 million, delivering John Major's surprise victory in the 1992 general election. Smith's Shadow Budget was widely blamed for the defeat, though the advertising campaign that did the real harm and structured the agenda of the election was actually more significant and was not in the least reliant on the real figures that Smith produced. His devotion to a didactic style of campaigning in an age of image was one factor amongst others – residual suspicion on European integration, Neil Kinnock's image and John Major's campaigning – which took Labour to its fourth consecutive defeat. Almost as soon as the results were known, Kinnock, having conceded defeat with dignity and passion, resigned as leader of the Labour Party. Smith was by an almost embarrassing margin, the front runner. His declaration of intent combines many of the features of his politics which we have seen in the speeches produced up to now and the clearest possible indication that the process of party modernisation – notice the emphasis on OMOV – would not stop.

Yesterday Neil Kinnock announced his intention to stand down as Leader of the Labour Party. Before I say anything else, I wish to express my very deep appreciation of all that he has done for our Party. In his decade as leader, Neil Kinnock modernised the Labour Party as a campaigning organisation and united it as a political force. I had the privilege of working closely with him and know for myself the warmth and generosity of his character, and the dedication and resolve which he brought to his responsibilities. There will be other opportunities for the gratitude of the Labour Party to be properly expressed to one of its great leaders.

I am today announcing that I will be standing for election as Leader of the Labour Party. If I am elected I will continue the work begun by Neil Kinnock of modernising the structures and procedures of the Party so that it can produce policies relevant to the society of today and tomorrow and can campaign effectively for them. I believe that we must continue to develop a wider democracy within the Party based, wherever appropriate, on the clear principle of one member, one vote. That is why in this leadership election I ask that every constituency party ballots all its members and that every affiliated organisation consults widely among its membership, using ballots wherever possible, before casting its vote. In deciding the timetable for this election the NEC must satisfy itself that it has provided adequate time for our democratic process. That is what I would wish.

The most important objective for the next Leader of the Labour Party must be to prepare to win power at the earliest opportunity. The immediate task is to lead a vigorous and searching opposition in Parliament. Following the general election the Conservatives have a sharply reduced majority. If elected, I commit myself to ensuring that a larger and stronger Labour Opposition will challenge ceaselessly policies which damage our economy and divide our society.

The more fundamental task will be to build on the principles and values of the Labour Party to produce policies which are relevant to modern society and answer the needs of Britain in a changing world. It is my strong conviction that an efficient economy and a fair society go together. Britain can – and must – have both. The Labour Party must produce policies which convince voters that their own prosperity depends on a government which takes active responsibility to promote a strong economy and that their own security – and that of their families – is best advanced by a government which works for the welfare of the whole community.

I believe that Britain's future lies in Europe. Labour must stand for a positive partnership and active participation in the Community as the best means to secure the most benefit for our country. Our commitment to adopt the Social Charter should remain a priority objective so that employees in our country can achieve the same rights and opportunities as their Community counterparts.

I want to see Europe and the world seize the exciting opportunities presented by the end of East–West confrontation and I want Britain to lead a new international effort to tackle the new causes of international instability, environmental decline and poverty in the Third World.

I believe also that we need to modernise our system of government and our constitution. Government must be brought closer to the people and the communities which it is elected to serve. Modern government should be both pluralistic and decentralised and should be underpinned by recognition of individual rights. That is why I favour devolution to the nations and regions of Britain and the introduction of a Bill of Rights. Labour should fully examine the issues of electoral reform currently being considered by the Committee chaired by Professor Raymond Plant. While the Labour Party must be free to reach its own conclusions, we should listen to the contributions which others wish to make to what now must become an important national debate.

The challenge for Labour in this Parliament is to broaden our appeal to the whole community and to convince those who did not support us in the recent election that we have policies which will benefit them and their families through the creation of a prosperous economy and the efficient provision of high class public services. At the same time the Labour Party must always be the party which is committed to lifting people out of poverty and out of unemployment.

I joined the Labour Party because of its commitment to the elimination of injustice. I believe that in a modern society we must achieve both the creation of a strong economy and a society of justice and opportunity for all.

I invite the support of all those in the Labour movement who share that vision of our future.

Smith won the leadership election as followed:

Section	John Smith	Bryan Gould
MPs and MEPs	23.187	6.813
Trade Unions	38.518	1.482
Constituency Labour Parties	29.311	0.689
Total	91.016	8.984

PART FOUR

Leader of the Opposition

INTRODUCTION

Smith's ascendancy within the Labour Party at the time of his election was soon matched by his ascendancy over the Prime Minister, John Major. Gallup regularly asks voters their views on the performance of the Prime Minister and the Leader of the Opposition, Smith overtook Major in October 1992 and stayed ahead for the rest of his life. (The full figures are shown in a graph in the introduction). These figures were reflected in the Labour lead over the Conservatives and began a virtually unbroken run of positive opinion polls for the Labour Party which continues at the time of writing, eight years later. Smith was the beneficiary of a reformed Labour Party but he was also one of the key architects of an electable party of government. He laid out his plans in his speeches as leader.

He did not make great Labour conference speeches and we do not reproduce any here for that reason. The key conference speech of his period as leader was made by John Prescott. Smith indicated in his first speech of the leadership campaign, reproduced below, that he wanted to move forward with the agenda that had been pushed by the gang of three, Williams, Rodgers and Owen, at the special Labour Party conference at Wembley in 1980, the prelude to the formation of the SDP. This agenda included the use of one member one vote for the election of leader and a reduction in the use of block votes. The block vote was duly reduced from 90% to 70%, a decision first made in 1990 and implemented at the 1992 conference. The following year the method for electing the leader of the party was altered to give equal weighting to the three parts of the electoral college – MPs/MEPs, Trade Unions and Constituency Parties were each given a third – and both trade unions and CLPs had to ballot their members before casting a *vote. The extension of OMOV to the selection of parliamentary candidates, which was designed to weaken the power of activists over their MPs, was much more controversial. The democratisation process of the early 1980s had empowered activists, as distinct from ordinary party members, and the activists and trade unionists at conference saw the mandatory re-selection of MPs as a key way of retaining some measure of control over a future Labour government. Kinnock began trying to reform the system in the mid-1980s and gradually won over the CLPs but some key left wing unions remained opposed and threatened to defeat the measure at the 1993 conference. Smith made it an issue of confidence in his leadership, the MSF union was pressured to abstain and Prescott made a rousing speech in defence of Smith which won over delegates in the hall. Smith's leadership position was never in serious trouble; this was not Scarborough in 1960, but the events made Smith even more disinclined to force the pace of change on the party. His settled view became that Labour should fight as it was in the next election.*

The job of leader of the Opposition demanded that Smith take a wider view of politics and he began to make more foreign policy speeches than he had done before. These tended, as the ones below illustrate, to focus on Europe but they reflect a growing concern with environmental issues and Third World debt. On the environment he maintained that growth and conservation could be compatible and on Third World debt he foreshadowed the leading role his then shadow Chancellor, Gordon Brown, has taken on the issue. He also took time to spell out the underlying elements of his political philosophy, especially the moral basis of his belief in positive government action.

A Commitment to Change

Royal Horticultural Hall, London, 18 July 1992

Smith's election as leader was generally welcomed and seen as another inevitable move towards the modernising wing of the party. It is important to remember that the Constituency Labour Parties were balloted in this election and voted overwhelmingly for Smith. Many of the myths of the nature of the Labour membership and the constituency for which the left was said to be speaking were laid to rest in this election. But Smith always tried to speak to the whole party and in his first speech as leader he made it clear that change in the party had been necessary but that the real challenge was to change the country.

Let my first words as Leader of the Labour Party be thank you. Thank you for electing me to be your Leader. Thank you for the trust you have placed in me. I joined the Labour Party when I was 16 years of age. I have served in Parliament as a Labour MP since 1970 and as a Cabinet Minister in the last Labour Government. Today, though, you have done me the greatest honour by electing me as Leader of the Labour Party.

I thank the party for its trust and confidence. Not just those of you who are sitting in this hall, but the thousands of party members who have taken part in this leadership election. In the past two months half a million members and supporters, who pay a political levy to the Party, have been balloted by constituency parties and affiliated trade unions. Half a million. That is real evidence of Labour's commitment to the democratic process. Half a million people making a democratic choice. No other British political party can match that mass participation in the choice of its leader. And we should be proud of it.

I also want to thank Bryan, my opponent in the leadership election, and all the candidates in the deputy leadership election. We have all conducted our campaigns without rancour and without personal attacks. I am grateful to Bryan Gould, John Prescott and Margaret Beckett for showing how an important election can be fought in a way which, far from damaging our party, has brought credit to it.

I'm sure that you will have noticed that some newspapers have from time to time complained that the candidates did not attack each other often enough to make the contest exciting. There was not enough blood on the floor for them. I am sorry if we disappointed them, but this election was not fought to provide entertainment for the press, but to choose the new leadership of the Labour Party. And both for myself, and on behalf of the whole Party, I want to thank Neil Kinnock. I believe the judgement of history will be that Neil had the courage, conviction and resolve to lead a party from the edge of the precipice to the verge of victory. I do not believe any other Leader could have done that. For nearly nine years, Neil – and Glenys – have been in the front line for Labour and day after day on our behalf they have endured, with impressive dignity, personal attacks which have been as frequent as they have been unfair.

In taking over the responsibility of leadership today, I am deeply conscious of the debt which we owe to Neil Kinnock for his achievements in transforming and modernising our Party. Our future victory will be built upon the sure foundations that he has laid.

I joined the Labour Party, as did most of us here today, because of its values – the values of democratic socialism. I admired its rejection of injustice and the deep commitment to provide, by the action of the community, real opportunity for every citizen in the land, regardless of their background, income, race, colour, gender or creed. That is still, for me, the mission of our party. Our task in the years ahead is to affirm that message in clear and confident terms.

The Labour Party has always been the party of change in Britain. It was our commitment to change that brought in the 1940s the creation of the Health Service and the building of the welfare state. It was our commitment to change in the 1960s that brought the extension of educational opportunity, not least the Open University. It was our commitment to change in the 1970s that led to the Sex Discrimination and Equal Pay Acts which gave new opportunities to women. And in the 1990s again it will be through our commitment to change – to match fairness with prosperity, to guarantee individual rights and devolve power, to give people more power over their own lives – that we will prepare this country for the new century ahead.

And the party of change must be ready to change itself, to be the best and most effective vehicle for realising our values. In each age and every generation, as we advance and grow, as we attempt to achieve more and always to reach higher – it has been the Labour Party that has led the quest for progress. Yet today our country is not able to reach higher. Progress is held back by a Government that has no direction or purpose other than to remain in power.

I look around and in every part of our country, in every walk of life, in our schools, at work, in our streets and towns, I see opportunity denied, potential unfulfilled and talent unused.

I remain convinced that the Labour Party must be the party that speaks for the people who are denied opportunity and are excluded from prosperity. But it is not just people who live in poverty who will gain from our commitment to social justice and fairness. We all live in the same society. It is a poorer society if it is diminished by unemployment, homelessness and poverty. We all gain in security, in a sense of identity, and shared achievement from knowing that we all belong to one community. We will all lose in our quality of life if we each look out only for ourselves, but no one looks after the community.

We know that it is only through an active government prepared to use the strength of our community, to stand up and advance the interests of each one within it, that we can open the doors, unlock the potential of our people and set their talent free.

Freedom is our goal – not just the abstract and theoretical choices of Tory privatisation – but the practical ability to make the choices that can lead to personal fulfilment: the ability to choose that comes from high class schools and hospitals, and from high wages and highly skilled jobs.

I say to the people of this country – it is right that we are ambitious for ourselves and our children. It is right that we should aspire for better lives and a better Britain. But let the ambition and the aspiration of our people be matched by the commitment and action of their government.

Labour's clear purpose is to build a fair society and a strong economy. Poverty, unemployment, low wages and low skills do not only deny opportunities to our fellow citizens: they are roadblocks on the way to economic success. It cannot be acceptable for us to continue to neglect our most precious resource. That is why Britain can have no future as a low-cost, low-wage bargain basement economy. It is why Mr Major is so wrong when he seeks to attract investment on the basis of low wages and the inevitable concomitant of low skills.

Why on earth should this productive and inventive country and people seek to position itself at the bottom of the wages league, at the bottom of the skills ladder? Why in Tory Britain are our ambitions so low? Does it never occur to the British Tories that when they are isolated in the European Community by their rejection of the Social Chapter, that all the other eleven nations might just be right and they might just be wrong?

It is not just a matter of giving the rights of ordinary people a proper place on economic and social policy, important though we consider that to be. It is also a total failure to comprehend the realities of the modern world. Investment does not follow low skills and low wages. It is attracted to high skills, and the expertise of individuals that can cope with modern technology and respond to the challenge of innovation.

That is why we must aim high for a combination of high technology and high skills. That is why we must encourage continuous investment in innovation and in the talents of our people. Labour's enduring belief in the extraordinary potential of ordinary people is not just an article of social policy: it is the only way to achieve sustained economic growth, and to create the wealth which will underpin our jobs and our prosperity. It is the best way to provide the resources to sustain both our public services and a caring and decent society.

What is absolutely clear today is that Conservative economic policy is failing to achieve either economic growth or create the resources necessary for our vital public services. We are enduring the longest recession since the 1930s – with record levels of firms going out of business, people without jobs, and families without homes. This year Britain will once again be bottom of the league table for growth, investment, and jobs among the major industrialised countries.

Whatever happened to the much promised recovery from recession which we were told would be the direct result of a Conservative victory? Do they remember Norman Lamont's assurance that the recession would be 'shallow and short-lived' and the promise that recovery would occur at the end of the first half of 1991? The Chancellor was so convinced of his forecast that he claimed that the 'green shoots' of economic recovery were sprouting all over the Tory Party conference last October. Well here we are, smack bang in the middle of 1992, one year on, and you don't have to be a paid-up member of the Royal Horticultural Society to know that the Chancellor's green shoots and his promised recovery are as far away as ever.

As manufacturing output, investment, and growth continue to fall, as unemployment and business failures go on rising, the recession goes on and on and on. That is why it must be our task to force growth, investment and jobs to the top of Britain's economic agenda.

But our argument with the Conservatives is not just about

economics. It is about the change that Britain needs to revitalise our democracy and to modernise our constitution.

We are a democratic movement. To the Tories democracy is only of interest as the means to power, and any form of democracy that threatens to put a limit on their power is suppressed. To Labour democracy is not just the means to an end but one of our basic values. It is the expression of our belief that all citizens are equal and power must rest not on the authority of the establishment but on the consent of the people.

We are one of the most centralised states in Europe. Labour's mission must be to challenge that immense concentration of power in Whitehall and open up the process of government by decentralising decisions to the regions of England and devolving policy to the nations of Scotland and Wales. We must lead a renaissance of local government. Our task must be to restore to local authorities not just the ability to provide decent local services, but the freedom to pioneer new ways of meeting local need. Local democracy must be encouraged as a creative, innovative force for change, not constantly disciplined by the state as a threat to central power.

Labour's role must be to expose the secrecy blanket behind which ministers shelter and offer a Freedom of Information Act that will give people the right to know what their government knows. I will believe the promises from John Major that he is going to be more open with us when he drops the new gagging clauses being imposed on hospital staff to stop them telling the public about the damage to their Health Service. I will believe they have changed their spots if they change the decision to sack this week Dr Christopher Chapman from a hospital trust because he exposed management incompetence. You cannot run a public service on the principles of a secret service. The best spur for improvement is the public's right to know what has gone wrong. I do not accept the argument that the issue of public democracy is of no interest to the people. We are all hurt if our democratic rights are diminished, and the weakest and the most disadvantaged members of society will suffer most if power is concentrated in fewer hands more remote from them.

I believe that the public are more likely to trust us with power if we convince them we will share that power with them by widening democracy. But if we are to convince them of our democratic credentials we must begin by modernising the democracy of our own party. That is why I believe we must base our internal democracy on the principle of one member, one vote, and not on the basis of block votes. Trade unions play a vital role in the democracy of Britain. Their role in protecting working people is as relevant as ever before, as increasingly jobs are put on a casual basis and as the legal rights of working people against unfair dismissal or to negotiation through wages councils, are stripped away by this Government. Labour's links with the trade unions are important to us because they are Labour's link with the millions of working people who join them. Our support from unions that have a real mass membership is a source of strength not weakness to Labour. But we must modernise that relationship. And I believe that in modernising our democracy we will strengthen not weaken our direct links with millions of individual trades unionists.

Labour must also be the party of internationalism. The patriot of today is an internationalist. I want Britain to take the lead in a Europe that has overcome the divisions of the Cold War. After 40 years in which the world has been divided into two conflicting blocs we now have the tremendous opportunity to build a new world order in which power is no longer the preserve of the superpowers, but is shared by the international community. I want to see Britain playing a leading role in tackling the new threats to international security – environmental decline and poverty in the developing world. The Labour Party will lead the debate about the issues of the environment and development.

This is not just our duty as democratic socialists, it is an intelligent response to a growing concern among our people.

Sustainable development is after all about the security of our planet, about its viability as a human habitat in which the world's people and future generations can live healthy and fulfilling lives. Nothing can be more basic than the air we breathe and the water we drink. These are not simply what some people condescendingly describe as 'Third World' or 'Green' issues. They are problems at home and abroad which matter to everyone – rich and poor alike. They are ultimately as important to our own community as they are beginning to be to the community of nations.

The Conservatives cannot give the lead that is needed on environmental protection because they believe that the market will of itself solve all the problems. The market will not, cannot, protect us from the environmental dangers which threaten the quality of life of future generations.

Today Labour has for the first time in our history elected a woman to our leadership team. I believe that Margaret Beckett will be a great asset to our Party, not just because of her own formidable ability, but in showing that women are valued and are influential in the Party. I will want to ensure that in the presentation of our policy she is supported by the widest possible use of the many able women who now represent Labour in Parliament.

Labour has policies of vital importance to women. And yet the polls reveal a growing gender gap as a result of our failure to win support among women. Labour is the party of equal rights. It was a Labour Government that legislated for equal opportunities in the 1970s and it was the Labour Party that offered a comitment at the last election to a Ministry for Women.

We must not hide the attractiveness of these policies to women by a macho style of debate. We need each to remember that when we use the rhetoric of confrontation we are often more successful in alienating our own support than in changing our opponents.

Today we have just brought to an end the Labour Party's leadership election campaign. Today we now begin the Labour Party's General Election campaign. Not only will the Labour Party under my leadership relentlessly prosecute this government in the House of Commons, but in and to all areas of this country we will popularise our Labour vision of the future. As Leader of the Opposition I will seek to speak out not just for the 35 per cent who voted Labour, but for the 58 per cent who voted in opposition to another Conservative government – and for the many who are already begining to regret voting Tory on April 9th.

I am certain that our agenda for change and our values of freedom and fairness, and of citizenship and community, are far more relevant to the needs and aspirations of the British people than are the dogmas of *laissez-faire* and privatisation that continue to dominate the Conservative Party. John Major is vainly trying to monopolise the language of choice and freedom but the reality beneath the rhetoric is an over-centralised state that is consistently limiting the access and availability of health care, education and employment – undermining the basic needs of people which are the very foundations of their potential for freedom and self-fulfilment.

Today we are embarking on a great journey. A journey to eliminate poverty, injustice and homelessness. A journey to build lasting sustainable prosperity. A journey to persuade millions of the strength of our vision, the relevance of our policies, the urgency of our demand for change. And to make Labour the party of Government in this country again – a journey that, to succeed, will require tough decisions, unity of purpose, a willingness to discard what is wrong and a commitment to change – a journey we can undertake with confidence because our values, our commitment to fairness, justice and strong communities –

the enduring Labour values – are even more relevant as we approach the great challenges of the years ahead.

Today Labour – the party of change in Britain – is not just electing a leader. We are re-dedicating ourselves to be at the service of the British people. And I know that by doing that we can be certain that the very best years for Labour – and for Britain – still lie ahead.

Reforming our Democracy

Strathclyde University, 23 October 1992

The rhetoric of constitutional reform that Smith had learnt from necessity in the 1970s was by the 1990s part of a settled conviction about what needed to be modernised in Britain. In this lecture given to a Strathclyde University audience, Smith pulled together his constitutional thinking at a national and local level with the European context of modern democracy. As mentioned in the introduction, some of the speech will make uncomfortable re-reading for the present Labour government.

It is an honour to be invited to give the first Richard Stewart Memorial Lecture. Dick was the most remarkable man I have ever known. He was my agent in six general elections and I think that everything I know about electoral politics I learned from Dick. He also worked for my predecessor as Member of Parliament, Peggy Herbison, whom I am pleased to see here tonight. Neither of us could have wished for a more consummate political strategist or a more loyal and devoted friend. Dick began his working life down the Lanarkshire pits where he worked underground until a serious injury forced him to leave the industry. After a period without work he became Labour Party Agent for the North Lanarkshire Constituency where he served right up until the constituency ceased to exist in 1983.

But his greatest contribution was in Scottish local government. After a period on the old Lanarkshire County Council, Dick came into his own when he was elected the first Leader of the Administration in the new Strathclyde Regional Council and during the twelve continuous years of his leadership he became a byword in Scottish local government – among members and officials alike – for his unerring instinct for what were the crucial issues and his deft administrative skills. It took a man of unusual political talents to weld together the very diverse personalities and interests which came together to form Strathclyde but his success was such that in every election his administration increased its majority.

He was motivated by a deep desire to improve the life opportunities of the ordinary people of Scotland, and this was always evident in his work. He added to that strong sense of purpose a sharp analytical brain and rock-like integrity which made him a formidable and highly successful leader. He was modest and unassuming in his life and manner, but when he was disturbed by, for example, incompetence or deception, he could be fearsomely effective. On such occasions he was capable of extremely direct expression in what came to be known as 'Harthill Latin.'

I learned from him the crucial distinction between popularity and respect and how, whilst one may be pursued, the other has to be earned. His family, whom I am glad we have with us tonight, was rightly proud of his formidable achievements. They and he took special pride in the Honorary Doctorate of Laws with which this University perceptively honoured him. I am sure Dick would have approved of an annual lecture which would provide a forum for fresh thinking and challenging ideas on all aspects of our political and social life. And it is in that spirit that I have chosen as my subject 'Reforming our Democracy.'

I wish this evening to offer some new thoughts on the way forward for our democracy.

It is clear to me that we need to re-examine the relationship between individuals in our society and the institutions that purport to represent them. I will argue that, in our over-centralised democracy, it is not only the style of government but also its structure that has led to this over-centralisation. And I will propose that we need a new system of government, appropriate to a modern European state, which puts the citizen at the centre of the picture and which has levels of government that are sensitive to individual needs and aspirations. I do not think that in these troubled times, and particularly after the events of this week, it needs much argument to demonstrate that all is not well with the governance of this country.

Of course, as Leader of the Opposition, I have not been reluctant to point out that the problems arise from the policies being pursued by the particular government that we have. But the unease which recent events have caused throughout the nation have illustrated that there is also public concern at what our system of government permits to happen. The initial decision to close 31 pits, leading to the direct loss of 30,000 jobs and the abandonment of our country's coal reserves, was made with scant regard for public opinion, without consultation, without even a full Cabinet meeting. It appeared that the few ministers involved in that fateful decision had forgotten that they were in fact accountable for their actions and ultimately dependent on the people's consent.

It is an astonishing way of conducting government. The government thinks, or thought, it could get away with anything. Consultation on the pit closures? Unnecessary. An independent analysis of comparative fuel costs? Waste of time. Full Cabinet meeting? Why bother. This is the arrogance of power, but it is only the latest glaring manifestation of what is by now a familiar feature of government. In this, Mr Major is continuing a pattern set by his predecessor. A pattern of clawing power back to the centre, of stifling the voice of dissent, of closing down the channels of open and accountable government.

It is an irony that those who talked about rolling back the state have done more than anyone else in our peacetime history to increase the powers of instruments of central government. And the increase in the power of the central state has been accompanied by the growth of an attitude of mind which considers that once an election victory has been secured, anything goes. The public outrage over the pit closure programme was triggered not only by feelings of sympathy for the miners and anger at a misguided and damaging energy policy, powerful though these feelings are. Underlying these sentiments, and shared by millions of ordinary people across Britain, was a sense that the government had broken its bond with the people. Not so much that it had decided to fly in the face of public opinion, but that it had considered it irrelevant.

There is yet another disturbing feature of the use of central power, and that is the abuse of the power of appointments. This occurs in two ways. New *ad hoc* bodies are instituted to perform functions which displace democratically elected local authorities. And on these – and the whole host of other bodies in respect of which Ministers have powers of appointment – this government has placed its own partisan nominees. The purpose of course is to strengthen the range and power of central government. But it gravely weakens the plurality and diversity of our national life, if it is necessary to be a partisan adherent of the ruling party to be considered for appointment.

Across Scotland, across Britain, people are losing faith in our democracy. This is largely because government has become so remote. People feel increasingly isolated and powerless. Disillusionment and cynicism spread. It must be understood that it is not only the style of government that is at fault. Mrs Thatcher's and her successor's determination to retain power at the centre is only possible because the structure of government allows it. The experience of the last thirteen years has merely exposed the weakness at the heart of the system itself.

Three separate factors have convinced me that new structures have to be found for the reform of our democracy here in Britain. The first is the experience of recent years under a government that has centralised as much power as possible, largely at the expense of local democracy. The second is the European dimension – an additional layer of government which calls for a radical reappraisal of existing structures and competences. The third is a discreet but significant sociological shift: a movement away from the traditional perception of ourselves as subjects to a more modern view of ourselves as citizens.

The time is now overdue to reverse the process of centralisation, by the conscious devolution of power to the nations and regions of the United Kingdom. That can best be achieved by establishing a Scottish Parliament and a Welsh Assembly and by moving towards regional government in the regions of England. Since I am addressing a Scottish audience, I can best argue the advantages of such a change in the Scottish context. We are all familiar with the administrative devolution which is the guiding characteristic of government in Scotland. The Secretary of State has responsibility over a very wide range of functions. He is Minister of Education, Health, Agriculture, Local Government, Housing, Environment, Home Affairs, and to some extent Transport and Industry.

The Scottish Office is a powerful instrument of state. But despite the steady increase in administrative devolution over the last hundred years, there has been no devolution of political control over Scottish affairs to the Scottish people. This is surprising in itself but perhaps it is even more remarkable when we consider that the areas of policy covered have a very direct impact on the lives of people. I venture to think that in no other European country would such extensive admin-istrative devolution not have been accompanied by a parallel transfer of political responsibility.

For more than twenty years, I have held the view that a Scottish Parliament is essential to the democratic governance of our nation. Much of my ministerial career in the 1970s was devoted to this end, and I regard this as unfinished business. But decentralisation of power cannot simply be a matter of reforming the institutions of central government. No modern working democracy worthy of its name can function properly without a robust and self-confident system of local government. That is why the persistent and relentless undermining of local government which has gone on for a decade and more is deeply inimical to our democracy. This is the level of government closest to the people: it represents most directly the democratic voice of the communities. Any reform of our democracy must seek to restore a proper level of independence to local government as part of the necessary and desirable plurality of our political life.

And yet, what have we in Britain? The history of local government over the past thirteen years provides a sorry insight into the condition of our democracy. The relentless centralisation we have experienced is a trend entirely at odds with the wishes of the people and, moreover, contrary to the pattern of government in the rest of Europe. Scotland may so far have escaped some of the damage that local authorities in England and Wales have suffered. Nevertheless, we have seen, and continue to see, a steady undermining of local government – wholly deliberate – let there be no doubt about that. And its result has been to unbalance the State. When we talk about reforming our democracy the starting point has to be the individual. Any democratic change must have at its heart the active engagement of the people. It was Goethe who asked: 'What government is the best?' And his answer was: 'That which teaches us to govern ourselves.' This has to be the starting point of reform.

In this context, let us examine the proposals set out by the current Secretary of State for the reform of local government in Scotland.

I will not go into the detail of all the arguments against the proposed reforms. I am well aware that they are already familiar to you all. I would however like to stress two fundamental weaknesses, in addition to the patently obvious lack of any public enthusiasm for these changes. First, the reforms can in no way be seen as an extension of local democracy. I challenge the Secretary of State to show me where in his document this entirely central issue is advanced. It is not. Indeed some of the proposals, if they were implemented, would achieve the exact opposite. The second weakness, as I see it, is that the proposed reforms entirely fail to address the real problems facing local government in Scotland. Who but this government could put forward a package of reforms that completely side-stepped the real issues, the real needs of the people whose concerns they are supposed to address?

The looming crisis of the council tax. The 70,000 homeless people on the streets of Scotland every night. The impact of public expenditure cuts on essential services. The threat to service quality, and to jobs, of compulsory competitive tendering. These are the real issues, and not one of them is addressed in the government's document. I am afraid that the Secretary of State's point blank refusal to establish an independent commission to consider the matter of reform is, once again, consistent with the current government's view of democracy. The case for an independent commission is overwhelming. The case against it – and the reason for Mr Lang's rejection of it – is that it would be unlikely to support the government's proposals. Even the Scottish Office's consultation exercise backfired on them. Instead of unearthing a mountain of criticism of the current system, which is what the Tories had hoped for, the exercise actually brought together some unlikely allies and served only to highlight the achievements and successes of the existing local authorities. This must have been a big disappointment to Mr Lang and is probably at least partly responsible for his refusal to allow any impartial consideration of the reform question.

On launching the latest consultation document with its four possible structures two weeks ago, Mr Lang pledged that he would give the final say over the changes to the people of Scotland. I sincerely hope he will keep to his word but I confess I do not feel too optimistic about that. I have touched on some of the main weaknesses of these reform proposals. What is most disturbing is the idea that something as important as local government reorganisation could be decided in such an *ad hoc* and overtly political manner. I would ask you to compare the present process with the Wheatley Report of the late 60s which, as you all know, established the structure we have in place today. Then, there was a thorough and balanced inquiry. Successful constitutional reform must proceed from such a basis. The contrast with Mr Lang's inadequate document is all too apparent.

As my good friend Alan Alexander has reminded us elsewhere, local authorities are the only Scottish democratic institutions which directly reflect the political aspirations of the people of Scotland. Therefore it is our duty to defend and advance their role, and to do our utmost to safeguard the future of our local democracy.

It is simply wrong, in my view, to seek to make extensive changes to local government in isolation. It is a mistake to attempt entirely to separate one level of government from another. In a successful democracy the different levels are interlinked, there is a clear rationale in the distribution of powers between them and, crucially, each level acknowledges the integrity of the others. Mr Lang's expressed wish to treat local government separately reflects his party's piecemeal approach to the overall structure of government in Scotland.

It is this approach which has led to the present wholly unsatisfactory state of affairs, where we have a Scottish Office which covers large areas of policy but does not deliver any major public service and does not reflect the voice of our communities; a plethora of agencies and boards answerable only to the Secretary of State; and a system of local authorities battling to maintain their integrity in the face of a relentless political onslaught. There is no rational allocation of functions between these different branches of government. There is no cohesion. The distribution of powers is, to put it mildly, haphazard.

What is needed is not a piecemeal approach to reform, but a full reappraisal of the relationship between the people and the political structures whose function it is to serve us.

This is why the Labour Party does not think we should look at the future of local government in isolation. The case for reform at this level has not been proven. But even if there were a consensus for reform, it should be part of a wider restructuring, and a restructuring that begins with the establishment of a Scottish Parliament.

I mentioned earlier the experience of our partner nations in the European Community. It is striking how many of them have decentralised systems of government and how, instead of seeking to undermine their local government, they take pride in its success. If we choose, as I believe we should, the path of decentralisation we will find considerable advantages in moving in the same direction as the rest of the Community.

The unit of government in other parts of Europe which is most obviously increasing in power and influence is not the old nation state as we thought of it in the 1950s and 60s, but regional government – often, as in Bavaria and Catalonia with long and proud independent histories. It is these levels of government which are increasingly important in providing the best means of intervention in industry, and for dealing with issues such as health, education and the reorganisation of local government. The common experience is that this level of government can best bridge the gap which can so easily open up between individuals and communities on the one hand, and the government which is meant to serve them on the other.

I have no doubt that this process will continue. The Committee of the Regions, which is envisaged in the Maastricht Treaty, is but the start of what I believe will be a dynamic process. It is at best deeply ironic that John Major should have chosen to come later this year to Edinburgh to tell the Scots and our fellow Europeans why subsidiarity is important because it removes powers from Brussels to London but that this principle stops at the Scottish border.

Mr Major's restricted notion of subsidiarity is a convenient and deliberate misinterpretation of a principle which is central to the Community's future development and which most people understand to mean devolving power down to the closest practicable level to the citizens. Not just from Brussels to Whitehall, but from Whitehall to the regions and from the regions to the localities. With Europe, as with our British institutions, we must start with the people and see how we can build the right structures to respond effectively to their needs throughout the Community. Real subsidiarity is entirely consistent with the Labour Party's view of the future direction of our democracy. It requires a reassertion of local government, the establishment of a Scottish Parliament to legislate on matters that concern us uniquely as a nation, government in Westminster to address the wider concerns of the United Kingdom as a whole, and power at the European level to deal with the broad environmental, economic and social issues which demand a Community-wide approach.

What we must do is restore people's faith in their system of government, and convince them that their participation is not only welcome but necessary. To do that the machinery of government must be seen to work effectively on their behalf, and the structures of government must be seen to respond to their individual needs, at the local, regional, national and supra-national level.

What is clear is that there is a need for fresh thinking on this subject. People are looking for alternatives because they see the deficiencies of the present system and they have experienced its injustice: over the poll tax, over the pit closures, over all manner of decisions that leave them feeling ignored, overruled, irrelevant. And this thinking must in my view come from the Left. Why? Because our concern as a Party and as a movement is the attainment of individual freedom and social justice. We approach this question of democratic reform from the standpoint of the individual, of the little man if you like, seeking greater freedom, better opportunities, a fair start in life. We do not approach it from the standpoint of authority or the vested interest of wealth, or from the position of a privileged elite.

It is for this reason that the Labour Party is the natural party of constitutional reform.

We came into being as a movement at the end of the last century to bring about change; to reform a system that assured the supremacy of a ruling elite and the tyranny of private capital. The Labour Party was born out of the determination of ordinary citizens to claim for themselves the opportunities enjoyed by others and to participate fully in the public life of their country.

Since its beginnings, therefore, Labour has been a vehicle for individual aspirations, a vehicle for social justice, and consequently a vehicle for democratic reform.

But democratic reform must extend beyond the reform of government. Our people need better protection against the kind of arrogance of power that puts vested interest before the national interest and ideology before need.

Britain is no longer a society at ease with itself. It is a society where fear of crime keeps people behind locked doors and barred windows. A society where growing numbers of young people sleep in doorways and beg on street corners. A society which denies us information on issues that affect our lives. A society which tolerates racism, and discriminates against women and against people with special needs. The democratic agenda must be widened to address these abuses of our rights as citizens. Because the right to walk our streets without fear, and to breathe clean air, and to expect fair job opportunities, and to have access to information that concerns us, are rights that can no longer be taken for granted.

It is the right of citizens in a modern society to know what government does in their name. That is why we should have a Freedom of Information Act. And I believe we need to give fresh consideration to the idea of a Bill of Rights which guarantees the rights of citizens against arbitrary government. We need wider scrutiny of our secret services, and we need a charter of environmental rights that holds the polluter responsible for damage to our environment. A mature democracy requires a notion of citizenship that has as its premise the idea that we are all participants in the democratic process and not observers or passive recipients of it. Democratic reform must take us in one clear direction, the direction of engagement, of making people more involved in the decisions that affect their lives. The approach must be: not how do we bring people closer into the political process, but how do we build structures that best meet the needs of the people. The structures must bow to the people, not the other way round.

And not only must we devise structures to reflect different levels of need, but also to reflect different levels of identity. People see themselves as members of a local community, as inhabitants of a region, as having separate national identity, as part of a wider community beyond that. All of these levels of identity should be respected and represented by our democratic structures.

Any attempt at democratic reform must make a better job of engaging people than the present system. Unless you achieve this, you lose the argument. You lose the people's consent.

I have sought to show that an over-centralised system of government, in which individual rights are inadequately protected, has serious defects. It can be too easily exploited and abused. The more fundamental question, however, is whether it is suitable for the type of society we should want for the next century. I am convinced that it is not and that we need to make fundamental reforms.

We should aspire to a more mature democracy in which a conscious effort is made, not just to create rights against the abuse of power, but also to create opportunities for citizens to participate in the decisions of government which affect their lives.

We can choose to reform central government, to make it less monolithic and more accountable. We can choose to make it more open and more subject to the rights of individuals. We can choose – together with our partner nations – to embark on an imaginative development of the democratic potential of the European Community. We can choose to enhance local democracy through a sustained and genuine commitment to local government. The time has surely come to make these choices.

Europe and the World

Lothian Lecture, University of Edinburgh, 20 November 1992

After nearly 20 years concentrating, with the exception of the European issue, on domestic politics in his detailed briefs, Smith, as leader, had the freedom to roam more widely. He seemed to relish the opportunity of thinking beyond the confines of Westminster politics and addressing issues that reflected the complexity of the world scene in the early 1990s. The Lothian Lecture and the Robert Kennedy Lecture he gave a year later, show a politician who was growing into the shoes of a statesman. The sub text of the Lothian Lecture is the history of the Labour Party since the founding of CND. Though Smith does not spell it out, he is as much criticising the Right for their Cold War nostalgia, as he is the Left for continuing to respond to the problems of the new world with rhetoric forged in the battles of the old. This is a multilateralist supporter of the Atlantic alliance and NATO, surveying the scene after

the conflict which dominated his adult life is over. What shines through in this, and in
his other foreign policy speeches, is an astonishing, though never naive, optimism
about the potential for the world to get better.

It is now three years since the people of Berlin tore down the concrete wall that had divided their city for nearly thirty years and which so powerfully symbolised the division of an entire continent. In 1989 the largely peaceful revolutions that swept throughout the former Communist countries of Eastern Europe not merely liberated the peoples of Poland, Hungary, Czechoslovakia, Rumania and East Germany, it changed all our lives. It was an extraordinary moment in European history, a triumph for democracy and the determination of ordinary people to assert their fundamental human rights. It was a moment of euphoria and inspiration for all Europeans.

The breaking of the wall in 1989 and what has flowed from it, the reunification of Germany, the break-up of the former USSR, and the end of the Cold War are nothing less than a total transformation of Europe and of our world. All the parameters have changed: political, social, economic, military. And not surprisingly, today, just three years since the revolutions of 1989, we are still unable to fully comprehend or anticipate what these changes will mean for the future not just of Europe but of the entire world.

And I believe it is because of this sense of uncertainty that the public mood in many countries of Europe is much more subdued today. The euphoria and enthusiasm of 1989 has given way to anxiety and the fear that Europe may once again repeat the mistakes of the past with all the terrible consequences that we have seen in the first half of the twentieth century. The tragic reality of what is happening in former Yugoslavia has provided a grim reminder of a terrible European past. Like a recurring nightmare we are again witnessing violent persecution and the horrors of so-called ethnic cleansing. It is perhaps not surprising that to some the stability and simplicity of the Cold War era is now being looked back on almost with nostalgia as some sort of golden age. A Europe divided between two superpowers was a Europe easy to understand and to manage, provided that everyone knew their place and which side to be on. The military stand-off between the East and the West was like a giant game of chess, played out over Europe. The board was carefully marked out in black and white; the rules were mutually agreed: US Pershing missiles matched Soviet SS20s – and we all know that the Americans and the Russians produce great chess players. So we in the West could relax, and even at times enjoy the Cold War watching the latest Bond movie or reading a new Le Carré novel. Occasionally, of course, the Cold War turned uncomfortably hot, but these events happily occurred outside Europe, in Korea, Vietnam and Afghanistan.

Today the chessboard in Europe has gone. Thankfully so too have many of the pieces – the massive nuclear arsenals that were always the most alarming and dangerous aspect of the relative stability of the Cold War era. But in place of chess, Europeans now find themselves in a land of a three dimensional game of snakes and ladders. The focus has shifted away from problems of military strategy in a world dominated by the super-powers, to an infinitely more complex set of social, economic, environmental and political problems that involve a wide diversity of countries both in Europe and all around the world. These are the new challenges facing Europe and the world as we prepare for the twenty first century. And no matter how intractable, I believe it is infinitely preferable to confront these new problems rather than to tolerate the military stalemate of the Cold War. This evening I would like to outline some of the major issues which I believe will shape our lives and those of future generations in the years beyond 2000.

A central dilemma we face today is how to reconcile the growing demand of people, of regions and of nations to self determination, with the fact that we live in an ever more interdependent world. It is the problem of safeguarding national sovereignty at a time when the ability to act both economically and politically increasingly transcends the power of any individual country. Whether we like it or not the reality of the modern world is that matters of vital importance to our lives such as our economic prosperity, our military security, and the protection of our environment all depend on international collaboration and agreement between and beyond the traditional nation state.

In Europe, in particular, we are ever more interdependent both economically and politically, but at the same time as individual people we remain deeply committed to our own national identities. And whilst we are determined to defend what we perceive to be in our national interest, we are also increasingly aware that to do so we must work in partnership with other nations.

I believe the European Community has been extraordinarily successful in achieving an agreement between independent nations to pool aspects of their sovereignty and to exploit the economic and political opportunities of interdependence. Of course, that success has been built over the last three decades upon shared prosperity. And it is that which has been absolutely vital in securing the democratic consent of people throughout the European Community.

Today, as we are poised on the edge of the Single Market and in the midst of the ratification process of the Maastricht Treaty, the problem of combining interdependence and self-determination could not be more obvious. The narrow rejection of the Maastricht Treaty in Denmark and its similarly narrow acceptance in France shows just how delicately these issues are balanced. Many people in Europe are anxious about the threat to sovereignty and sceptical about the potential economic benefits of further integration. If the public begin to believe that inter-dependence is a source of economic weakness and not strength – that it will diminish the opportunities for employment and prosperity – then the clamour for purely 'national' solutions, however misguided, will grow.

In far more dramatic form the same dilemma has come to the forefront in Eastern Europe. The collapse of Communism has released a wave of nationalist feelings and ambitions both in the former USSR and elsewhere. In one sense the Russian revolution stopped history in its tracks. Totalitarian government froze over ethnic, regional and nationalist tensions which, with the thawing of the Cold War, have re-emerged almost precisely as they existed before — or worse — exacerbated by the experience of Soviet domination as one ethnic group was deliberately set against another.

Last year there were more than 160 border disputes in the former Soviet Union. We are all too well aware of the problems in Georgia, of Armenia and Azerbijan, in Moldavia and Uzbekistan, and of the problems of minorities such as Slovaks in Hungary, Germans in Poland, Hungarians in Romania and other examples throughout Eastern Europe.

This tide of nationalism has coincided, of course, with the collapse of the former COMECON economies. Economic dislocation has caused a severe economic slump throughout Eastern Europe. Since 1989 the Bulgarian economy has shrunk by about thirty per cent, that of the Poles and Czechs by about a fifth. The Russian economy was reduced by about 14 per cent in the first quarter of 1992 alone. Under such economic conditions it is all too easy for the pain and hardship of ordinary people to ignite the fires of extreme nationalism, of unrest, persecution of minorities and civil war. I am sure that we all agree that it would be ghastly if what has happened to Yugoslavia becomes not a grim reminder of old European history but a foretaste of things to come.

There is no question, I am certain, that Western Europe can ignore or remain unaffected by such developments in the East. Whether driven by political unrest or attracted by the prosperity of the European Community, there is already a significant pressure for migration from East to West. Pressure which has raised tensions and provoked political extremism and the reappearance of the far right in Western Europe. Whilst it may have been possible to hold back the threat of Soviet expansionism during the Cold War, I am far from certain that it would be as straightforward to stop rising levels of economic chaos and civil disorder in Eastern Europe from spreading across borders into the European Community.

If there is any doubt about the significance for us of the changes in Eastern Europe, just look at the way in which we have all been affected by German unification. The impact of the absorption of East Germany into West Germany has been immense. The economic shock of unification has been transferred directly through to the economy of Western Europe as a whole with consequences for levels, of growth, trade and employment throughout the Community. And, of course, it was the combination of higher German interest rates and the failure to agree a general realignment of the European Exchange Rate Mechanism, compounded by the weakness of our own domestic economy, which provoked the currency crisis that caused the devaluation of the pound on September 16th. In this way we can see quite clearly how the events of 1989 have already had a profound affect on arrangements at the very heart of the European Community. The lesson of these events is that we in Europe must respond more imaginatively to the new political challenges which have arisen since the end of the Cold War. And that means that, whilst we continue to deal with important issues of the European Community's internal economic and political structure, we cannot afford to neglect vital questions about our role in a wider Europe and a wider world.

It is perhaps an accident of history that the blueprint for the next phase of internal change in the Community – the plans for Political and

Economic and Monetary Union – was drawn up just before the full extent of the changes of the last three years were known. As a result, the Community has sometimes given the impression that, like those hankering after the Cold War, it would have preferred not to have to worry about Eastern Europe just now.

And I believe it is unfortunate that discussion about the future of Europe in the last few years has been so dominated by debate about the Maastricht Treaty. After all no one knows for certain whether or not a single European currency will be agreed by the end of this century.

The Community will clearly be financially and industrially more integrated not least because of the impact of the Single Market. That in itself will underpin the rationale for EMU although, I suspect, on a timetable less ambitious than that envisaged in the Maastricht Treaty.

In passing I am reminded of a remark by the former President of the Bundesbank Karl Otto Pohl who wondered if it was significant that EMU was named after an Australian bird that had no wings, couldn't fly but would not go backwards. But whatever happens to EMU there are other urgent and equally important concerns for the Community to consider.

My plea, therefore, is for the Community to put greater emphasis on Europe's external role in a world that is transformed and continuing to change rapidly. I believe that this is important not simply as a selfless act on the part of good Europeans – as a kind of moral imperative to look kindly on our neighbours, entirely honourable though that would be – I believe Europe needs to look outward in its own best interests and as the only sure way to achieve the peace and prosperity which has been our very good fortune over the last forty years.

The external agenda that I believe should receive the concentrated attention of the European Community includes aid and support for the reform process in Eastern Europe, new efforts to overcome the crisis of debt and deepening poverty in the Third World, greater European responsibility for management of the world economy and a deeper commitment to safeguard the international environment. The description I have already provided of the severe difficulties facing many of the emerging democracies in Eastern Europe raises the obvious question of whether we in the West are doing enough to help the process of reform. The answer I am afraid is almost certainly no.

There is growing unease that the scale of our response to the crisis in Eastern Europe is totally insufficient to secure the great advance for democracy that occurred after 1989. Release of credit and measures of debt relief have been very slowly disbursed and the International Monetary Fund has been given the decisive role in administering the reform process in Russia and throughout Eastern Europe. Whilst I do not dispute for one moment the legitimacy of a role for the IMF alongside the World Bank and the European Bank for Reconstruction and Development, I am not alone in questioning the wisdom of their policy advice, which invariably proposes severe reductions in social expenditure and austerity measures applied almost regardless of the political consequences.

The IMF suffers from two critical weaknesses: it lacks resources and it lacks political skill. The Fund's quota increase is still held up in the US Congress, just at the moment when more and more countries, particularly from Eastern Europe, have taken up membership – placing increased demands for its borrowing facilities. What the IMF needs is political leadership from the Group of Seven. Without it I fear the IMF will fail to develop a reform programme in Eastern Europe that is both economically and politically feasible.

The contrast with the experience of the post-war reconstruction of Western Europe is striking. Consider the sheer scale of the Marshall Plan initiative launched by President Truman in 1948. Aid from the US amounted to a staggering $70 billion in today's prices. Political leaders on both sides of the Atlantic, including the then Labour Foreign

Secretary Ernest Bevin played a crucial role in mobilising the political will for an unprecedented act of statesmanship and generosity. Above all they recognised that failure was unthinkable and the Americans, in particular, appreciated that their own security depended on prompt and decisive assistance.

But where is the George C. Marshall of 1992? The best the West can offer are IMF officials bearing privatisation plans. It would be far better, I believe, for the Group of Seven leading industrial nations to appoint a leading statesman or woman to provide the political flair, leadership and judgement that is needed to galvanise our assistance to the East.

In fact help on the scale of the Marshall Plan is probably far in excess of what is needed. Eastern Europe is not lacking in natural resources. To take one important example, Russia is an oil rich country with the potential for substantial economic growth. The problem for most countries in Eastern Europe is severe economic dislocation and the collapse of the COMECON trading system within the former Soviet Bloc. What they all need most of all is the ability to earn hard currency through international trade.

I have spoken of the great upheaval in Eastern Europe and of the massive consequences of this change for us in the West. But we must, at the same time, look farther afield. Because similar problems also bedevil the developing world. The debt crisis, now more than 20 years old, is still shackling many countries in Latin America and in Africa. Both regions have endured a lost decade of falling per capita incomes and severe social decline. The hesitant and delayed efforts to reschedule and write down the debt burdens of the so-called middle income countries of Latin America are, of course, welcome but long overdue. And in comparison, Africa's debt burden, owed overwhelmingly to Western governments, rather than to private banks, is still seriously neglected.

Our failure to come up with a concerted response to the debt crisis is not just a human tragedy for millions living in poverty, it has acted as a drag anchor on the world economy. For the poorest countries, prospects remain grim. There is still lack of agreement to implement fully official debt relief under the so-called Trinidad Terms which was first proposed more than two years ago. And to make matters worse it looks likely that negotiations currently underway to replenish the World Bank's fund for very low interest loans will fail to secure any increase at all. This at a time when the World Bank forecasts for the year 2000 at best minimal, and more likely negative, levels of *per capita* income growth in sub-Saharan Africa.

The rich countries, I believe, have a moral duty to provide a combination of debt relief and generous levels of official aid. But a commitment to aid alone is not enough, 'trade is better than aid' is an old saying but it is true nonetheless.

That is why it is absolutely vital to overcome the crisis that has hit the current round of international trade talks. The risks to the world economy are far too great to allow brinkmanship over the GATT to degenerate into a trade war. A compromise agreement between the European Community and the United States must be reached now, which will provide a solution to the enduring problem of agricultural protectionism. A trade war would not just be a disaster for us. It would deal a fatal blow to the emerging democracies of Eastern Europe and it would be a catastrophe for the debt-ridden Third World.

It is important to realise just how important agriculture is to most developing countries. Agriculture accounts for about 40 per cent of the economic output of the poorest countries and provides work for over 70 per cent of their people. Compare that with Europe, where agriculture accounts for less than 3 per cent of output and employs less than 10 per cent of the workforce.

It really would be absurd if – after all the staggering changes that have occurred over the last three years – the only institution that remains unchanged and immutable is the EC's Common Agricultural

Policy. The CAP must be reformed and we must abandon protection of agriculture which makes our own food more expensive and impoverishes millions in the Third World. Trade wars and recession threaten a downward spiral into a global slump and political disintegration. That was the awful lesson of the 1930s. In Europe we have, I believe, a special responsibility to prevent anything like that ever happening again.

Serving to remind us of our past mistakes is a favourite political cartoon of mine which although published in 1932 contains a powerful message for us all today. The cartoon by David Low depicts a boat called the World Money Problem, sailing in very rough seas and leaking heavily. At one end of the boat the 'big three' leading economic powers sit on the bow with not even their feet wet. At the other end sit the smaller nations with their heads barely above water. One of the big three says to the other: 'That's a nasty leak – thank goodness it is not at our end of the boat'.

The same characteristics of complacency and shortsightedness are still with us sixty years on. Today, the reality of the modern world is that we are all in the same boat – and the rough seas of recession are threatening to drag us all down. Interdependence is a double-edged sword. We share, the rewards of economic progress, but we also share the consequences of our mistakes. That is why we must insist that the only solution lies in international economic co-operation and action to ensure growth, employment, and investment, which remain the best guarantees of peace and prosperity for all people across the world.

The threat of world-wide recession is real. Britain, first into recession, remains seemingly stuck with no growth and rising unemployment. The United States has experienced a very weak recovery, and now Germany is drifting from slow growth into recession itself. The economic slowdown is most acute in the European Community. Growth in the Community has fallen sharply and unemployment has risen dramatically. I cannot stress too strongly the urgency of the need for action to reverse this trend.

That is why the Labour Party has been insisting that, during the British Presidency, recovery, growth and jobs, be put at the top of the European agenda. We believe there is considerable scope for joint action at the Community level to tackle unemployment, to increase support for training and spending on European-wide projects for infrastructure and investment. On the initiative of the European Commission President Jaques Delors, it now seems possible that these issues will be discussed at the European Summit here in Edinburgh next month. What is astonishing is that the British Government has not already used its period in the Presidency to push them to the forefront of European decision-making.

We must also put growth back on the agenda of the Group of Seven leading industrialised nations. We will certainly find a willing partner now following the election of President-elect Bill Clinton. Similarly, the Japanese, also experiencing an unusual period of sharply reduced growth would be, I believe, receptive to a strategy for growth. They have in fact already undertaken a significant boost to public investment to stimulate their own economy. The time is ripe for a Group of Seven summit to consider a co-ordinated strategy for growth that replicates what I hope will be agreed for Europe in Edinburgh next month.

The emphasis I have placed on growth this evening may raise concern that protection of the environment must inevitably take a lower profile; that a growing world cannot be a green world. But I have long rejected the view of some in the environmental movement that growth and conservation are incompatible. In fact, I believe sustainable growth and rising prosperity are the essential pre-conditions for effective international action to protect our environment.

It is far more likely that industrial and agricultural systems that pollute and degrade our environment will remain unchecked and unre-formed whilst the threat of recession hangs over so many countries in the world today. The necessary adjustments that we must all make to reduce greenhouse gases and to curb global warming will be far easier in an economic environment of development and rising prosperity. And that, of course, was the explicit understanding of this year's Earth Summit in Rio di Janeiro. The Summit's full title was the United Nations Conference on Environment and Development – with a significant emphasis on the 'D' for development as well as the 'E' for environment.

Many of the high expectations of the Rio Summit were unfulfilled. It was always overambitious to expect a single gathering of world leaders to provide solutions to the complex problems and threats to our environment today. Nevertheless, the Summit was an important breakthrough and there is a real opportunity for Europe to take a leading role in setting meaningful targets both for environmental protection and for advancing development.

Above all we must avoid the situation in which disagreement between the industrialised nations and developing countries causes a new international stalemate. It would be tragic if, having so recently overcome East-West tensions, we then stumble into a bitter new North-South divide. New patterns of international co-operation must be agreed and Europe should point the way forward.

It should be possible, I believe, to construct a 'green alliance' of countries from the North and the South that are committed to practical measures that encourage sustainable development and environmental protection. An alliance willing to lead by example, rather than wait for a consensus which can only be achieved at the lowest common denominator. Once again, I hope the election of Bill Clinton and Al Gore as his Vice Presidential running mate will ensure swifter progress in following up the agreements already made in Rio last June.

The end of the Cold War gives us all tremendous and unprecedented opportunities. The chance, as a truly international community, to devote our economic and political resources to tackle the world's most serious underlying problems. That is the agenda which we in Europe should grasp with imagination, energy, and leadership.

For the choices we make today, here in Europe, will profoundly affect our future and the future of the world in the next century. The choice, I believe, is stark. We can turn our backs on these opportunities and treat them only as problems to be avoided. But I am certain that any attempt to lock our prosperity inside a Fortress Europe is bound to fail. We would be repeating the mistakes of the past which caused such havoc for so many people in our continent earlier this century.

Or alternatively we can seize the opportunities of a world transformed. It is within our grasp to close the gap between the North and the South and arrest the slide into poverty and despair that is still the fate of many millions of our fellow human beings. We have the opportunity to respond to the great challenges of the environment. And we have the responsibility to strengthen democracy, to defend human rights and extend social justice. That is the agenda of opportunity that faces us today – opportunities we simply cannot afford to miss.

That we have these opportunities is because of the courage and sheer determination of the people in Eastern Europe who destroyed The Wall in Berlin and brought the Cold War to an end. If we begin building a new Europe for the 21st Century with the same determination and the same enthusiasm with which they inspired us all in the Autumn of 1989, we will not fail.

The Standards and Practice of Government

Labour Finance and Industry Group, 28 January 1993

Though Europe was the theme that occupied immense amounts of parliamentary time in the 1992–7 parliament, it was sleaze which defined the era. In this speech Smith combines an attack on the personal probity of the Chancellor of the Exchequer, Norman Lamont, with the conduct of government itself and the accountability of government ministers for their actions. Smith's moral authority was such that the Labour Party was never associated in the public mind with sleaze or even a hint of scandal during his leadership. But he tries to raise the level of the debate, delivering the necessary political hits but also outlining the need for reform in democratic structures, a theme he had developed in speeches reproduced earlier in the collection.

I have not known a time when there was such genuine disquiet throughout the country about the standards, practice, and attitudes of government. It is a time of growing disillusion and increasing cynicism which, if it continues unchecked, will eventually corrode public confidence in our whole political system. It is not just that a particular administration is at odds with public attitudes over a whole range of important policies, or that its arrogant style and often cavalier disregard for contrary opinion is regarded as profoundly unattractive. The problem is much deeper than that. There is mounting unease in Britain today about the declining standards of government. It would be foolish to ignore this widespread unease in the hope the problem will correct itself. We must recognize that it exists and we must tackle it, if we are to prevent the crisis of political authority which is in danger of taking hold.

In the House of Commons last week, when I questioned the payment of tax-payers' money towards the Chancellor of the

Exchequer's legal fees in the matter of evicting a tenant from his London house, the Prime Minister's response was as follows: 'It says a great deal that the day after our servicemen have been in action in Iraq and we have troops in Bosnia, that Mr Smith raises this matter in the House.' This reply by the Prime Minister was revealing. It revealed how out of-touch he is with the public mood, completely failing to grasp the depth of people's anger and concern over this issue. My question, he said, was 'uncharacteristically cheap'. Yet the British people are truly outraged by such a disgraceful misuse of public money. Indeed large numbers of them have written to my office urging me not to let the matter rest. As so many people have pointed out most eloquently to me in letters over recent weeks, hard-working British people do not pay taxes in order that they should be used to bail out a Tory minister from some wholly private embarrassment for which he himself was responsible. I have no doubt the Prime Minister and his Chancellor have received similar correspondence. Indeed I know they have since I have received copies of some of it. I quote from one letter sent to the Prime Minister, a copy of which was sent to me.

Dear Mr, Major,

I am profoundly upset by the continued decline in standards of honour and honesty in public life. John Smith was not only right to raise the matter of questionable use of public funds for private expenditure. He would have been failing in his duty had he not done so. I am deeply saddened to find that you seem unable to recognize legitimate concerns when they are raised, and resort to such degraded tactics in trying to deflect public attention therefrom.

I would suggest to the Prime Minister and to Mr Lamont that they read some of the letters that have been coming into their offices recently. They should see what ordinary people are writing and hear what they are saying. They should listen to the mood of the people. They are angry. They are disappointed. They are demanding better standards from the government elected to serve them.

It is of course particularly unacceptable to have Treasury legal aid proffered to the Chancellor and accepted by him when the government of which he is such a prominent member is in the process of dismantling our system of legal aid by imposing the most swingeing cuts in its history. I might also observe that the ordinary citizen has never been entitled to any legal aid to pay the bills of libel solicitors. What a curiosity that the Superintendent of Public Expenditure should be offered, and should accept, such a privileged and exceptional form of legal aid. If this payment was considered to be as routine and uncontroversial as the Treasury sought to pretend in evidence to the Public Accounts Committee, why was it concealed under a general heading called 'Expenditure on economic, financial and related administration'?

The conclusion I draw from this sorry set of events is that the money should never have been offered, should never have been accepted, and should now be repaid. This unfortunate affair is, however, only the latest in a series of events which, seen together and following in close succession, paint a very sorry and disturbing picture of the present government and its activities. I will run through these briefly and ask you to reflect on whether such conduct would have been considered acceptable fifteen years ago.

The pit closure programme, when it was first announced, was fiercely defended by both Michael Heseltine and John Major. The Prime Minister insisted the closures should take place 'cleanly and quickly'. 'That', he said, 'was the right way to do it'. Shortly afterwards, as we all know, the government was forced by an explosion of public anger and parliamentary pressure to climb clown. The government got it wrong. The nation as a whole was not prepared to tolerate such a decision with all its devastating and inhuman consequences. And yet, despite having to go into humiliating reverse, there has been no contrition shown on the part of the government. No apology for the anguish caused to tens of thousands of families. Not even a minimal recognition of its mistakes.

And let us recall the bizarre behaviour of the President of the Board of Trade in this fiasco. Not only did Michael Heseltine, in reaching his initial decision fail to consult those affected; not only did he, in the unanimous view of the All-Party Commons Employment Committee, fail to take sufficient account of the employment consequences of his plan; not only did he (if we believe Mrs Shepherd's friends) fail to consult his colleague the Employment Secretary; in reaching his decision to close thirty-one pits the President of the Board of Trade broke the law. The High Court judged that the plan was illegal. And yet Mr Heseltine, totally discredited and humiliated, clings to office and – one must assume – retains the support of his Prime Minister, if not of his colleagues.

Let us recall the Matrix Churchill trial, when it emerged that senior ministers had knowingly misled parliament over the government's policy on selling arms to Iraq. This in itself was a very serious matter. There was also the disturbing possibility that three businessmen could have been sent to jail for doing nothing other than following the advice of ministers. The affair turned the spotlight on the government and gave us a highly revealing insight into its internal dealings. It sharply exposed ministers sliding about, running for cover, giving false answers, ducking their duty to parliament and behaving in an altogether shabby way.

On the subject of Iraq, my colleague Jack Cunningham, the shadow Foreign Secretary, has shown me a letter he has received from Douglas Hurd in which the Foreign Secretary admits that he has authorised Iraqi businessmen to visit Britain to discuss possible telecommunications deals with a British company here. Is it not deplorable that, at a highly delicate time when strict United Nations sanctions are in force against Iraq, and when we are sending our airplanes to the Gulf in support of UN Security Council resolutions, at such a time, the British government is saying to the Iraqi regime: 'By all means let's talk business.'? Is it any wonder that Saddam thinks he can act in defiance of the UN when he receives such wholly contradictory signals from a leading member of the Security Council? I strongly condemn such practice from our government at this time.

Let me turn to the continuing question of the management of the British economy. I'm sorry to have to return to Mr Lamont again. I have nothing personal against the Chancellor who, whilst lacking in other skills, has to be admired for his staying power. But these are matters of national concern. Mr Lamont's entire economic policy has been a complete failure. He cannot deny it – it's already part of political folklore. Whatever the rights and wrongs of the government's economic strategy in the run-up to Black Wednesday, and whatever the circumstances of the devaluation, Britain was humiliatingly forced to pull out of the Exchange Rate Mechanism which had been the very cornerstone of Mr Lamont's economic strategy. Since then he has been a lame duck. How could he be otherwise? His credibility vanished in a puff of smoke along with the billions of pounds in foreign reserves that were lost in a bungled attempt to save sterling from inevitable collapse. How can a Chancellor whose entire economic strategy has been blown to pieces remain in office? He has only to open a newspaper any day of the week to know that the financial and business communities have no confidence whatsoever in his stewardship of the economy. There was a time not so long ago when ministers resigned over events which left them seriously diminished in the eyes of the British people.

In April 1982 Lord Carrington, then Foreign Secretary, resigned from the government because his department had failed to anticipate the Argentine invasion of the Falklands Islands. Mrs Thatcher spent a long time trying to persuade him to stay on. But, according to a *Times* report the day after Lord Carrington's resignation, 'he felt that he had been Head of the department responsible for the policy, the policy had failed and therefore it was a matter of honour that he should go.' It was as simple as that. No ducking and weaving. No excuses. No long interviews on Walden. The policy had failed and therefore it was a matter of honour that he should go. That's what people expect. They expect the government to act in their best interests and, when things go wrong, they expect someone to take responsibility for it. But when did we last hear a member of this Cabinet mention the word 'honour'? Somewhere along the line the concept of responsibility has been thrown overboard by this government; and it has been replaced by a different code – survival. Survival by any means, at any cost, until the last possible moment.

This is a government from which nobody resigns unless absolutely forced to do so by overwhelming pressure from the public, the media and their own backbenchers. They mislead parliament, they break the law, they jettison policies which once formed the cornerstone of their entire programme, they use public money to pay private legal bills, they are forced into retreat by the anger – the anger – of the British people, and nobody takes responsibility. One is forced to ask the question: what on earth does it take for a minister to resign from this government?

There can be little doubt that this attitude, this hanging on at all costs, is the hallmark of a party too long in power. But the arrogance of power that we are witnessing today has more serious manifestations. Lines have been crossed that leave decent people feeling uneasy and poorly governed. It has become standard practice under this government for Tory politicians to move from senior positions in the Cabinet to influential posts in privatised industries. It is even the case that ex-ministers accept directorships – in industries for which they themselves established the regulatory environment. Should former ministers be allowed to benefit in such a way from policies they themselves implemented when in the privileged position of government? I think not.

The too-close relationship that has developed between this government and the private sector, and particularly those industries privatised by this government, is unhealthy and improper. Similar questions arise from the revolving door which increasingly sees senior civil servants pass directly from top jobs in Whitehall to top jobs in industries closely connected with their former departments.

It is little wonder that people in the country see a government out of touch with the nation's needs, refusing to take responsibility for its actions, and operating on no fixed principle but that of its own survival.

It is a government whose action on virtually every front is at odds with the wishes of the British people. On which of its policies does the government actually have the nation's backing? On pit closures? On rail privatisation? On its approach to unemployment? On its training policies? On its handling of the economy? The truth is, in a few short months this government has lost the support of the country. At the election, the people gave them the benefit of the doubt. But since then they have done nothing but break promise after promise. And in the process they have conducted themselves with an arrogance and an insensitivity which has appalled the nation. It is this that has led to such widespread disillusion and despair. And in case the Prime Minister and his colleagues feel tempted to think these criticisms come exclusively from the Labour side of the fence, let me say this: even among loyal supporters of the Conservative Party, as I know from my own correspondence, there is embarrassment, bewilderment and anger at the government's performance.

What is equally, if not more, worrying than the declining standards of government is the effect of single party rule on our civil service. Many senior civil servants have never worked under another political party or another political philosophy. The implications of that are far-reaching, and, as I will seek to show, potentially extremely damaging. Speaking recently on this subject, Lord Callaghan pointed out that

John Major is the first Premier of this century never to have served in Opposition. The same is true of nearly half the present Cabinet. Lord Callaghan attacked what he described as 'the irresistible tendency for ministers to regard the Civil Service as their own fiefdom.' By the same token, civil servants may be forgiven for sometimes forgetting that they have a role and a duty above the service of the government of the day, which is the service of the country. There is all the difference in the world between a duty to the national interest and a duty to the political interest of the party in power.

Let me say at this point that I am a genuine admirer of the civil service and of its traditions of impartiality and public service. I have had the privilege of working with civil servants at the highest levels of government, and I know how deep is their desire to identify and to serve the national interest. But the truth is that, increasingly, their impartiality is being compromised and many civil servants will, I am sure, share my discomfort at what I will call the poor judgement of some of their most senior officials in recent weeks and months.

Sir Peter Middleton and his successor at the Treasury Sir Terry Burns were wrong to allow public money to be put towards Mr Lamont's legal bill. The fact that the two men, when called to explain their actions before the House of Commons Public Accounts Committee, could see no impropriety in what they had done is in itself revealing. Perhaps just as revealing, from the standpoint of controlling public expenditure, is Sir Peter's throw-away line that £4,700 for eighteen hours' work by a posh firm of libel lawyers was 'astonishingly good value for money'. If this is the Treasury's idea of cost control, no wonder we have a multi-billion pound deficit in the public accounts.

The behaviour of officials in the Matrix Churchill affair was equally questionable. When the relevant documents finally came to light they painted a picture of civil servants blithely discussing how best to circumvent official guidelines and protect their ministers if their misdeeds became public. This is not the kind of behaviour civil servants should be expected to deliver. They should not be required to find ways round official guidelines, and they should certainly not be expected to protect ministers from fair scrutiny. One final example: in the run-up to the American elections, it emerged that Home Office officials searched confidential immigration files to see if Bill Clinton had applied for British citizenship to avoid the Vietnam Draft. What on earth were these civil servants doing trawling through files for potentially damaging information on the US President-elect, contravening official guidelines and, it goes without saying, without the consent of the individual concerned? We do not know who initiated this request for information, nor who authorised it. Isn't it worrying that, under our system of government, it seems impossible to get an answer to such elementary questions? In any event, it should never have been allowed to happen.

This is no small matter. It was an attempt to infringe an individual's civil rights. It was an attempt to interfere in the democratic process of one of our major allies. And it has created what must be an embarrassing impediment to relations with a new President and his administration.

Anyone who has had dealings with government departments in recent times will have wondered at the reluctance of officials to impart information – information to which any citizen ought to have a right – that may reflect in any way badly on the government. I know that a great deal of civil servants' time is wasted trying to find facts and figures that will present the government's policies in a favourable light – an increasingly challenging task. But it is surely not the role of civil servants on the one hand to deny access to information and on the other to put a gloss on it. That these things do happen exposes a civil service becoming confused about its role and unclear as to its obligations. The civil service has always prided itself on its impartiality. This impartiality is central to its functions and to its effectiveness. Ministers above all others should respect and value this principle. A government that cannot tell the difference between party interest and the national interest has missed a very important point about the British constitution. It is crucial that this distinction should be maintained. Under this government it is becoming increasingly blurred. Civil servants must be assisted in preserving that distinction, and resisting ministers who seek to abuse it. So where do we go from here? What remedial action can we take to halt the slide?

First of all, it is extremely important that we recognize and discuss openly the problem we have and the dangers it represents. To diagnose the sickness is the first step towards restoring good health. Secondly, specific measures can and should be taken to clarify the role of civil servants in relation to their ministers. I believe we need now to draw up a clearer definition of the responsibilities of civil servants. There must be protection in our system for a civil servant who correctly identifies a distinction between the national and a party interest, and who seeks to resist the pressure to cross that line. We surely need a published code of conduct setting out clearly and unambiguously the respective roles and responsibilities of ministers and civil servants. I am sure that would be widely welcomed within the civil service itself. There is evidently also a need for a clear definition of the purposes to which public funds can be legitimately committed. However, I believe there are also much deeper failures in our constitution which need to be tackled. Having the same party in power for fourteen years, and the abuses of that power which we now witness, have served to expose serious systemic weaknesses. The over-centralisation of British government which has gone on apace over the last decade seriously accentuates the problem in our country, with too few checks and balances against the arbitrary use of power. We need to strengthen the power of parliament over the Executive. We need to devolve power to the nations and regions of Britain. We need to revive and restore local government as a vibrant part of our democracy.

It is also clear to me that the individual in Britain has too few rights in relation to the state – or indeed as against the abuse of private power. A first step should be the enactment of a Bill of Rights to protect and defend the individual. We also need a Freedom of Information Act which gives us all – the sovereign citizens of this country – the right to know what government knows and what it does on our behalf; and the overriding precept must be openness. The mature democracy towards which we must strive will be a democracy in which there is wide participation, keen debate, and open decision-making. It is ultimately the only way to ensure accountable and responsive government.

To conclude, let me return to my office correspondence. Although the outrage expressed in so many of these letters makes depressing reading, the strength of feeling and prevailing sense of morality and fair play they convey has impressed me greatly. I would like to think that we are, to borrow the words of Woodrow Wilson, 'witnessing a renaissance of public spirit'. Perhaps it has taken the recent catalogue of events of which I have spoken this evening to rouse the nation's indignation, and that this will indeed prove a catalyst for change. I hope so. It is certainly my intention to campaign for that change; to assert the rights of ordinary people to hold their government to account; and to start to fashion a new constitution for a new century.

Reclaiming the Ground

R.H. Tawney Memorial Lecture, 20 March 1993

John Smith was a Christian socialist who believed in an ethical and moral approach to public life. In this speech he matches the ideas of Christian socialism with the needs of public policy in a statement of his political faith. These underlying moral standards

LEADER OF THE OPPOSITION

were in sharp contrast to the political culture of the Conservative Party under John Major and contributed to Smith's ability to expose the sleaze at the heart of government. But the speech was much more about a positive statement of political faith than simple Tory bashing. The centre of the speech returns to some of the themes developed in the 1980s in the critique of Thatcherism. In particular the speech attacks the notion of the individual which the rational choice theorists of the new right had elevated to a position of political orthodoxy in that decade. In sum, Smith rejected the notion that individuals are composed only of wants and needs. Here, yet again, Smith's optimism about the human condition and lack of cynicism about human potentialities comes across. This was a homage to political heroes, like Tawney himself and William Temple, and a message to the Labour Party that their Leader had a mature and well developed political philosophy.

R. H. Tawney was, throughout the whole of his long and productive life, an uncompromising ethical socialist. He founded his political outlook on the moral principles of his Christian commitment. From that strong redoubt he assailed the deficiencies of both communism and capitalism and espoused the cause of a democratic socialism. This sought to enhance individual freedom in a framework of collective common purpose and opportunity, in which fellowship was the bond of a community of equality. He saw British socialism as ethical, individualistic, and pragmatic.

Were he alive today, I do not think he would have been surprised by the failure of communism, or the disillusionment at the results of unrestrained market forces. Throughout his life he was a vigorous opponent of both ideologies, both of which he saw as antithetic to his vision of a society founded on fraternity and solidarity. His Christian faith, which I am glad to share, was the foundation of his approach. But he did not claim – nor should any Christian – that Christianity could provide the only moral framework for an ethical approach to politics. Our own experience tells us that an ethical approach to life and politics can be held as firmly by people of other faiths and by those who hold no religious conviction. Nor should Christian socialists ever seek to suggest that Christians must be socialists. Just because we, like Tawney, see our Christian faith as leading towards democratic socialist convictions, we must always recognize that fellow Christians might properly arrive at different conclusions from ourselves.

Having established these caveats, let me assert my profound conviction that politics ought to be a moral activity and that we should never feel inhibited in stressing the moral basis of what we believe.

But of course this is not all. We have to undertake the intellectual task of applying our moral principles in a way which results in practical benefit to our fellow citizens. And we must never be afraid of saying that we will adopt a policy because it is, quite simply, the right thing to do.

Let us not underestimate the desire in our society, a desire which I believe is growing, for politics based on principle. And let us not deny the tide of opinion which I believe is beginning to flow towards a recognition of the value of society and away from the destructive individualism of so much of modern Conservatism.

Instead of making promises which will not be kept, pledges which will be betrayed, let us deal honestly and courageously with the many problems which grip our country today. We could replace cynicism with faith, despondency with expectation, despair with hope.

And at a time when the moral values of our society are coming under increasing strain, we could be taking the first steps in a social revolution by encouraging, through conviction and example, a return to the standards of integrity and honour our society deserves.

Fifty years ago there was such a recognition as, in the throes of a World War, two major thinkers were reflecting on the needs of a nation. Beveridge, whose seminal report was the basis of the social action programme of the great post-war Labour Government, called for a war against those five giants – want, disease, ignorance, squalor and idleness.

At the same time, William Temple, Archbishop of Canterbury, published *Christianity and the Social Order* which strongly asserted the duty of the Christian churches to concern themselves with the application of Christian principles to the needs and problems of society.

Temple did not advocate a Christian social ideal; indeed he was sceptical about ideal states from Plato onwards. But he believed Christianity could provide something of far more value – namely principles which could guide our action. He identified three guiding social principles – freedom, fellowship and service.

Freedom, for Temple, meant freedom 'for' something as well as freedom 'from' something, and was the primary object of all political action. But he recognised that human beings are naturally and incurably social, and freedom is best expressed in fellowship. The combination of freedom and fellowship resulted in the obligation of service; service to family, to community and to nation.

Temple drew an important distinction between personality and individuality. 'Every person is an individual, but his individuality is what marks him off from others; it is a principle of division; whereas personality is social, and only in his social relationships can a man be a person … This point has great political importance, for these relationships exist in the whole network of communities and fellowships. It is in these that the real wealth of human life consists.'

The theme that unites the writings of Tawney and Temple and which makes them so appealing to democratic socialists is their insistence on situating the individual in society. Individual freedom for them is only meaningful and achievable within society. This explanation of human experience is, of course, a core belief of democratic socialism.

It provides an organising principle around which we believe our social order – both politically and economically – can and should be built. It is the way in which we believe individual freedom – our ultimate goal – can best be secured.

In this lecture, I will try to explain why I believe that real freedom depends on the interdependence of the individual and society, and why this idea – which has long remained at the centre of democratic socialist thinking – retains its intellectual force and its capacity for popular appeal.

For despite the considerable electoral disappointments that many parties of the Left have experienced in Western democratic societies throughout the 1980s, there remains strong public acceptance for many of the principles and achievements of democratic socialism. I am thinking in particular about the National Health Service in Britain and the framework of social and employment rights that are widely supported in most countries in Western Europe.

Indeed, it is surely a paradox that despite their electoral achievement since 1979, the Conservatives have really achieved so little in reshaping public attitudes in their own *laissez-faire* self-image. The Thatcher revolution in this respect is looking far less revolutionary today – particularly as John Major's Conservative Party struggles to find a post-Thatcherite agenda amidst the economic and social ruin that fourteen years of Tory rule have brought.

What I believe to be certain is that the flaws in the free market doctrines of the radical right are becoming more widely appreciated and more easily exposed than ever before. Their vision of humanity consists of individuals as decision-making units, concerned exclusively with their own self-interest, making transactions in a marketplace. It is a theory which makes very ambitious moral and economic claims; for example, that it alone preserves freedom and promotes prosperity. I believe, however, that it is a doctrine based on an absurd caricature of human behaviour, which grossly misunderstands the nature of freedom, and seriously ignores the value of society – even to the extent of denying its very existence.

Its roots go back to the classical writers of the eighteenth century, to utilitarians like Jeremy Bentham who argued that human conduct is solely motivated by the pursuit of pleasure and the avoidance of pain, and who believed that 'the community is a fictitious body, composed of . . . individual persons.' A comment to be compared with Mrs Thatcher's, notorious remark that there is 'no such thing as society'.

Here, if proof were needed, is conclusive evidence to support John Maynard Keynes' famous warning about the power of the ideas of economists and political philosophers 'both when they are wrong, and when they are right' to influence future generations. 'Madmen in authority,' wrote Keynes, 'who hear voices in the air, are distilling their frenzy from some academic scribbler of a few years back.' In such a fashion were the extreme anti-government polemics of Friedrich Hayek disinterred – from near oblivion – to be put to the service of Mrs Thatcher, Keith Joseph and others.

The fundamental flaw in the individualism of the classical writers, and their modern counterparts in today's Conservative Party is, I believe, their assumption that human beings conduct their lives on the basis of self-interested decisions taken in radical isolation from others. This thesis grotesquely ignores the intrinsically social nature of human beings and fails to recognize the capabilities that all people have to act in response to commitments and beliefs that clearly transcend any narrow calculation of personal advantage.

Of course people have a natural and powerful regard for their own interests and that of their families. That is certainly a dominant and entirely necessary feature of human experience. As Archbishop Temple warned, 'a statesman who supposes that a mass of citizens can be governed without appeal to their self-interest is living in a dreamland and is a public menace' (adding the wise advice that 'the art of government in fact is the art of so ordering life that self-interest prompts what justice demands'). But although Temple accepted that 'man is self-centred', he also believed that 'this is not the real truth of his nature. He has to his credit both capabilities and achievements that could never be derived from self-interest.'

Providing perhaps unexpected support for this line of argument is none other than Adam Smith who, in the *Theory of Moral Sentiments*, wrote: 'How selfish so ever man may be supposed, there are evidently some principles in his nature, which interest him in the fortune of others, and render their happiness to be necessary to him.' The fact that this insight of Smith's is difficult to reconcile with his later and more famous study of economics has caused many of his recent followers to overlook his earlier work. Just as they also tend to ignore his support for public investment in infrastructure, in education and the arts, which are hidden gems of intervention that can be found alongside his thesis of the invisible hand in *The Wealth of Nations*.

Human beings are therefore, I believe, much more than the '*homo economicus*' of classical theory. They are people – people living in families, in communities, in regions, and in nations. People sharing languages and cultures which in themselves shape our aspirations and ideals. People living in societies which profoundly affect our individual ability not merely to make commercial transactions, but to co-operate in ways which crucially determine our capacity for personal freedom and spiritual fulfilment.

In Temple's words, 'people are not just individuals – they are person-alities too'.

Similarly, markets do not enjoy the total supremacy that is envisaged for them by neo-classical economics. Market systems, whilst remaining an effective and useful means of enabling choice and distribution of myriad goods and services, exist alongside and are embedded in other social and political institutions which also contribute to human welfare, and which themselves shape and modify the way markets actually work.

Implicit within so much laissez faire theory is the idea that a perfectly functioning unregulated market is the natural state of humankind. And that this system has occurred somehow spontaneously 'as if economic man was a biological-psychological miracle, born fully formed, say in his mid-twenties with his preferences 'immaculately conceived'.'

The truth, of course, is that markets are social institutions created within communities that have already developed complex structures of co-operation and common identity; structures which have been characteristic features of human existence from the earliest days of civilisation to our own modern day industrial democracies. And it is within these civil institutions, held together by bonds of mutual trust and consent – absolutely crucial elements of human co-operation – that the business of markets is able to take place at all.

It surely follows that, if the neo-classical explanation of both human behaviour and of markets is seriously flawed, then, I believe, so are the political and economic systems that are erected upon it. That is why, in my view, the modern Conservative concept of individual freedom is so incomplete and the role they ascribe to government is so inadequate. For it is upon these same neo-classical assumptions that they adopt a highly restrictive conception of what it is to be free and they base their case for radically limiting the role of government. Hence we arrive at the model of a minimal state – in its most idealised form with the authority only to protect property rights and enforcement of contracts of exchange.

If, as I strongly believe, the moral goal of our society is to extend and encourage individual freedom, then it is certainly not enough to rely simply on a minimal State charged with defending negative liberty – the freedom from coercion by the State. For, as Tawney himself observed, 'A society, or a large part of it, may be both politically free and economically the opposite. It may be protected against arbitrary action by the agents of government, and be without the security from economic oppression which corresponds to civil liberty.'

What Tawney realised was that meaningful freedom depended on real ability. That for millions of people citizenship was empty and valueless if squalor and deprivation were the reality of a society only theoretically free. What was needed was positive liberty – the freedom to achieve that is gained through education, health care, housing, and employment. An infrastructure of freedom that would require collective provision of basic needs through an enabling state. It is this richer conception of freedom for the individual in society that is the moral basis of democratic socialism.

It is also a vital theory of citizenship, just as concerned as any neo-classical writer with protection from coercion by the State and with the values of democracy. And, of course, in this important respect it is sharply distinguishable from the anti-democratic and totalitarian forms of socialism against which Tawney was such a steadfast opponent.

For Tawney, Marxism was a 'barbarous inhuman sordid doctrine' as amoral and materialistic as *laissez-faire* capitalism. He was scornful of those who believed that the Labour Party had something to learn form Marxist collectivism, accusing its supporters of a 'credulity so extreme as to require, not argument, but a doctor.' He saw quite clearly that liberty-creating socialism was only possible in a context of political democracy and freedom of speech and thought. After the collapse of the former Soviet Union and its satellites, I think Tawney is shown to have had an insight, and a percipience which saw through the deterministic philosophies which took so little account of the moral influences on humanity. it would also, I am sure, be a considerable source of pleasure to Tawney, if he were, alive today, to know that his arguments for social justice, freedom and democracy retain all their persuasive power even after a decade dominated by Conservative ideology. For despite the supreme arrogance of their period in government, the so-called triumph of Thatcherism and the radical Right has been remarkably short-lived. Its narrow conception of freedom and its adamant support for unfettered free markets is being challenged not merely by traditional opponents such as the Labour Party but from within its own ranks.

A striking example of this trend was the publication last year by the Institute of Economic Affairs of a study by the Oxford philosopher John Gray entitled *The Moral Foundations of Market Institutions*.

Gray, previously closely associated with the ideas of the New Right, now argues that freedom requires the creation of an enabling State, meeting the basic needs of its citizens and which is modelled on European (particularly German) ideas of a social market economy.

His IEA pamphlet, deploying arguments not unfamiliar to Tawney, exposes the inadequacy of negative liberty as advocated by supporters of *laissez-faire* capitalism and offers in its place as 'the only principled position' an enabling Welfare State 'which confers on people a variety of claims to goods, services and resources.'

To be fair to Gray's work I should add that he is critical too of the egalitarian arguments of democratic socialists. He is dismissive of concerns about fairness and social justice on the grounds that, in his view, the basic needs that are necessary for individual freedom are readily satisfied. This is a critical and controversial point of debate which is disputed in an interesting commentary on Gray's paper written by Raymond Plant and which the IEA have helpfully included in their publication.

I believe it is significant that some honest advocates of the radical Right are having to come to terms with the limitations of their theories and that this is just another sign that the intellectual ground is moving-steadily towards the democratic Left.

The conclusion I reach is that the goal of individual freedom and the value of society, which we advocate as democratic socialists, is a theory of sustained intellectual force. When tested in the experience of humanity it can be found to be a better explanation of the lives and purposes of men and women than its rivals on the *laissez-faire* Right or the Marxist Left. We ought, therefore, in the battle of ideas which is at the centre of the political struggle, to be confident in the strength of our intellectual case.

But I believe we must also argue for our cause on the basis of its moral foundation. It is a sense of revulsion at denied opportunity, injustice and poverty, whether at home or abroad, which impels people to work for a better world, to become, as in our case, democratic socialists. The powerful contribution of Christian socialists in all the denominations of the Church has always focused on the moral purpose of political action. How true it is that the Labour Party has owned more to Methodism than to Marx.

But it was that great Anglican William Temple, who identified what he called 'the real wealth of human life', who saw that the individual was best fulfilled in the context of a strong community. That is the truth I want to re-assert today with confidence and conviction. That is why I believe the Labour Party must be bold in demonstrating our commitment to enhance and extend individual freedom by building a society which is dynamic and responsive to the aspirations of all our people.

Temple defined the relationships which constituted our real wealth as existing in terms of family, community and nation. We ought to support family life as one of the foundation stones of a good society and in consequence fight determinedly against the unemployment, poverty and lack of opportunity by which it is so often menaced. When Labour founded the National Health Service we lifted a great burden from the shoulders of ordinary families who were set free from the financial perils of ill health.

In 1993 we ought to reflect that in this year a new American President is following in the footsteps of a pioneering Labour government forty five years ago. Let no one tell me that the principles of democratic socialism – of which the NHS is a fine example – are dated. They are, as in this comparative example, often ahead of their time.

By the same token we must strengthen our communities and our sense of community. The undermining of local government which is part of the deliberate down-grading of all alternative power systems to the central State means that communities are being weakened by having no means to advance their own ambitions and to tackle their own problems in their own way.

That is why I urge a renaissance of local government in the context of a more pluralistic and diverse society. It is why I believe that devolving power from an over-centralised Westminster and Whitehall to Scotland, Wales and the regions of England is a necessary part of the refurbishment of our democracy. Democracy has to be a vital and constantly refreshing element on our socialism.

We also want to build a society which strives always to unlock the talent and skills of its own people, to harness what Tawney once magnificently described as 'the extra-ordinary potential of ordinary people'. More and more we realize, as deskilling and lack of training inhibit our economic capacity, that a policy of social opportunity also makes the most obvious economic sense.

As we near the end of the twentieth century our horizons must extend well beyond our own national frontiers to our new relationships which are developing fast in the European Community and to our obligations and opportunities in the exciting, but also perilous, circumstances of the post-Cold War world. Thanks be to God that we now perhaps have the opportunity of diverting our resources from the piling up of armaments which threaten our planet's existence, to tackling the profound injustices and deprivations of the North/South divide.

There is no doubt whatever where our obligations lie both as Christians and socialists. We must never allow the needs of the developing world, where live the majority of our fellow world citizens, to be anything but central to our political purposes. There is no good reason why Britain should not have emulated the achievements of the Scandinavian countries which, profoundly influenced by their social democratic tradition, have set standards which in recent years our country has fallen well below.

In Britain and in the world of the new century which approaches, we will need to give the enhancement and protection of our environment a prominence which simply did not enter into the consciousness of earlier generations.

The earth upon which God has placed us should be for us a special trust from one generation to another. The need to develop effective action to implement that trust is a dramatic illustration of how economic forces need to be contained and controlled for the good of the world community right across both frontiers and generations.

We must approach our politics with a sense of optimism for the future. There is so much of good that can be done if we seize the opportunities which the modern world makes available. Instead of carrying the miserable burden of mass unemployment, we could be investing in new technology and in new skills. Instead of witnessing the crumbling of our education system and the fracturing of our health service, we could be building high quality public services which provide security and opportunity for every family in the land. Instead of allowing our society to become diminished by the violence and dishonesty of crime, we could be building strong communities which provide protection for every citizen. Instead of savagely increasing unfair taxes which will further damage so many lives, we could be investing in people, investing in infrastructure, investing in manufacturing industry. There is so much we could do. There is so much that needs to be done.

The Second Commandment calls upon us to love our neighbours as ourselves. It does not expect a frail humanity to be capable of loving our neighbours more than ourselves: that would be a task of saintly dimension. But I do not believe we can truly follow that great

Commandment unless we have a concept of care and concern for our fellow citizens which is reflected in the organization of our society. In this vital way we can ally our Christian faith to our democratic socialist conviction. In the pursuit of both we can aspire to lead our country to find the real wealth which only a good society can provide.

Maastricht

Hansard, 22 July 1993

John Major celebrates as one of his finest achievements the negotiation of an opt-out from the Social Chapter of the Maastricht Treaty. From the perspective of Conservative political philosophy and from the necessity of managing the Conservative Party with a small majority, this judgement is sound. It was a remarkable piece of political gymnastics which kept his party in power and delayed the implementation of workplace reforms until after the 1997 General Election. The complexity of the treaty and the fierceness of the politics that surrounded it are reflected in a small selection of the interventions left in the text reproduced below. There were many more. The Conservatives set out to wreck Smith's speech almost from the outset, but he pushed on and, in the end, as so often in his career, he mastered the House of Commons. His case was simple: All other governments in Europe, plus those waiting to join, and European employers endorsed the Social Chapter, only Britain was alone and isolated because of misapplied dogma and political opportunism. There were a number of speeches from these long debates that could have been chosen, this is representative of Smith's impact on the debates.

The Prime Minister made a curious start to the debate when he complained about the fact that we were debating the resolution and the amendment at all today. We are having the debate because of section 7 of the very Act to which he drew attention. He claims that the Act has been passed by both Houses of Parliament, which is certainly true – it has received Royal Assent. Section 7 makes it clear that the Act cannot come into force until the House of Commons comes to a resolution.

The Prime Minister described the debate as if it were an irritation to the Government – a devious ploy by the Opposition. However, the debate is a requirement of the Act of Parliament which he used to justify most of what he said. In addition, when discussing the Bill in Committee, the Foreign Secretary said that the Government had no difficulty in accepting new clause 74 – which became section 7 of the Act. The Foreign Secretary said that the Government accepted the challenge presented by the proposals contained in the new clause. On 22 April he said:

It is reasonable that the House should want the opportunity to vote on the principle of the social protocol.

I have discovered why the Foreign Secretary is not winding up today's debate. It would be too inconvenient to have a Government apologist who had agreed to the procedure which we are now adopting speaking alongside a Prime Minister who is seeking to condemn it. It is nothing other than a requirement of the Act which both Houses of Parliament have passed, but it gives the House the opportunity which the Government sought to avoid in Committee – a vote on whether we should have the Social Chapter and the Social Protocol as part of the British version of the treaty.

It took the Prime Minister a little while to get round to it, but once again he today advanced the startling proposition that measures of social protection which are thought to be desirable by all 11 of our partner nations in the European Community are in some curious way a threat to British prosperity. As the argument has continued throughout the

Bill's consideration, the Government have persistently sought to misrepresent the content and effect of the Social Chapter provisions. A deliberate campaign of misrepresentation by the Government has reached new peaks of exaggeration as each day passes. Therefore, it is vital for the House to consider what the Social Protocol is and what it is not. The other 11 states have agreed that there should be a modest extension of the Community's competence in social affairs – matters such as the protection of the health, safety and working conditions of people at work, workers' rights to information and consultation, and equality for men and women in relation to work opportunities and treatment at the workplace. The argument is all about those sectors where qualified majority voting applies.

There are other extensions of competence to social security and social protection where unanimity would still be required. There are sectors – which the Government have consistently failed to acknowledge – which are specifically excluded from the agreement. They include pay, the right of association and the right to strike.

I shall remind the House just what the Social Protocol is about. I do not make any enormous claims for its proposals, which are fairly modest. But the Government say that the proposals are a sinister threat to our economic future, a deadly plot by the Brussels bureaucrats to destroy jobs and economic growth from which, in the nick of time, our heroic Prime Minister has rescued us all. The irony of the Prime Minister posing as a job protector will not be lost on the millions of people who have been victims of the economic policies for which he has been responsible as Chancellor and Prime Minister. That self-styled saviour of jobs and growth has the worst record on jobs and growth of any British Prime Minister since the war.

It is when one examines the provisions of the Social Protocol that the absurdity of the Government's claims is revealed. In what sense and in what way does the improvement of the working environment to protect workers' health and safety or the improvement of working conditions impede economic growth? How on earth can equality between men and women in labour market opportunities and treatment at work be considered economically harmful in a civilised, modern state? It becomes even more absurd when one appreciates that the purpose of the agreement is to have similar rights and opportunities in every Community country to create a level playing field of social opportunity. We hear much about level playing fields from Conservative Members who mention them nearly every day in the Chamber. It is odd that they will not adopt that concept in relation to the rights of working people and men and women.

That concept is fully understood by the rest of the Community, which is why all the other 11 member states readily agreed to the social charter of 1989 and the social action programme that flowed from it. It is why they have consistently resisted British Conservatives' attempts to prevent further progress in the social sphere. They agreed to the protocol because they all understand what the British Conservative party is incapable of appreciating – that economic success and social progress go hand in hand. [*Interventions and Interruptions*] We should make more progress if Conservative Members were to calm down a little. They get very excited when remarks of the employers are quoted, but they never think of consulting the employees about any of their rights. The general secretary of UNICE, the employers' organisation in Europe said: 'If we look at the costs of employment only or social costs only, we're looking at one very small part of the picture. So it's really a gross over simplification to reduce the whole thing to the costs of labour.'

He is right. That is the view of UNICE, just as it is the view of the European TUC. If the Conservative party is so right on this subject, why is it that the only political party in the rest of the Community that supports it is Mr Le Pen's National Front? [*Interruption*] Why is it that even right-wing Governments do not perceive the menaces and the threats which the Prime Minister and his colleagues see on all sides? [Long and frequent interruptions] The fundamental point is why, if the employers were so compelling in their arguments, they have not been able to persuade Chancellor Kohl, Mr Balladur and Mr Lubbers, the right-wing Conservative figures in Europe, to listen to them. It passes belief that these people are involved in a nefarious plot to destroy their own prosperity. Are these right-wing Conservative leaders so muddled and confused that they have become socialists by accident? Do we really believe that, when the Prime Minister goes to meet these colleagues at meetings of the European People's Party and other such gatherings, he bangs the table in his commanding style and warns them that they are closet socialists?

Is it not passing strange that 11 Governments of many and different political complexions are all incapable of discerning the weaknesses in the Social Protocol? Why is it that not one of the four countries seeking entry into the European Community wants to opt out of the Social Chapter? Fifteen countries in Europe – those in the Community and those wanting to join – are all of one opinion; only one party and one country is on the other side – all out of step except our John. The Prime Minister must believe that they are all deluded.

Surely the truth is that it is the Prime Minister who is deluded about the nature and effect of the social chapter which elsewhere finds such widespread favour. After all, it requires quite an acute form of delusion to claim a triumph of negotiating skill in getting one's country isolated and excluded from a decision-making process of great importance to the Community and, inevitably, of importance to this country. What kind of success is it to have engineered a situation in which, when social affairs are on the Community's agenda, British Ministers will be bereft of influence over legislation which many believe will come to apply in Britain as a result of decisions by the Court of Justice, whether or not there is an opt-out.

Only in the Walter Mitty world that the Prime Minister increasingly inhabits could such nonsense be thought to be an achievement. Of course, we know that the Prime Minister wants the country to believe that, whatever the mess at home, he is really an ace negotiator abroad. Like the comic strip hero, Clark Kent, as soon as he leaves our shores behind, the Prime Minister is transformed into a diplomatic megastar. There he is, Britain's diplomatic megastar, his Superman shirt tucked neatly into his underpants; there he is, a very special kind of hero, shaping the very destiny of Europe, clutching his Maastricht opt-out as his colleagues gently take him to the door marked 'Sortie'. The Prime Minister and the Government do not understand that their opt-out is Britain's lockout – a lockout from decisions. I could not understand how the Prime Minister could argue that we had to be involved in decision-making in the Community while also arguing the justification for an opt-out. Once again, decisions will be arrived at and policies forged in Britain's absence.

One should not be surprised to hear that the views that I have quoted were expressed by the President of the Board of Trade. One also hears them from Conservative Members of the European Parliament. In a debate in the European Parliament on 27 May this year, Sir Christopher Prout, whom I understand to be the leader of the Conservative MEPs, could not have put matters more plainly. What he said is on the record of the European Parliament:

'The Conservative Party is in favour of the social dimension' – [*Interruption*] I thought that Conservative Members might all agree with that, and I hope that they will also agree with what Sir Christopher said next. He added, for good measure:

'We all hope once Maastricht is ratified that a suitable intergovernmental agreement can be reached on this matter which will include all Member States.'

The Conservatives will come back to the subject. I am sure that some hon. Members will have spotted their tactic. I find it fascinating that Sir Christopher Prout seems more determined to opt in than to opt out.

Mrs Edwina Currie: It may assist the right hon. and learnéd Gentleman to know that Mr Bill Newton Dunn is the leader of the Conservatives in the European Parliament and that many of us have no problem with the social dimension; it is the details of the protocol that we dislike and wish to vote against.

Mr Smith: I hear what the hon. Lady says, but I wish that she would weigh in the balance the comments that I read in newspapers such as the *Sunday Telegraph*. Last week that newspaper quoted a Dutch Christian Democrat, Jean Penders, on the attitudes of Tory MEPs. Mr Penders said that at first he was doubtful about his new British colleagues in the European People's party, but that now he is full of praise: 'Oh, they all believe in the Social Chapter, all of them.' [*Hon. Members*: Who ?] The Tory MEPs. The article, by the Brussels corre- spondent of the *Sunday Telegraph*, went on to discuss the dilemma over the manifesto being drafted by the European People's Party for the European elections next year, in which I believe the hon. Member for Derbyshire, South (Mrs Currie) hopes to stand. Will the British Tories be bound by it? According to the European People's Party, the manifesto will be based on its policies and positions and the British Tories will have to defend every word. It seems that quite a lot of talking will have to take place. The problem for the Tories is that the European People's party has not been reticent about its views on feder- alism and the Social Chapter. I shall quote from the Athens declaration of the ninth congress of the European People's Party [*Laughter*] Conservative Members should not mock their continental confederates in that way. The declaration, approved in Athens in November last year, comes straight to the point: 'The main political aim of the European People's Party is European unity. The party advocates European unification on the basis of democracy'

So far, so good. I can see the Tories looking at me. But the declaration adds the words 'and federalism.' Even worse, federalism is described as 'the ideal for Europe.'

But it is when dealing with social policies that the European People's Party, the Tories' new friend in Europe, really gets motoring. It says: 'the European People's party declares its support for the implementation of the European Social Charter, the introduction of minimum standards for working conditions and social benefits, and workers' participation in decision making and company profits.' Few of us could have put that better than the European People's Party did.

Let no one tell me that the EPP is not having a positively beneficial influence on the Conservative Party. I know that it has friends and admirers in the highest reaches of that party, because of a speech made earlier this month by the Secretary of State for Employment, (David Hunt) in which he declared himself glad to be a Christian Democrat. He said:

My own background in politics is a very European one, and I have always, willingly described myself as a Christian Democrat as well as a Conservative. As the Union between the peoples of Europe, inch by questioning inch, grows ever closer, we will need to look for new alliances. I believe that political and ideological alliances between like-minded parties from different countries will soon come to complement – or supplant old national rivalries and friendships. Our admittance

he means the Conservative party's admittance

to the European People's Party in the European Parliament puts that scenario into perspective.

I am grateful to the right hon. Gentleman for having said so clearly where the Conservatives stand. Revealingly, he also said: 'There is already far more common ground than people imagine'. Hon. Members may wish to ask him more about that when he speaks later and makes his second intervention in the debate.

Lest there be any doubt about the increasing influence of the European People's Party on the Conservative Party, the Secretary of State for Employment drove his point home by saying: 'There is even now an EPP office at Smith Square.'

Gosh. That must be where Conservative Members can get their personal copies of the Athens Declaration. But for the convenience of those attending the meeting of the 1922 Committee tonight, I have caused a copy to be placed in the Library. They can pick it up on their way.

Mr Garel-Jones: I am the only one who has a copy.

Mr Smith: Precisely. It was a document for which wide circulation was not desired. However, it is now in the Library and hon. Members can obtain it. When they read it they will find out how much they have signed up to in Europe. It is a case not so much of socialism by the back door as of federalism by the front door – the front door of Tory Central Office.

At the heart of the debate is a profound difference about the kind of policies that Britain needs if we are to succeed and to hold our own in a competitive world. The Conservative Party, as the Prime Minister's speech confirmed, wants to persist with the failed policies of the 1980s, for which the people of Britain are paying such a heavy price today. It wants to persist with those policies despite the accumulating evidence of their failure.

For example, the World Economic Forum recently published its *World Competitiveness Report* on the countries of the OECD, which showed that over the past five years the United Kingdom has fallen down the league. That is the sharpest deterioration in competitiveness of any EC country. The truth which must someday dawn on this Government is that their policies simply have not worked. Even the expurgated version of the Government's own Department of Trade and Industry report shows that Britain is still 25% below France and Germany in terms of productivity.

The evidence shows that the member states which embraced the Social Chapter, when Britain rejected it, have more impressive records of competitiveness and productivity. The Conservatives fail to understand that low wages, inadequate skills and persistent under-investment are the real drag anchors on Britain's economic performance. We have no future as the sweatshop of Europe. If we persist in the policies of social devaluation which lie behind the opt-out from the Social Chapter, I fear that our relative decline will continue. Indeed, it will accelerate.

Warburg's briefing last week on competitiveness among the leading industrial countries stated: 'Despite having the lowest labour costs per working hour, Britain struggles with the highest unit labour costs.' That is proof surely, if it were needed, that having the lowest wages does not, as the opt-out merchants maintain, lead necessarily to competitive advantage. That is the answer to the question that I was asked at the beginning of this debate.

The Warburg study shows – sensible people know this – that improvement in productivity depends critically on capital investment, the pace of innovation and the quality of the labour force. That is the new economic agenda which Britain and Europe must embrace – not the bargain-basement techniques of wage cuts and skills depression. That is how we can best achieve the competitive edge which is vital to our economic success.

There is another view, the view adopted by British Conservatives that by depressing wages and undermining the conditions of the work force, a relative advantage can be obtained. We have seen a grotesque example of that in the destruction of the wages councils which, for decades, offered protection to the lowest-paid workers in this country – the people at the greatest risk of exploitation.

The wages councils legislation was introduced at the turn of the century by Winston Churchill to protect the low-paid worker and the good employer. It has been swept aside by the mean-minded men and women of this Administration. Winston Churchill put the point forcefully to the House in 1909; I remind the House of his comments, as it has seldom been put better:

Where you have no organisation, no parity of bargaining, the good employer is undercut by the worst where those conditions prevail you have not a condition of progress, but a condition of progressive degeneration.

What a contrast that is with today, when a British Government actually place adverts in the German business press advertising Britain as a low-wage economy. Not for our skills, technology or productivity are we to be recommended – we are to be recommended just for our low wages.

There are low wages in a society in which income equality has dramatically widened over 14 Conservative years. Let me just remind the Prime Minister [*Interruption*] He may want to look at my notes and I hope that he will listen carefully to what I am going to say. I want to remind him of the wages that are actually being paid in the Britain of which he is Prime Minister today. A 28-year-old care assistant working in a private nursing home works 60 hours for £1.33 an hour. A coach driver works 60 hours a week for £2.10 an hour. A forecourt attendant in a petrol station works 70 hours a week for £1.40 an hour. That is the philosophy of the Conservative Party and that is how it affects real people in the real world.

How many Conservative Ministers would contemplate accepting those rates of pay for themselves or for their families? If it is not acceptable to them, why should it be thought acceptable for anyone else? What makes it even harder to stomach is the constant rise in salaries, pensions and perks for the highest-paid executives at the same time as the exploitation of vulnerable people proceeds and the Government walk away from their responsibilities to those people. It is that weird Tory double standard on incentives: poor people can be motivated only by the thought of even greater poverty, but the rich are to be inspired by the lure of even greater wealth.

The Government's approach to international competition is just as crude. It is to compete against Taiwan on wages rather than against Germany on skills. The Government say that if our competitors pay low wages, we must follow them down. If there is no employment protection in countries against which we compete, such protection apparently cannot be afforded here either.

We in the Labour Party believe that that approach is wholly flawed. Not only is it totally unjust to our people, it is not related in any way to the dynamics and realities of today's world economy. Investors at home and abroad today are seeking skills, technology and a highly motivated and self-confident workforce. We hear a lot from the Government about inward investment and how that investment would be afraid to come near us if we were to sign up to the Social Protocol. How strange that, in a recent study carried out by Arthur Andersen of Japanese inward investment, wages and social costs are not mentioned by Japanese companies as a factor determining decisions to invest in Britain. The problem which is highlighted and described as most important by Japanese enterprise is 'the difficulty in recruiting skilled or qualified employees.' The Nissan director of personnel gave evidence the other day to the Select Committee on Employment. He dismissed the Social Chapter as a significant factor in respect of inward investment. It is also highly revealing that many Japanese firms in Britain bring with them much better working practices than are common in British firms and which far exceed anything that would be required by the Social Chapter. A recent survey – [*Interruption*] It would benefit Ministers to listen to some of this evidence instead of, like the Chancellor of the Exchequer, rudely interrupting from a sedentary position.

The Chancellor of the Exchequer (Mr Kenneth Clarke): I was merely provoked by the logic of the right hon. and learned Gentleman's position. Having used a 1909 quotation and 1909 sentiments, he went on to describe the attractions to this country now of Japanese investment, to a deregulated economy which is outside the Social Chapter. He illustrates that the Japanese are not creating a sweatshop economy here. It is a modern, thriving economy, and the Japanese are coming here because we are attractive outside the Social Chapter.

Mr Smith: I am surprised at the Chancellor of the Exchequer. Surely the point about the 1909 quotation is that it is astonishing that someone in 1909 understood something which members of the Conservative Party have not yet realised in the 1990s. Churchill said that when he was a Liberal. Apparently Conservatives only pay attention to what Churchill said when he was a Conservative, such is the narrow and partisan view of history and reality adopted by the Conservative Party.

What the Chancellor of the Exchequer should understand – [*Interruption*] I hope that he will listen carefully to this – is that a recent survey of the pay and employment conditions in eight major Japanese-owned companies employing 15,000 people in the United Kingdom found that wages, maternity and paternity leave and fringe benefits in those companies were far more generous than those in Britain [*Hon. Members*: What is the point?] I hope that the Chancellor of the

Exchequer will finally get the point that companies as progressive as that are not worried about a Social Chapter because they will easily be able to comply with its provisions.

I hope that some British companies will copy Nissan, which recently agreed two-year pay deal increases with maternity pay of up to 100 per cent of average earnings for up to a maximum of 18 weeks. Maternity leave has been extended to 40 weeks after birth with existing rights of return to work maintained. Matsushita Electric, Sony and Komatsu have introduced parternity leave for their workers. Although Conservative Members often jeer at that, what in some ways is the most successful economic country in the world is showing us a better way forward in terms of social provision. Far from being put off by the Social Chapter, the Japanese are ahead of it.

In the real world, the new economic agenda requires a new approach − a positive combination of skills development, decent standards, humane standards, and ever-widening employment opportunities. That must mean giving greater opportunities at work for women on the basis of equal rights and adequate provision for maternity leave and child care − not just because that is their right, but because our economy needs the indispensable contribution that women can make to our future prosperity.

I see the Chancellor of the Exchequer nodding. That is why I find it odd that the Government should object to a Social Chapter which provides for 'equality between men and women with regard to labour market opportunities and treatment at work.'

In rejecting that provision, what message is the Conservative Party giving to the women of this country? That is why the Conservative Party is seen as socially the most backward in Europe, even by its own party colleagues. It is now entirely clear that the whole of this argument about opting out of the social dimension of the treaty is not about Britain's national interest or our future prosperity. It is much more about the internal politics of the Conservative Party and increasingly about the tattered reputation of a discredited Prime Minister. One day he tells us that Britain must be at the heart of Europe – that is to keep his Chancellor and his Employment Secretary on board. On another day he warns of the insidious socialist threats inherent in the European scheme – words to please his Home Secretary and his Secretary of State for Social Security. One thing to the 1922 Committee; no doubt something else to the European People's Party. We are, of course, accustomed to and indeed sometimes entertained by the right hon. Gentleman's increasingly desperate games with his own party, but, at the end of the day, that must be a matter for them. What is an entirely different matter is the Prime Minister's attitude to Parliament. It must be a matter of astonishment that he has not readily accepted that the decision on the Social Chapter is for this House to take. Throughout our deliberations on the European Communities (Amendment) Act, the Government sought to avoid the House coming to a decision and agreed to section 7 of the Act, under which this resolution is debated, only when they faced the prospect of inevitable defeat if they did otherwise.

Over the Conservative years we have seen the checks and balances of our system of government being persistently undermined in favour of the power of the central state. We see that, for example, in the deliberate diminishment of local government and in the creation of ministerially dominated quangos on an unprecedented scale. But I warn the Prime Minister that, if he seeks to take it even further and seeks to defy the will of the House, he will have exceeded the power of his office.

I urge the House to vote for the Social Chapter. It is our responsibility in this House to make the decision and, when we have made the decision, it is the unavoidable responsibility of the Government to accept and to implement what the House has decided.

Re-inventing the United Nations

The Robert F. Kennedy Memorial Lecture, 4 November 1993

The failure of the West, Europe in particular, to make a co-ordinated or appropriate response to the civil war in Yugoslavia and in particular the failure of Douglas Hurd to give any sort of lead in Europe on the issue, dominated foreign policy debates in the early 1990s. Coupled with the Gulf War and Maastricht, foreign issues were at the forefront of British politics to an unusual extent. Smith responded to the times and to the increased scope of the leadership with a number of key foreign policy speeches. In this speech he argues for the reform of the United Nations, still at the time of writing not properly implemented, as the key to the policing of the new world order.

Robert Kennedy was a man of passionate conviction and of vision for the future. His death in June 1968, just as he was on the verge of winning not only the Democratic nomination but probably also the Presidency itself, was a tragic loss for the people of the United States and for many more all around the world. He would have made an impact on the world stage as great, and perhaps greater, than any post-war President.

He was a man prepared to take risks for peace. He wanted an early end to the Vietnam War. He wanted new efforts to control the then burgeoning nuclear arms race. And most passionately of all, he wanted to heal the divisions of his own great nation – to reduce the gap between the rich and poor, between black and white, and build a new society of freedom and social justice.

His assassination in Los Angeles twenty five years ago meant that we can never know if a second Kennedy presidency would have lived up to the high hopes that he inspired in 1968. He was in many ways a controversial figure, but there can be no question that he was a courageous man. Courage best exemplified, I believe, on the night of that other terrible assassination in 1968, the murder in Memphis of the Rev Martin Luther King. That evening in April, as riots broke out in more than 100 cities around the US, Kennedy was scheduled to speak at an open air rally in a black ghetto in Indianapolis. Against police advice, he insisted on going to the meeting which had not yet heard of King's assassination. He himself broke the news to the crowd, and then spoke movingly about his sympathy and understanding for the feelings of the black community their sense of anguish and loss. A loss he compared with his own after his brother's similar death five years before. The speech was short, but highly effective, and the crowd, despite the anger they all felt at King's death, went home peacefully in Indianapolis that night.

During his '68 campaign Kennedy often repeated a famous phrase adapted from George Bernard Shaw – 'some men see things as they are and say 'why' – I dream of things that never were and say 'why not'?' Tonight in the spirit of Robert Kennedy's thirst for a better future I would like to explore how things could be in this new world order that we live in today. I would like to focus in particular on the role of the United Nations. I will set out why I believe the UN is so important and central to any vision of international progress. But I will also explain why I believe change in the structures of the UN is now imperative if the institution is to remain a dynamic and effective force for peace and progress.

Today people seem to be overwhelmed by the difficult realities of our modern world. Prompted by the harrowing scenes of disaster, famine and civil strife that so frequently dominate our television screens, it is easy to become pessimistic and defeatist. The euphoria that greeted the end of the Cold War has certainly dissipated very rapidly indeed. In just three years the mood has swung from a facile optimism that we could instantly build a new world order, to a foolish pessimism that the international community can do nothing at all.

Such pessimism, I believe, is unrealistic, naive and unreasonable. The world today is, without doubt, a much better place than it was at the height of the Cold War. And I believe that it is entirely justifiable to be sensibly optimistic about the state of the world; to view the cup of the international community as half full – not half empty.

Of course, the world is also a very different place. The Cold War era was like an elaborate game of chess. A contest between the superpowers in black and white, with clear rules, and all the games apparently ending in a draw.

But it would be foolish to be nostalgic for the relative stability of the Cold War – for it was based on a nuclear powder-keg – an escalating arms race that not merely wasted resources on an unprecedented scale but which threatened the very survival of our planet. And as we see all too clearly today, the Cold War merely suppressed, and in many cases intensified, a number of long-standing ethnic and nationalist tensions that have erupted all too quickly into violence and civil unrest. But despite the absolute horror of the war in Bosnia, the dreadful conflict in Somalia, the problems of Georgia, Azerbaijan, Haiti, and Angola, we should not overlook the real progress that is being made elsewhere.

I believe there is much that is being done and can be done to build a better world. This positive agenda was reinforced for me very powerfully at a meeting of the Socialist International that I attended in Lisbon recently. Speaking at the conference were Shimon Peres, the Foreign Minister of Israel, Abdel Latif, the representative of the PLO, and from South Africa, Nelson Mandela, Leader of the ANC. The progress reports they gave us on the Middle East peace settlement and on the forthcoming non-racial elections in South Africa were truly remarkable. They were reports of agreement, conciliation, and negotiation between Jew and Arab, between whites and blacks in South Africa, that would have seemed unimaginable just a few years ago. Of course, there is still a long way to go in both the Middle East and South Africa – a lot of fear and hatred still to be overcome. But the evidence of progress – real progress – cannot be denied.

And there have been other successes too – successes in particular for the United Nations and, surprising as it may seem, in its peace-keeping activities. Unlike the well known problems of Bosnia and Somalia, the UN's peace-keeping work in other countries has not been widely reported. TV shots of ballot boxes being used, of new constitutions being agreed, of refugees going home, are not in the current idiom as newsworthy as the scenes of destruction and human misery that we see from Mogadishu and Sarajevo. But this year there have been some highly successful UN peace-keeping operations.

In Cambodia the UN deployed 21,000 military police and civilian personnel to organise the repatriation of more than 360,000 refugees and arranged a successful election this summer which has been endorsed by the Security Council as free and fair. This in a country which all too recently experienced genocide on a scale to match the Nazi holocaust. And take another example – El Salvador. The UN has successfully mediated a peace agreement between the Government and the rebel FMLN after more than ten years of civil war. The agreement involves complete reform of El Salvador's judicial and electoral systems and will culminate in elections due to be held next Spring. I cannot recall a single television news item on the UN's involvement in El Salvador – a country that seemed to be far more newsworthy during the height of its bitter and violent civil war.

And there is more besides – the United Nations and its specialised agencies play a key role in development in the Third World. Here too there has been spectacular progress. A few weeks ago UNICEF the UN Children's Fund published a new report *The Progress of Nations* which presents some remarkable facts about human development in the late twentieth century: that in little more than one generation average real incomes in the developing world have more than doubled;

child death rates have been more than halved; malnutrition rates have been reduced by 30 per cent; life expectancy has been increased about a third; primary school enrolment has risen from less than 50% to 75%; and the percentage of rural families with access to safe water has risen from ten to more than 60%

Of course, there are billions of people still living in conditions of appalling poverty all around the developing world. Some regions – especially sub-Saharan Africa – are struggling with desperate problems of debt, economic stagnation, and social decline. And there is still too little recognition by the powerful states in the world of their moral obligations to the majority of their fellow human beings, still denied even a minimum standard of living.

But UNICEF is right to demonstrate that progress is possible. Proof that the international community can achieve social and economic progress, and together build a more prosperous and peaceful world. Now as the end of the Cold War opens up new opportunities for international co-operation in a truly world community, we should be bold and ambitious to achieve much more. And if we are to achieve much more then we must, I believe, put much more effort and, commitment into strengthening the United Nations. For the UN is the body that best represents the international community. It must be right at the centre of our blueprint for international relations in the years ahead and the new century to come.

The Labour Party has always insisted that support for the United Nations must be a key component of British foreign policy. The post war Labour government and, in particular, its distinguished Foreign Secretary Ernest Bevin, played a critical role in its foundation. In fact the Labour Party is the only major political party in Britain that includes support for the United Nations in its constitutional objectives. It appears in a clause which is usually discussed by political pundits who have little idea of its real content. It is clause four of the party constitution. So the next time some worthy commentator calls for the abolition of clause four perhaps they would like to read it first.

But, of course, support for the UN does not mean that we should be reluctant to make changes to the organisation. Quite the opposite. For as one of its strongest supporters we in the Labour Party want to encourage change and reform. There is clearly a need to cut out waste and streamline the administration of this very complex organisation. However, I have no time whatsoever for those critics of the UN who are constantly on the attack, denigrating and scapegoating an institution which can only be as effective as its member states allow it to be.

Just think for a minute about a world in which the UN did not exist. There would, I believe, be extraordinary and justified demands to create an institution of the world community with objectives almost exactly the same as those set out in the UN's own Charter.

What I believe the international community should be doing now is 'reinventing' the United Nations – bringing it up to date and refashioning its roles and responsibilities to meet the needs of a new world entering a new century. I think that we must learn a lesson from the confidence and vision with which the architects of the immediate post-war world planned for the future. For it was during the Second World War, before the Allies were certain of victory, that plans were laid for a new international order. The Atlantic Charter of 1941 and the Bretton Woods Conference of 1944, for example, were events that tried to anticipate the political and economic systems of the new world that was to come.

Today, events have moved so fast and so unexpectedly – who for example predicted the reunification of Germany and the largely peaceful collapse of the Soviet Empire? – that we are still trying to catch up with the tide of history rather than running ahead of it. So the time has come to think ahead and propose reforms that will ensure that the UN can adequately respond to an uncertain but exciting future. There are three main issues that I want to address this evening: reform of the Security Council; peace-keeping operations; and the organisation's role in economic and social policy.

First, the Security Council, the UN's most senior decision-making body. At the moment it has a rotating membership of ten member states and five permanent 'veto' powers – the UK, France, China, Russia and the United States. This structure clearly represents the political settlement of 1945 rather than the political realities of today. The issue of reform is, however, firmly on the agenda. The UN Secretary General, Mr Boutros-Ghali has invited member states to consider the issue which may be decided as early as 1995 on the occasion of the UN's fiftieth anniversary. It is widely accepted that Germany and Japan should be included in a reformed Council. Their extraordinary post war economic record, and their major financial commitment to the UN makes them prime candidates. But accepting Germany and Japan clearly raises other questions. What, for example, about India, Brazil and Nigeria? All of these have strong claims as major powers in the developing world not yet permanently represented in the Security Council. I believe all these countries should be considered for membership provided that they are prepared to accept the full responsibilities of senior representation within the UN. The problem is how to accommodate new members without weakening the effectiveness of the existing Council. It is certainly unrealistic to expect any existing permanent member to surrender their place. Clearly, Britain, having played a key role in the foundation of the UN and with a strong history of international diplomacy and co-operation should retain its place in the Security Council and its veto power. But it is surely possible to achieve a solution that accommodates the aspirant members, which is acceptable to the existing members without jeopardising the effectiveness of the Council. One approach would be to increase the number of permanent members but without giving them the power of veto.

Because achieving reform is difficult some would like to postpone this issue indefinitely. I believe this is unrealistic. Inaction will ultimately threaten the credibility and authority of the UN itself. For the UN must be representative of the world community. There are great risks if it is widely believed to be dominated by a single region or a single nation. The underlying principle of the UN must be a firm commitment to multilateralism – to international co-operation by nations with common goals working together with shared responsibilities. It is this sense of international partnership that needs to be reflected not just in a modernised Security Council but in all the UN's activities.

Nowhere is this more important than in the UN's peace-keeping role. This is another area that is ripe for new thinking. New approaches are, urgently required if we are to catch up with events that have already sent the UN into new, delicate, and dangerous areas of conflict. Traditional UN peace-keeping activity has concentrated on placing blue helmeted forces in buffer zones, by mutual agreement of the parties in conflict. The long-standing UN presence in Cyprus is a classic example of this traditional peace-keeping role. But in recent years the kind of conflict in which the UN has been asked to get involved has changed dramatically. There has been a shift from peace-keeping to peace enforcement. The UN is now involved in countries such as Somalia and Bosnia where agreement between the conflicting parties is almost impossible to achieve; and where the distinction between the provision of humanitarian relief and peace enforcement is also very blurred. There is clearly disquiet and concern that the international community has not yet given the UN either the resources or the effective command and control over peace enforcement operations. This has been most obvious in the case of Somalia in which the US-led humanitarian effort has become so sadly embroiled in the brutalities of a dreadful civil war. With hindsight it is easy to recognise the mistakes in the UN operation in Somalia. Action was taken too late and was led too visibly by the US who retained absolute military control over their own forces. An independence so complete that UN personnel did not have any advance knowledge of the unsuccessful raid by US forces against General Aideed's compound last August.

In my view this state of affairs makes it extremely difficult, if not impossible, for the UN to fulfil the mandate it has been given in areas of bitter internal conflict like Somalia. So we need to strengthen the UN's peace-keeping activities and adhere to some very basic principles. For a start, the UN must retain an effective system of command and control over all the forces at its disposal. This may well require improving the UN's command structures and logistical capability both in the field and in its New York headquarters. It is also important that, wherever possible, UN peace-keeping operations should be based on forces from member states in the region of conflict itself. For example a stronger African presence in the UN operation in Somalia would have been desirable – especially since a number of African countries have participated in successful peace keeping roles in Namibia, Chad and elsewhere.

There is also the critical question of resources. The international community must ensure that the UN has both the financial and military resources at its disposal to be able to tackle the growing range of peace-keeping duties that it is being asked to fulfil. There is under-standable frustration within the UN at the continued build-up of arrears and delayed payments to the organisation at a time of unprece-dented additional demands for both humanitarian relief and peace-keeping activities. I am glad to say that Britain has a good record of prompt payment of our contribution to the UN.

Where I believe Britain can do more is in the area of peace keeping. In our last general election manifesto, the Labour Party proposed that the UN should work to establish a permanent peace-keeping force. A recent proposal on this subject has been made by Britain's distinguished former Under-Secretary General of the UN, Brian Urquhart. This summer Mr Urquhart proposed the concept of a specially trained volunteer unit that could go in to areas of conflict at short notice and with a specific remit to enforce peace. Interestingly the idea has been endorsed by Britain's former ambassador to the UN, Anthony Parsons.

There are, of course, many practical difficulties with the creation of such a force. There would have to be very clear and agreed rules covering military command, financing and deployment for instance. But these should not be treated as fundamental objections to the idea in principle.

Following a suggestion made by Field Marshal Lord Carver I think the Security Council should create a working party to prepare a detailed proposal for such a volunteer force.

In the meantime we believe that Britain should be willing to designate specific units of our military forces to be available for UN operations, and to offer to support the development of centralised military command structures for the UN. NATO, similarly, I believe, could adapt its force structures to make them more relevant to UN requirements and participate in joint training exercises.

My third suggested area of UN reform is not about military issues but it is about security – human security – the security that comes from economic and social progress. During the Cold War and even today the UN's role in promoting economic growth and sustainable development is too frequently overlooked. But the UN was always intended by its founders to be an important forum for international economic and social policy. In fact the Charter of the UN states that 'all members pledge themselves to take joint and separate action in co-operation with the organisation for promoting higher standards of living, full employment, and conditions of economic and social progress and development'.

Today I think it is time to reinvigorate the UN's economic and social roles. After all the economic challenges of the world today are immense. Much of the industrialised world is struggling to escape from recession. Growth is too weak and unemployment is too high – expected to reach 36 million in the OECD countries next year. The emerging democracies of Eastern Europe and the former USSR are coping with massive economic shocks at the very same time that they are trying to consolidate their new-found freedom. Our open international trading system is threatened by beggar-my-neighbour policies of protectionism. And levels of aid and assistance for the poorest countries remain stagnant and far from adequate. Many developing countries are still burdened with debt, poverty and disease.

Against such a background, can we be satisfied with the way in which the international community tackles the economic challenges of our day? I think not, despite a plethora of international meetings held by the OECD, the World Bank, the IMF, the GATT, the UN itself and, of course, the Group of Seven leading industrialised countries. It is an international economic merry-go-round which in recent years has very little to be proud of. Just look for example at the long overdue conclusion of the GATT trade talks, or the still unfulfilled commitments made by the Group of Seven to write off the debts of the poorest countries in Africa.

I think the time has come to try to consolidate the efforts of the international community to develop a coherent global economic strategy. And it is right, I believe, to consolidate this work within the UN.

In July this year, just before the Tokyo summit I suggested that the Group of Seven leading industrialised countries should consider becoming a permanent core of an economic equivalent of the UN's Security Council. Such a body could take on the existing work of the G7 but with a slightly expanded membership that better reflects the changing dynamics of the world economy. For just as the UN Security Council still reflects the world of 1945, the G7 is beginning to look a little outdated as well, for the Asian-Pacific and Latin American countries are beginning to make their own very distinctive mark on the world economy. And before long they will demand a seat at the top tables of international economic policy.

Simply rearranging the structures of policy-making does not, of course, guarantee better policies. But I do believe that there could be positive gains from focusing the attention of the international community on an UN Economic Council which would gain greater status than that enjoyed by the current G7, and which would have clear authority over the major international financial institutions, such as the World Bank and the IMF. A restructured UN could also provide an additional feature of policymaking that I believe is of central importance – to restore a social dimension to the international economy.

In Europe, I profoundly believe, we cannot build a market for business without creating a community for people too. And the same argument applies just as forcefully anywhere else in the world. For me, economic progress and social justice are intertwined and inseparable. That is why I want to see economic policies that encourage growth, employment and investment in people. It is an approach built on the idea that our most precious resource are the skills and talents of people. In the jargon of economic theory it is an investment in human capital. And it is an approach that I believe that is just as applicable to the most advanced industrial country as it is to the least developed country.

For how are modern industrial economies going to remain competitive and create jobs if they do not invest massively in training and the skills of their workforce – when all the evidence shows that higher levels of technology require greater flexibility in the workplace? And how are poorer countries going to escape poverty if they do not invest in the health and education of their own people – when all the evidence shows that reduced rates of infant mortality, and higher literacy rates are not merely inter-related but are the very foundations of development itself?

This evening I have set out what I believe to be an agenda of change for the United Nations which would make it a powerful force for peace and progress in the years and decades ahead. Cynics will no doubt look for the pitfalls. But they will always find a host of reasons why change is impossible, even undesirable. Surely the lesson of history is that we must be grateful that the cynics were outnumbered by the people of vision back in 1945 when the principles of multilateralism and international co-operation were so successfully set in motion. Because it was these principles and the institutions that embodied them which generated an era of economic progress and prosperity never seen before.

So let us do what Robert Kennedy challenged the American people to do in the Spring of 1968. Instead of accepting things as they are, think about the way things could be. For we are living at a time of great change. A time of enormous challenge and opportunity. It is this generation that must shape the new post Cold War world. It is up to us to reforge the institutions of the international community. We are the architects of the twenty first century – trying to build a world that will be more peaceful and more prosperous than ever before. And if we are to provide a blueprint for a better future, we must be ready to change and to think how things could be different. And instead of asking 'why?' ask 'why not?'

The Queen's Speech Debate

Hansard 18 November 1993

There are a number of annual set pieces in Parliament. Smith replied to many budget speeches during his years as Shadow Chancellor, but they are very much of the moment in content and style. Autumn statements also provided larger stages than the

normal run of debates. However the reply to the Queen's Speech is a key moment for
the Leader of the Opposition. Smith was much better at large set pieces in parliament
than anywhere else. His reply to the 1993 Queen's Speech was one of his finest House
of Commons performances. It combined the sharp jabbing of political attack with some
reasoned alternatives to the current plans laid out in the Queen's Speech. Though
kicking a governing party that was languishing at 25% in the polls was easier than
attacking Thatcher in her prime, the 1992 election had taught the Labour Party that
nothing could be taken for granted, and it is the obvious preparation and planning
coupled with the speed of thought on his feet that comes over in this speech.

It is a pleasant convention of the House that the first duty of the Leader of the Opposition today is to congratulate the mover and the seconder of the Loyal Address (*See introduction to this volume*). The mover and the seconder referred to some parts of the Gracious Speech. I shall start, on the lines of the mover, by referring to foreign policy. There are some important developments which I am sure all hon. Members will welcome. In September this year the momentous agreement between Israel and the Palestine Liberation Organisation signalled a new start in the Middle East. It is vital that those who have taken risks for peace receive the whole-hearted support of the international community as they grapple with the formidable tasks which they have set themselves.

Yesterday, as the mover noted, Mr Mandela and President de Klerk made a historic agreement about a new democratic constitution for South Africa. On 27 April next year, the first – and crucial – non-racial elections in the history of South Africa will be held. It is vital that Her Majesty's Government give all possible assistance to ensure that those elections are both free and fair.

We welcome the commitment in the Gracious Speech to strengthening the United Nations' capacity for peace-keeping and preventive action. That cannot be achieved without greater support by the international community in terms of financial and military resources, if the

United Nations is to make a more effective contribution to the solution of acute and deeply distressing situations such as those that are occurring in Bosnia, Somalia and elsewhere.

Opposition Members warmly welcome the signing of the chemical weapons convention and we agree with the Government about the importance of an indefinite and unconditional extension of the nuclear non-proliferation treaty. The cause of non-proliferation will be immeasurably assisted by early agreement on a nuclear test ban. The continued moratorium on tests, led by the current United States administration, is encouraging and the time is overdue for Her Majesty's Government to give the initiative their full support.

We welcome enthusiastically the early accession of Austria, Finland, Norway and Sweden to the European Union. In making their applications they have not sought to opt out of the Social Chapter of the Maastricht Treaty, which they all strongly support. Once they are members, Conservative Britain will be isolated, not just as one among 12, but as one among 16.

In Northern Ireland a window of opportunity now exists to achieve a lasting and peaceful settlement. The Government must grasp this opportunity and work with the Irish Government and the constitutional parties in the Province to create the conditions for peace. The speech by the Tanaiste on the principles that should be applied has rightly been recognised as an important step forward, particularly his acknowledgement of the importance of recognising the legitimate concerns of both communities in Northern Ireland.

We agree with the Government that if the IRA genuinely and clearly abandons the use of violence, there should be no objection to the participation of Sinn Fein in constitutional discussions. We believe also that the elected representatives of Northern Ireland have an obligation to respond to calls from all sections of the community to enter into discussions to agree a peaceful settlement. The British Government should not hesitate to call the parties back to the negotiating table. Compromise and concessions will be required from both sides. All the parties involved, including the British Government, must not be afraid to take risks for peace. They must all be prepared to transcend the old dogmas that stand in the way of reconciliation, which is passionately desired by the vast majority of people throughout the whole British Isles.

At the Conservative Party Conference the Prime Minister launched his big idea – 'back to basics'. It is true that those magic words do not appear in the Gracious Speech itself. We should perhaps be grateful that Her Majesty was not obliged to repeat the mantra, but there is no doubt that that is the right hon. Gentleman's chosen course. He could not have been clearer about it at Blackpool. The Conservative Party, he told us, is now going back to basics. Ever since then political commentators, some bewildered members of the Cabinet and millions of incredulous electors have been trying to work out what the Prime Minister means. The first thought that occurs to them, perhaps not surprisingly, is that the Conservatives have been in government for 14 years. If now we have to go back to basics, what on earth has been happening over 14 years of Conservative Government? Or is this perhaps another coded attack on the glorious achievements of the former Tory leader – another oblique reference to 'the golden age that never was', to quote the Prime Minister's own revealing description of his predecessors's achievements? I hope that there are still some loyal souls on the Tory Benches who will be prepared, as a matter of honour, to rebut such a surreptitious attack on the Thatcher Downing Street years.

We know, of course, that the Prime Minister is haunted by those years and even more troubled by the recent flood of memoirs from former Cabinet Ministers all bearing the same title, 'How I almost stood up to Mrs Thatcher'. Her memoirs rather stole the show at the Conservative Party Conference. Even the Prime Minister's speech could not avoid them. At the start of his speech to the conference he said: 'memoirs to the left of me, memoirs to the right of me, memoirs in front of me volley'd and thundered'. He borrowed the quote from Tennyson's great poem, *The Charge of the Light Brigade*. Perhaps he should have read on. The poem continues: 'Boldly they rode and well, Into the jaws of Death, Rode the six hundred'. I know why the Prime Minister did not finish the quote – there are only 332 Tory Members facing obliteration at the next election. We all know that, after 14 years of Conservative Government, 'back to basics' is no more and no less than an appalling admission of failure. The Conservative Party and the Prime Minister have clearly reached the conclusion that they can no longer plausibly defend their record in office, so they are seeking to wipe from our consciousness the fact that they have been in power for the longest single period of any Government since the Second World War and that they – and they alone – after all these years, are responsible for the state of Britain today.

Let us look at the record of failure from which the Conservatives seek to shy away. Since 1979, economic growth on average has been only 1.7% per year – worse than the preceding decades of the 1960s and the 1970s. Now, after all those years, we have an economy weighed down by the burden of two massive deficits in our public finances and overseas trade. Worst of all, the 14 Conservative years have seen the return of mass unemployment, with millions of our fellow citizens denied the opportunity, dignity and responsibility of work.

Let us look at the other dismal record-breaking achievements of the Government. Record levels of crime – up by a massive 120% since they came to power; record levels of homelessness; record numbers of families living in poverty; and the gap between the rich and the poor wider now than in Victorian times. [*Hon. Members*: 'Rubbish.'] With a record like that, it is no wonder that they want to divert attention from their own responsibility. Their means of diverting attention is the oldest trick in the book – create a diversion, search out a scapegoat and put the blame on someone else. They know that it is no longer convincing to blame the last Labour Government or the trade unions [*Hon. Members*: Why not?] Why not? There are still some brave souls prepared to try that one on. Well, let them try. The public will not listen very carefully to that. They cannot use the last Labour Government or the trade unions as an excuse; it is doubtful that they can any longer blame the Government of the right hon. Member for Old Bexley and Sidcup (Sir Edward Heath). After 14 years in power, the Government know that those excuses are unconvincing. The Prime Minister in particular knows they are unconvincing.

This summer the Prime Minister gave an interview to the *Los Angeles Times*. He was asked directly about the unpopularity of his Government so soon after they had won an election, and he replied:

Fiddle-de-dee! I said immediately after the election, sitting up the day after we won the election with a number of people around me: 'within the next twelve months the Government will be the most unpopular we have seen for a long time!' Nothing in the interim has changed my judgment about that.

It was staggeringly prescient. It perhaps hasn't come about in quite the way I had myself imagined, but it has. We have been here for 14 years. There is no-one else one can blame for anything that has gone wrong.

Let me repeat the Prime Minister's revealing conclusion – 'there is no one else one can blame for anything that has gone wrong.' The Prime Minister's conclusion, hidden until now in the columns of the *Los Angeles Times*, deserves a wider audience. I suggest that he circulates the remarks in a memorandum to his Cabinet colleagues, in particular to those who, for reasons of delicacy, have now become known as the B team – for they were the ones who were let loose at the Tory Party

Conference to target single mothers as the new enemy within. What a disgraceful exercise that was. It was an exhibition so odious that it drew a stinging rebuke from the right-wing commentator, Mr Simon Jenkins of *The Times*, who described it as: 'Mob oratory of the worst sort.' Let me quote his assessment. He wrote:

Ministers paraded the Tory Party in its least attractive mode: lecturing the working class on personal morality. No single parent, no homeless teenager, no dole recipient, no immigrant refugee was free of a sneer from somebody on the platform.

We all listened to those speeches and watched that conference and we all know how true that assessment is. What Ministers did at Blackpool, consciously and deliberately, for their own political purposes, was to exaggerate cynically a social problem. In doing so they insulted thousands of conscientious and caring parents, widowed as well as divorced. Simon Jenkins went on to say: 'Such sanctimoniousness is a measure of the insecurity and desperation of some in the Tory party.'

That desperation is nowhere more evident than in the bizarre theories of the Home Secretary that rising crime and what he calls moral decay can be traced back to the Second World War when fathers were absent in our fighting forces. Of course that was a time described by a former Conservative leader as 'Britain's finest hour'. No evidence is produced for the Home Secretary's wild assertion, but with this lot evidence is not required.

Apparently it is not enough to blame it all on Harold Wilson and the 1960s; now it is all Winston Churchill's fault. Do the Government really believe all this? Do they seriously expect anyone in the country to believe it? Clearly it is not just a few Conservative back-benchers who are barmy. I do not know to which of the two B teams the Home Secretary has been assigned. For all I know he may have sought to qualify for membership of both.

I mentioned evidence. The Government's view is clearly that not only [*Hon. Members*: 'Get on with it.] Hon. Members do not like it when 'back to basics' is challenged. All I am asking for is some evidence for the assertions that the Government have been making. They do not believe that it is necessary to have evidence when one is making a constant appeal to prejudice. If they get contrary evidence, what do they do with it? They have a simple solution – bin it. Even the evidence of their own advisers at the Home Office, the Department for Education and the Cabinet Office is treated to the same response – 'Just bin it'.

Perhaps they should also shred it, for sometimes it comes out. In the leaked memorandum from the Cabinet Office [*Interruption*] Hon. Members do not like reference to be made to that memorandum from the Cabinet Office. I am glad to say that it has now made its way into the public domain despite the fact that every single page has stamped at the top, 'Policy in Confidence'. [*Interruption*] It is wholly in the public interest that what I am about to say has been revealed to the public. Having in mind what I am about to say, it would be disgraceful for it to be prevented from reaching the public because that memorandum dealt with the assertion of the Secretary of State for Social Security that young ladies get pregnant just to jump the housing list.

The facts that the Cabinet Office produced are these: only 5% of lone mothers are teenagers; 88% of pregnancies are unplanned; most single mothers do not know the benefits to which they are entitled; and 90% of 16 and 17-year-old mothers live at home with their parents. That was what was contained in the evidence given to Ministers in the Cabinet. But what have facts to do with Tory prejudice?

Despite the evidence, the Secretary of State for Education ploughed on with his ill-considered plans for tests in schools. Two senior advisers resigned and this week he even lost his Permanent Secretary.

Undeterred by those failures and, once again, with no evidence whatever to back it up, he proposes to begin the de-skilling of the teaching profession. He would be much better employed if he had plans to provide nursery education for all children and the Queen's Speech would have been much better if it had contained such plans. As the report of the National Commission on Education shows only too clearly, investment in the education of the under-fives is the right sort of basic investment in education and provides real benefits for children, families and society. Typically, the Commission's evidence was not good enough for the Government. It is not just Ministers who ignore evidence. In one of his recent essays on modern Conservative thought, delivered at the Carlton Club earlier this year, the Prime Minister – ever eager to scapegoat and to ignore evidence – sought to distinguish between the social problems of suburbs, small towns and villages on the one hand and inner cities on the other. It was, he said, in the inner cities that violent crime flourished. And that was not the fault of 14 years of Conservative Government but was down to socialism.

As the Home Secretary knows well, when the evidence is examined, it can be seen that crime in rural areas is, regrettably, rising much faster than in the inner cities. But when did facts ever get in the Government's way? [*Interruption*] The Conservative Party does not like discussing 'back to basics', but we shall have many such discussions. I fear that the abject failure to tackle the real problems that affect our nation is reflected all too clearly in the legislative programme that has been laid before us. Apparently, we are to have a Bill on deregulation which is to be presented to the House as part of the legislative programme. Apparently, after 14 years of Conservative Government, too many regulations have accumulated. How that happened during the years of the so-called enterprise culture, and and economic miracle, is hard to imagine. Of the 3,500 regulations apparently reviewed by the Government, 71% have been introduced since 1979.

There can be no objection to weeding out outdated and unnecessary provisions. What is to be objected to is a weakening of the proper protection for both employees and consumers in the name of the same misguided dogma which, last Session, saw the abolition of wages councils. Any weakening of safety standards for people at work will be fiercely resisted by the Opposition. Too many avoidable accidents already happen at the work place and it cannot be right to dismantle protection that would increase their number. Consumers too will be rightly concerned at any weakening of protection contained in, for example, fire safety regulations. It is right, is it not, that there are strict provisions controlling the manufacture of furniture and children's nightwear? To avoid horrific dangers, that protection should be not only maintained but enforced with vigour.

It would also be wrong, although I understand that it is being considered, to seek to reduce insulation standards for new houses. Energy costs for millions of people are being increased enough already by the imposition of VAT on fuel without extra costs being caused by a lowering of standards, which inevitably will cause greater energy waste.

Hard though it is to believe, I understand that one of the regulations being reviewed is the obligation on employers to provide toilet paper and soap in workplace lavatories. What kind of uncivilised nonsense are the Government engaged in? [*Interruption*] That may not sound important to Conservative Members, but it is extremely important to people who work in factories. The public, listening to Conservative Members' sneering reception of that, will draw their own conclusions.

Surely the basic truth is that this much-trumpeted deregulution programme is marginal to the real problems that confront our industry and our economy. Let me remind the House that Britain is still struggling to recover from recession — the greatest recession since the 1930s — and is still afflicted by mass unemployment. Neither in the Gracious Speech nor in any other manifestation of their policies do the

Government show any understanding of the real problems that lie in the way of recovery and prosperity. Our problem is persistent under-investment in industry, persistent under-investment in skills development and persistent under-investment in innovation and in our regions, causing structural defects in our economy, which cause low growth, high unemployment and a deficit in overseas trade which is unprecedented at this stage of the economic cycle.

The external deficit in the first half of this year is equivalent to 2% of national income. After 14 years of Conservative economic management, the wealth-creating core of our economy is simply too small to sustain our prosperity or to allow us to pay our way in the world.

Sadly, there is no sign that those vital and, if I may say so, basic strategic issues are being tackled by the Government. They are engaged, in contradiction of their election promises, in a series of tax increases which are not only unfair to millions of people but which threaten to undermine the consumer confidence that is necessary to any recovery of demand.

The discomfort that occurs on the Government Benches whenever tax increases are mentioned is quite noticeable because it is the party that told a lie at the general election. It said that it would not increase taxes and even told us which taxes it would not increase. Those are the very taxes that it is now increasing and it will cost a typical family in Britain an extra £8.50 per week. The Budget later this month needs to be geared to economic recovery that promotes investment and begins to tackle the deep-seated long-term problems that are the legacy of 14 years of Conservative Government. Instead of concentrating on those issues, the Government are intent on promoting irrelevancies. A prize example of that is to cause yet another upheaval in local government. Not only is there no demand in Scotland and Wales for the Government's proposals, but there is massive opposition across a wide spectrum of political views. An overwhelming majority of the hon.

Members who represent Scottish and Welsh constituencies are against the Bills that will only be carried by the votes of English Conservatives who do not represent the people in the countries concerned. I understand that it is proposed to introduce the Bill concerning Welsh local government in the House of Lords. That is a quite outrageous and reprehensible way for the Government to proceed.

Mr Phil Gallie (Ayr): The right hon. and learned Gentleman is suggesting that hon. Members from England should not determine issues in Scotland and Wales. Is not it the case that we are a United Kingdom Parliament? Does not everyone deserve to be able to speak on such issues?

Mr Smith: The hon. Member for Ayr (Mr Gallie) showed a sense of aptness in intervening at that point. I was about to point out that the change was especially reprehensible because the true purpose of the legislation in Scotland was to gerrymander boundaries in the interests of the Conservative Party. One of the most blatant examples occurs in the hon. Gentleman's constituency where there is deliberate gerrymandering to assist the interests of the Conservative Party. Everyone in Scotland knows that to be the case. Local government reform in both countries should be preceded by the devolution of power from central Government. That would be a genuine increase in democratic accountability. But of course a Government who are committed to a relentless increase in quangos and to the imposition of unelected Conservatives to administer our public services are hardly likely to be interested in democratic accountability.

There is one thing for which we should have a little gratitude. The Government were forced back from their plan to privatise water in Scotland because of a nationwide campaign led by the Labour party. They were forced into the curious halfway house of removing water from local authorities, and therefore from democratic control, and giving it to so-called 'public' boards which, of course, will just be another set of quangos. The only thing that can be said for that is that it is not privatisation. The Government should be warned that if it is intended to be a paving step towards privatisation, the passage of time will not diminish public opposition to the privatisation of water. Taxpayers in Scotland, Wales and England will continue to wonder why the Government spend hundreds of millions of pounds on another local government reorganisation when vital public services are being under-mined by a lack of finance.

In 1979, at the start of their party's years of power, the Conservatives complained loudly about the prevailing levels of crime. Their manifesto boasted that they would restore the rule of law. We know their record 14 years later. Crime is up by 120%, violent crime is up by 126% and burglary is up by 180%. Only one in every 50 crimes committed ends in a conviction in court. So much for restoring the rule of law!

We shall, of course, examine with care the Government's proposed legislation on criminal justice. We believe in a twin-track approach. While we should be prepared to be tough on crime, we should be equally tough on the causes of crime. We need to make far more effort to detect crime and to bring its perpetrators to justice. We also need to take more effective action to prevent crime from occurring in the first place. We need visible and effective policing in our communities. We need to take seriously the prevention of crime by better security for property and by better safety in public places. We also need to offer our young people in particular opportunities for employment and for personal fulfilment to counter the alienation from society which corrodes a sense of responsibility and which inevitably fosters crime. We have been told that part of the intention of the 'back to basics' policy is to teach people the difference between right and wrong and the impor-tance of the acceptance of responsibility. The problem for the

Government in that approach is their credibility as teachers and the example of responsibility that they have set. Surely it is wrong to break election promises as cavalierly as the Government have done. Surely it is wrong to impose a tax on the heating of every household in Britain when such an action was expressly excluded before the 1992 election. Surely it is wrong to scapegoat single parents and to stigmatise their children. Surely it is wrong never to resign voluntarily if major errors are made. Surely it is wrong to deny responsibility for policies which have led to mass unemployment and misery for millions of families. Surely it is wrong to have deliberately widened the gap between the rich and poor in our society.

Those are actions of a Government who purport to lecture others about getting 'back to basics'. I believe that 'back to basics' is easily exposed as a political sham, but there are basic needs and aspirations among our people. They want jobs for themselves and for their children. They want a truly national health service which is available to all and which provides the best possible health care proudly in line with the principles of the service's founders. They want well-equipped schools and well-trained and valued teachers to provide opportunities for their children to learn and to succeed. They want decent and afford-able homes for their families. They want our industry to compete with the best and to win, for they know that that is the best security for their prosperity.

I regret that the Gracious Speech is irrelevant to the real aspirations and needs of our people. It is so removed from those aspirations that, instead of going 'back to basics', the Government should be going back to the drawing board.

The European Candidates' Meeting

19 February 1994

This was one of the final texts put into the box files of Smith's speeches. It brings together many of the themes of his political life and the vision he had for a reforming Labour government. The speech was given to Labour's prospective candidates in the European elections held in June 1994. In that election Labour secured 43.5% of the popular vote. This was a campaigning speech in the only major election campaign of Smith's leadership. Labour won the election by a landslide.

I am delighted to be here with you today as we launch our campaign for the local and European elections. I am also pleased to speak to you in the presence of our friends in the media – unlike Douglas Hurd, who felt it necessary to address Conservative European candidates behind closed doors.

These are crucial elections for the Labour Party. We must carry our message to every corner of Britain. A message of revival and renewal. A message of confidence in Britain's future. A message of co-operation and partnership in Europe. A message of change. A message of hope.

Because there can be no doubt that the British people want change. They are sick and tired of the dishonesty, waste and incompetence of this Conservative Government – without doubt the worst government Britain has had this century. A government which has been too long in power and which has, through its own actions, totally lost the consent of the electorate and won nothing but their scorn, their anger and their contempt.

John Major has been under a lot of pressure recently to drop his Back to Basics theme. Understandably, some of his backbenchers are rather nervous about it. But pressure has also come from his colleagues in the Cabinet, who are sick to death of trying to explain a slogan which none of them agree about. Even his own advisers want him to forget it. For the whole idea has been a disaster from start to finish.

But the Prime Minister is adamant. He won't let it drop. Despite everything that's happened, he's determined to press on with it. And in the *Daily Express* on Thursday he wrote a long article explaining – again – what he really means by Back to Basics.

'Like a good family,' he writes, 'a great nation blends the wisdom and experience of the old with the vigour and challenge of the new.' A thought so compellingly bland that it could find its way into a Liberal Party Manifesto. He goes on to say that Back to Basics is about going back to grassroots beliefs. But there is one grassroot belief which is curiously absent from this lengthy statement by the Prime Minister. There is no mention of tax anywhere in the article. Not a paragraph; not a sentence; not a phrase; not even a word. Not a single reference to taxation.

And yet, two days before the last election, Mr Major said this: 'More tax cuts for all ... That is our basic Conservative belief.' So why, we ask, is low taxation no longer included in the Prime Minister's list of basic beliefs? Since, before the election, he said it was the basic Conservative belief? Could this be because his own Treasury Minister was about to reveal the true nature of the Government's massive tax hike? Now we know that, from this April, the typical family will have to pay £600 a year more in tax. And in 1995 they will have to pay £1,160 more in tax.

This is a disaster for hard-pressed families struggling to make ends meet. It is a tragedy for the British economy which is struggling to recover frorn recession. As the London Business School showed only yesterday, tax increases will seriously harm the recovery. That can only be bad for Britain. No wonder Mr Major has abandoned low taxation as a basic belief. He knows that no-one will ever believe him about tax again. And he knows that no-one will forgive him for having to pay more, but get less in return. Billions of extra pounds in taxation – not to improve our services but to pay for the economic failure of the past fifteen years.

In this revealing article, the Prime Minister insists that Back to Basics does have a moral dimension. His idea of morality does not apparently include telling the truth to the electorate about taxation. And there are some other passages in John's article which are so revealing that it is just possible he wrote it himself. He tells us of the drift away from common sense in law and order, schools, social services, and housing over the last 30 years – forgetting, in a burst of selective amnesia, that the Conservatives have been in power for nearly twenty of those thirty years and – as we know to our cost – for the past fifteen years in succession. And listen, if you will, to the thoughts of the great leader on education. I quote an astonishing passage:

In education the experts who drew up the National Curriculum took a commonsense idea and mangled it beyond recognition. So we have taken the pruning knife to the curriculum and the overblown assessment system.

Just pause for a moment and reflect on whose government it was which introduced the National Curriculum and the tests? Should not Mr Kenneth Baker and Mr John Patten step forward to claim the prize? But of course, it could not be they who were at fault – Tory Ministers can't be at fault – it's the mysterious experts once again. Funny though that they should be blamed for carrying out their Ministers' instructions.

People are getting very tired of a Prime Minister who constantly seeks to blame others for his Government's mistakes. A Prime Minister always looking for a new scapegoat to take the rap for his own failure. A Prime Minister always trying to opt out of his own responsibility and the responsibility of his Government. There is only one basic message I have for the Prime Minister: stop blaming everyone else and start telling the truth about the mistakes of the past 15 years.

Let us, in these elections, show people how things can be different. What we are experiencing after fifteen years of Conservative rule is not an inevitable process of decline. With the right policies, with the right vision, Britain can be a successful confident country again. I want the Labour Party in these elections to restore people's belief in themselves, in their communities, and in Britain's future. Let us show them what today's Labour Party stands for, and what we want for our country: economic revival; democratic renewal; and an opportunity society. Let us show them how these can be achieved. And let us show them how our commitment to Europe can help us achieve them.

There is one thing we need to make absolutely clear about the Conservatives in these elections. It is the dishonesty and contradiction at the heart of their position on Europe. I don't think we should allow the British people to be deceived by the Government over Europe. The people have a right to know where the Conservative Party stands, and what it stands for, because the Government speaks with a forked tongue about Europe. On the one hand you have the pro-Europeans, which includes the majority of the Tory MEPs. They are, as you know, part of the European People's Party in the European Parliament. The leader of the Conservative MEPs is vice-president of the group. The European People's Party even has an office in Conservative HQ in Smith Square. This group supports the Social Chapter and it supports federalism. But on the other hand you have the No Turning Back group of Conservative MPs who are violently opposed to Europe and everything it stands for. Peter Lilley, Michael Portillo, John Redwood – senior Cabinet ministers – are all keen supporters of this group.

And John Major hovers nervously somewhere in between the two. No-one knows where he stands or what he thinks, because he sends different signals depending on which group he's talking to. In meetings with European leaders and with the pro-European wing of his Party, John

Major claims to be in favour of Europe. Didn't he say that he wanted to put Britain at the heart of Europe? But to his anti-European wing he speaks a different language altogether – the language of isolationism and Euro-scepticism and xenophobia. So what on earth is the Conservatives' position on Europe? Are they in favour of European integration or are they not?

Do they want to work together with other European countries or do they not? Do they accept the need for co-ordinated action across the Community or do they not? How can the Conservative Party expect people to vote for them in the European elections when their MEPs say one thing about Europe and members of the Cabinet say the opposite? They need to sort out the line before they ask for people's votes. But they can't sort out the line because they are too deeply divided. The two sides will never agree.

And it is because the Prime Minister knows this that he speaks with a forked tongue about Europe. But it won't wash with the voters. And we will expose their hypocrisy at every opportunity, because the people have a right to know what it is they are voting for. The Labour Party has a clear simple message about Europe and it is this: Europe is good for Britain; good for British jobs; good for British companies; good for British standards at work; good for the quality of the food we eat and the water we drink; good for the environment; good for cracking down on drugs and crime; good for attacking racism; good for our relationship with the rest of the world; good for our own national security.

And Labour is the Party of Europe because we stand for the things that are most important to the British people: jobs; security; self-respect; a decent quality of life and a future for Britain's children.

The first plank of the Labour Party's message to the British people in these elections must be economic revival. Before we can do anything else we must make our economy strong again, so that we can bring about the steady growth and the high levels of employment Britain so desperately needs. Labour's Business Plan for Britain will achieve that. It is a programme of investment, of training, and of jobs – a Business Plan that will carry Britain forward with new confidence into the twenty-first century. Investment is the key to success – investment in people and in their skills; investment in new plants and the most advanced technology; investment in research and innovation; investment in the regions and in our public transport system; investment which has been so sorely lacking in Conservative Britain and which the next Labour government will begin to put right. The kind of investment set out in the Delors White Paper on *Growth and Employment*, which we warmly endorsed.

And training is critical to Labour's economic programme. We must give people the chance to learn the skills which will bring them jobs in tomorrow's world of work. We want to build a new workforce – a workforce that is highly skilled, confident, and equipped to meet the needs of a high-tech, rapidly changing, competitive economy.

Our goal must be full employment. Full and fulfilling employment. Of course we cannot guarantee work for every single man and woman in Britain, but we do accept the responsibility of government to work to maintain the highest possible level of employment for our people, because mass unemployment – the miserable legacy of this Conservative Government – drags people down, drags communities down, and drags the economy down.

It is our priority to get Britain working again. And we can do this by investing in infrastructure projects, by building new homes, by improving the environment, by training and re-training people, and by opening up opportunities for women to combine their family responsibilities with work outside the home. We utterly reject the view of the Conservative Party – the view that governments should stand back and do nothing – hoping that somehow market forces might put people back to work. For we know there is so much that can be done and should be done now to tackle unemployment in our country.

And it is by working together with our partners in Europe that we' can best achieve our goals. It is by acting together, combining our individual strengths, and putting the resources of the Community to work for the good of the people of Europe, that we will succeed in bringing unemployment down, and securing sustainable economic recovery. The Conservatives' way of winning votes is to try to frighten people. They tried to frighten people about Labour's tax plans before the last election. That was before they imposed the biggest tax hike on British families since the war. They tried to frighten people about the Social Chapter. And during this European election campaign they will try to use the same tactic again. They will say that by supporting the Social Chapter we are putting people's jobs at risk. This from a Government which has the worst record on jobs and growth of any government since the war.

We know they are wrong, as their disastrous policies have so brutally shown. And we will not let them frighten the British people with their false claims and wild distortions. It is right that the British people should have the same standards at work, the same conditions, the same employment protection, the same health provisions as people in the rest of Europe. If it is good enough for Germany, it is good enough for us. If French employers aren't put off by these rules, why should British companies be? And Japanese employers in Britain have said time and again that they are perfectly happy with the Social Chapter provisions.

The battle over the Social Chapter reflects a far deeper division between us and the Conservatives. A division which starkly exposes the difference between our two parties, and the kind of society we want to build. The Conservatives believe the route to economic success is by driving wages down, lowering standards, scrapping regulations, forcing people to work longer hours for less pay. That is why – alone in Europe and to Britain's shame – they refused to sign up to the Social Chapter. The Labour Party prefers a different route – the route of a highly skilled, highly motivated workforce. A workforce whose rights are respected and whose work is fairly rewarded. A workforce with the knowledge, the skills and the confidence to succeed in a rapidly changing world. And a workforce which can produce the high quality goods and deliver the high quality services which Britain needs to achieve lasting prosperity.

This is the difference between our two parties, and this is the choice we must present to the British people in the months ahead.

But as well as economic revival, we stand for democratic renewal. In Britain, people are losing faith in the democratic process. They see their own priorities and their own needs neglected and ignored by a ruling party which has completely lost touch with the people. The powers of local councils have been snatched from them and given to a new tier of Conservative quangos, unaccountable to the communities they serve, answerable only to their political masters.

And Government itself has become over-centralised, secretive and self-serving, undermining the high standards of public service which have been the pride of our country for more than a century. Is it any wonder that people have become cynical and disillusioned? But we must challenge that cynicism. We must show them that government can, and must, work for them, on their behalf and for the good of the whole community.

The Labour Party will give power back to people in their communities. We will revitalise local government. We will give new powers to the regions and nations of Britain so that they can respond to the differing needs of their own communities. And we will enable them to forge new links with other regions of Europe so that everyone can enjoy the very real benefits of closer ties with Europe.

We want to see more openness in government, and more accountability. This applies as much to the institutions of Europe as to the conduct of our government at home.

This message of democratic renewal is critical to the way the Labour Party wants to shape the future of our country, and our future in Europe. It is about empowering people, giving them more control over their lives, and creating a society in which everyone can participate and no-one need feel excluded.

And our third ambition for Britain is to build an opportunity society.

People need good schools; the National Health Service; a decent home; freedom from crime; the chance to learn a skill. These are the basic things which provide the secure foundations upon which everyone can mark out their own individual route to success.

An opportunity society in which women have the same chance as men to find fulfilling jobs.

An opportunity society in which people are well paid in return for hard work.

An opportunity society in which people can carry on learning and acquiring new skills throughout their working lives and beyond.

An opportunity society in which merit not privilege opens doors to advancement.

An opportunity society in which human dignity and respect for others are highly valued.

An opportunity society which offers everyone, whatever their gender, colour or creed, a real chance to succeed in their own way to the very best of their abilities.

An opportunity society which will be part of a strong and dynamic Europe, working together to improve the lives of each and every citizen. We are proud of our ambition for Britain, and proud of our vision of Europe. In the months ahead we will carry our programme to every corner of Britain. And at the local government elections in May, and at the European elections in June, the people will give their verdict on the past fifteen years and on the future we in the Labour Party offer them.

I look forward to this campaign. And I look forward even more to the day when we finally banish this clapped-out Conservative Administration – the worst government of this century – to the electoral oblivion it deserves.

The Opportunity to Serve

Speech at European Gala Dinner, London, 11 May 1994

This is an edited version of the final speech John Smith gave. The speech reflected the growing consensus that Labour would win the next election. The number of business people in the audience suggests this, as does Smith's confident tone. The was a long way to go and much would have been different, but here is the final political statement from a man ready for the top job in British politics, its themes, echoed throghoput this volume, were of social justice, european social democracy and the need for active government.

Tonight we are engaged in a European Gala Dinner and it is interesting that we have here tonight the Leader of the French Socialist Party, because we at the Labour Party are committed to the vision of the Europe that is most economically successful and socially just, which is why we are committed to the Social Charter. In the course of the campaign for the European elections, we will have the issues posed very clearly for the people of this country. On the one hand, we will have a Government which says the only way towards prosperity in Britain is to have the lowest wages, to have the poorest conditions and is hopeful that we will attract investment on that ground. But anyone who understands modern business and modern industry understands very clearly that that is the most foolish of views because there will always be people in the difficult world in which we live who will be able to undercut us on that assumption. Britain's future depends on investment in the skills of our able people, investment in our industry, particularly our manufacturing industry, and in a partnership between Government, industry and business that makes sure that this country succeeds because of consistent investment in the very best training that any country can provide for its people.

One of the ambitions of the next Labour Government is to create the best educated and trained workforce in the whole of Europe. In workforce, I include management. I believe 99 per cent of the people of this country would wish that as an objective. But what they have not had for 15 years is a Government that made that its objective. And if there is one single thing that the next Labour Government can do, it will be to make education and training the absolute star in the policies we propose so that at the end of our period of Government – I hope it will be ten years and perhaps it will be 15 years – but whatever it is, people will say at the end of it, 'this is the one country in the whole of Europe which does its very best for its young people'. Let everybody follow their abilities as far as they will take them and as far as their ambitions dictate.

There can be no better ambition for a Government to wish for its people and I cannot think there are not intelligent industrialists, financiers, bankers and managers who don't share that vision for the future, which is why I welcome tonight so many representatives from the world of industry, finance and banking, probably more than we have ever had at a Labour Party Dinner in our history. It is right that they should be here because the Labour Party is the party that understands modern industry, modern society, modern finance and modern economics but also understands that the crucial raw material of our future is the skills of our people. There is a new duality to be created, as

Gordon Brown, our Shadow Chancellor, constantly says. It is the connection between investment in technology and investment in people. And the investment in people has to be accompanied by the acknowledgment of the dignity of people. If we ask people to be responsible, we must give them rights as well. We must say to them, you are not to be exploited, which is why we are unequivocally in favour of a minimum wage, for the Social Charter, for decent conditions, because I don't think there should be an industrialist or financier who wants to employ people who are not employed under decent and reasonable conditions. Now, that is the message that we will be taking to our people in the European election. It is the message we have carried through all our campaigns and we will be taking it right through to the general election.

Now, we are going to go into the European elections, not arguing for referendums, not arguing for a sceptical view of Europe, not hesitant about our future in Europe. We are going to approach the European elections with a sense of vision and of purpose because we in the Labour Party believe that our future is truly in Europe, that the sum of the parts that we can create in the European Community is far greater than what we can achieve on our own and that the scale of events that the modern world requires, the intensive commitment it needs, the techniques it requires for effective government, require a proper European approach. That is why the Labour Party is now the European Party in British Politics. We are totally committed to it and we are going to sign up for the Social Charter which every other country in the European Community wants and which significantly the four new countries, whom we are proud to welcome, in the Community, also want, because we have a balanced view of Europe. We want a successful Europe for business. We have a single market. Let's make a success of it.

But it is not enough for business to be successful. No business can be successful without reference to the people it employs or the community in which it survives. We must let prosperity spread throughout all our people and that is one of the visions that the European Community brings to the world and one which we are happy to subscribe to and support in what we do. We will fight the European elections on these policies and we will fight proudly because we are clear and confident about the European mission not only of our Party but of our country, and when we have a Labour Government, it won't be a Government which the rest of Europe just looks at slightly suspiciously and says, 'What are they up to now?' It will be a Government that proudly takes its place because it believes in the concept of Europe as much as all the other member states gathered round the table.

I think there is a great hunger amongst our people. There is a great hunger amongst our people for a return to politics of conviction and idealism. The Thatcher years proved that it was not possible for people to be successful and content simply by being successful on their own part because there were so many that had not been successful and the menace of high unemployment still threatens our society. The mission of the Labour Party must be to get Britain back to work, to get the people who are unemployed now employed in the useful work that needs to be done in building houses for people without homes, in building a new transport infrastructure for this country, and starting regional development on a scale that has never been attempted properly in this country, bringing not only power but economic success back to every region in this country, empowering industry and local authorities by a participating Government, a partnership Government that says that, if you are prepared to commit yourself to the success of your country, your Government will be behind you. That applies at home and it applies abroad – a Government that supports British industry when it fights for orders abroad, supports the investment in technology and science which is desperately needed in our country.

I think we are one of the most able countries on the face of the earth, certainly one of the most able countries in Europe, and the skills of our people are underdeployed by our Government.

But it must not be a Government which imagines that it can decide everything for business or decide everything for people. It is above all an enabling Government. A Government which seeks to share power, to enable power, to give them the chance to give of their best. I think that is the style of modern society and it ought to be the style of modern Government. I think that Government has to insist on certain important qualifications to business effort. It must say to all our businesses and all our people, you must respect the environment in which we live. You must respect the social rights of our people, but you run your own business. You run them well and you run them successfully and we will be happy about that. But it will be in your interest to respect our environment and to respect our social rights and to give power to your people, and to clever and intelligent people working in your companies and in your industries. I think that is the message that Britain wants to hear. But there is, perhaps, the most important message of all: no society, no country can ever survive to be successful without a profound sense of social justice and unless we bring social justice back to this country this country cannot be healthy and cannot be successful.

When I go campaigning round this country and I meet the old age pensioners who are having to pay the VAT on fuel, I see the poor people who are struggling to make ends meet. One understands what social justice means when I meet the people who are dependent on state education for the future of their children, when I meet the vast majority of the people of this country who depend on the National Health Service for the health of their families, and they know – don't they know! – what is happening to our NHS. Ministers can produce statistic after statistic but our people who are connected to the Health Service from the moment they are born until the moment that many of them die, know the truth about our National Health Service and they know one wonderful truth about the Labour Party. If the Labour Party did nothing else in all its history, to have founded the National Health Service and lifted the care and worry from our people and founded a Health Service which was only to do with human need and not to do with money and access, or to do with privilege or anything else, they would know that the Labour Party had achieved a great virtue. But now we have to come back and restore it once again. So when you sum up all the issues we have in this country – social justice, economic justice, conquering unemployment, giving our young people the opportunities they ought to have in a modern Europe and a modern world, it adds up to a stunning case for Labour.

I am glad to say that our Party has been reinvigorated in recent years. This is now a confident Labour Party that you see meeting here tonight and can I say to those of our guests who may not be totally committed to our case, thank you for coming to us and thank you for listening to our case tonight. I think we have a strong, powerful and persuasive case. It is one which will be assisted by your contribution here tonight. It is one, I can tell you, which will be persisted in. Because this is a Labour Party that is determined to win. We believe in the idealism of our cause but we also believe it is not enough to be idle idealists who think we should just announce policies and hope that somehow people will come to them. We have to go out, argue fiercely, everywhere and in every town and hamlet and part of this country.

There is something fundamental happening in this country now. I suppose the academics would call it a circular shift in political attitudes. But we all know that it is happening. People who for years have been Conservatives have lost the faith and many people who sat on the edge of British politics have realized there is only one way forward for this country: a Government with purpose, pragmatism and economic determination and for social justice. I believe that everything is moving our way. We must never be complacent and must never take anything for granted but I believe the signs are set fairer for the Labour Party than they have been for a very long time.

Thank you all very much for coming here tonight and helping us perhaps partly to achieve that objective. We will do our best to reward your faith in us but please give us the opportunity to serve our country. That is all we ask.

CONCLUSION

Having read what I believe is a representative sample of John Smith's words, I hope you will judge him by what he did and not by what he did not do. Having done that, we can consider the counterfactual games of history, and the question I posed in the introduction: how would a Smith government have been different? The place of John Smith as the last great politician of the collectivist age is assured. The question is whether he would have been the first great leader of a post-collectivist social democratic government. That question will dog his historical reputation for all time.

In my view his greatest virtue as a politician was derived from the major element of his character: integrity. It was this palpable integrity that allowed him to transcend the reality of the political stable he emerged from. John Smith was a machine politician who was not defined by the morality of the machine. He was bigger than that machine. He was a Scottish politician who was capable of being the leader of a United Kingdom in a way that none of his contemporaries could match. He was a European statesman who understood the centrality of the European vision for the economic and social future of Britain. In all these respects he would have made a fine Prime Minister and an international statesman.

On the three greatest issues in the politics of the Labour Party which were revolutionised by the Thatcher era, Smith was as consistent as he was passionate in his beliefs. He was a pro-European, pro-NATO multilateralist who believed in the use of direct and indirect taxation to finance redistribution in the name of social justice. He also believed that general affluence was the best route out of sectionalised poverty. He did not have to change his position on any of these issues as the Labour Party went through the process of modernisation associated with the leadership of Neil Kinnock. Whenever a politician, like Shaun Woodward for instance, decides to leave a political party they are fond of saying that they have stayed still but the party has moved away from them. It is much rarer for the party to move towards the politician. In Smith's case he watched the party slowly move towards him on the core issues. Moreover, Smith was the last leader of the Labour Party to feel entirely at home with the traditional doctrine and ethos of the Labour Party, to sit comfortably within its conventions even as he set out to try and modernise them. But he was also the last great collectivist because he was the last fully active Labour politician to have run a major depart-ment of state in the dying days of the long boom. Perhaps the last British politician to have created a state-owned enterprise.

His consistency shines powerfully through the speeches reproduced in this volume. Especially on Europe, the issue that dominated his period as leader of the Labour Party, his unquestionable credentials as a pro-European actually gave him more freedom to manoeuvre in gaining political advantage from the Conservative's civil war over Europe. He was also a confident European Social Democrat. As such he never needed to apologise for endorsing the party's gymnastics on the issue.

Integrity and consistency made him largely immune to the bland-ishments of image-makers and the advice of spin doctors. He listened but he did not shape his approach to politics with the spinning of the message as the starting point of the analysis. Communication followed on from principle. In this sense he would not have secured as big a majority in 1997 because he would not have targeted as ruthlessly nor tailored and packaged his message as carefully. He would also have allowed himself more political room for manouevre by presenting his tax policy differently. I do not think he would have returned to the Shadow Budget of the 1992 election but neither would he have given up direct taxation for the duration of the parliament. In this respect he might well have proved that the electoral analysis of the 1980s – you cannot win from the centre left while advocating direct tax increases – has in practice been superseded. Not ruling out direct tax increases would probably have had a marginal effect on Tory turn out, inspiring some of the four million stay homes to vote for Major. It would not, in my judgement, have been a significant number.

Once in power the style of a Smith government would have been very different. Cabinet would have been much more central to the operation of government decision-making and the House of Commons might have returned as an important locus of political debate. The need for a Cabinet style of government would have reflected a greater attempt to maintain a political balance within the government. Smith's own style of working with people, respecting opponents, opinions and forging an agreed consensus would also have reflected this. Whether this would have actually made for a more successful government or not is an open question. Cabinet government, though beloved by many, is not necessarily a more efficient form of executive nor is the House of Commons, especially in an unreformed state, an especially democratically empowering institution.

The pace of constitutional reform and the main areas of economic policy would, I think, have been pretty much the same. Smith had long been a supporter in principle of the notion of independent central banks playing a role in the fight against inflation, but this belief might well have clashed with his residual desire for active government. It is an open question, impossible to answer, if Bank of England independence would have come. Smith could, of course, have blocked it and other economic policies not to his liking because his power in relation to his Chancellor would have been much greater. Indeed, his ascendancy over the government would have been based on experience and character as much as on being a proven election winner and popular politician. Therefore a number of early gaffes, the Peter Mandelson house saga and perhaps even the Formula One debacle, might have been avoided. But other problems would have arisen and mistakes would no doubt have been made. While the style and conduct of a Smith government would undoubtedly have been different, it is impossible to say what problems would have arisen, what issues well handled by the Blair administration would have stumped a Smith one.

There are two areas, however, in which the difference would have been clear. In one I will stick my neck out with a guess: Britain would by now have a timetable for membership of the Single Currency or at the least a definite date for a referendum this side of the election with a Yes campaign in full swing. I base this analysis on the direction of Smith's speaking and writing and on the centrality this issue would have had for him in personal political terms in a way that it does not for Blair. Such a decision might well have destroyed the government or at the very least allowed a much speedier Conservative recovery. Or it might have galvanised the Labour Party against the Conservative's narrow English-Powellite nationalism, around a vision of taking Britain into the mainstream of European social democracy.

The second area in which there would have been a clear difference is in the relationship between the government and the party. I am not going to suggest that Smith would not have tried hard to get his chosen candidates into the Welsh Assembly and as Mayor of London, he would have done. But he would have backed off quicker, been more prepared to compromise and more interested in bringing the party along with him on key issues rather than forcing it to follow him. If the OMOV experience is any guide then there would have been issues that he would have made ones of confidence but they would have been fewer and would have been managed with a greater eye on the need for compromise. This unity of the party might well have helped defeat people like Livingstone because he could have played a loyalty card more effectively with a membership that still felt in tune with the leadership.

Things would have been generally quieter, the pace of change slower and the relations between party and government closer. Whether this would have made any difference is a difficult question. On the core achievements of the first Blair administration: a stable economy, the new deal for and cut in unemployment, the minimum wage, NHS investment, devolution and constitutional reform, there is little to choose between what has happened and what Smith believed in. More industrial intervention, perhaps saving the odd car company, a greater emphasis on the need to help manufacturing and a surer hand in dealing with Scottish politics, would all have been in evidence, but to a remarkable extent the Blair government has delivered on the Smith promise. He might not have liked elements of the style of this government; he would not have bought into the importance attached to the packaging and he would have been less interested in the way new Labour sometimes follows fashions, especially in the media, but he would have approved of the substance, content and consistency of purpose that the Blair government has so far demonstrated on the issues which mattered most to him: education, employment health and, yes, the creation of an optimistic democracy.